Horizon Hunters

Horizon Hunters

a memoir of adventure

Clara Lukens Parks

WINGS
PUBLISHERS

Published by
Wings Publishers
3555 Knollwood Drive
Atlanta, Georgia 30305

Text ©1999 by Clara Lukens Parks

ISBN 0-9668884-1-3

Book and cover design by Robin Sherman
Composition by Marian Gordin

Manufactured in the United States of America

10 9 8 7 6 5 4 3 2 1
First Edition

Dedication

This true account is lovingly dedicated
to the memory of the late Bill Parks,
my husband and partner
during our fifty-four years
of adventure together.

Contents

1

An Introduction

"As Bill always says when the going gets tough, 'We'll be eatin' the bark off the trees if something doesn't turn up pretty soon.' But something always does turn up, even that time when we were down to thirty-five cents between us."

Those are the first two sentences in my article "Horizon Hunters" that was published in the August, 1947, *Ladies' Home Journal*. It was about my life of adventure, hard work, and hardship with my husband Bill Parks all over the Southwest after our marriage in Kingman, Arizona, on April 12, 1941. I received many wonderful letters of appreciation and interest from readers all over the country, some enclosing dollar bills to help us out, although I certainly wasn't asking for help. We wrote letters of gratitude to those who included their addresses.

At the time I wrote that article we were broke, in dire straits, and reluctantly about to try to borrow money, as I was pregnant with our first child. We were living on the desert at our little cabin we had built near Cave Creek, Arizona. The thousand dollars I received from the *Journal* saved our lives and enabled us to travel in our '28 Chevy to Grand Canyon where Bill would again have a job as bus driver/guide.

Now the story I am about to tell continues with my life and adventures for the next fifty years, but first this introduction concerning my background showing the contrast between my life before I met Bill and since our marriage until his death at age ninety-seven in the Prescott, Arizona, V.A. Medical Center Nursing Home, on June 15, 1995.

I was born on November 9, 1914, in Deadwood, South Dakota, in a house on Forest Avenue overlooking Calamity Jane's grave in Mt. Moriah Cemetery. It was hunting season, and the doctor phoned his office telling the nurse that he had just bagged another little "dear."

My father Edward French Lukens was born in 1884 in Fort Wayne, Indiana, to Alfred Thomas Lukens and Mary Melita Brandriff Lukens. They had six children: Alfred Brandriff, Clara Maria, Grace Emma, Lydia Moore, Martha, and my father. I was named after Clara who was born in 1874, the oldest child, my father's favorite sister, who died in her early thirties from kidney trouble and influenza, so I never knew her.

The family name Lukens was originally Lucken according to the account on page 361 of Volume II of the *Genealogy of the Descendants of Thomas French*. Copies of the two volumes are available in the New York Public Library. They cover a span of years from 1639 to 1913 and were compiled, published, and copyrighted by Howard Barclay French of the seventh generation.

Jan Lucken was one of the thirteen pioneer colonists who settled Germantown, Philadelphia, Pennsylvania, in 1683. Most of them had come from Crefeld on the Lower Rhine near the border of Holland. The Lukens family was actively involved with the Quakers, the Friends Meetings, although Jan Lucken's family members were originally Mennonites. My grandfather Alfred Thomas Lukens was the second son, third child, of Perry and Lydia Ann French Lukens. He was born in 1845 in Springboro, Ohio.

My dear little cousin Susan Hopkins, granddaughter of my Aunt Martha Lukens Hopkins, and daughter of my cousin Richard Hopkins and his wife Astrid, is an avid student of the genealogy of our family and belongs to several organizations studying the subject. She told me that she has traced our family clear back to the English Barons and Charlemagne. She lives in New York and works at West Point.

During the Civil War, my grandfather Alfred Thomas Lukens served in the Union Army, first as a drummer boy at age sixteen, and then with the Ohio Volunteers. He later became an editor of the *Fort Wayne News Sentinel*. My father, Edward French Lukens, attended Columbia University in New York for six years and became a mechanical engineer. But he didn't receive his degree as, a rebel back then, he refused to take Physical Education, a requirement. He was a member of Phi Kappa Psi fraternity.

After my father left New York, he traveled to Deadwood, South Dakota, for adventure, and worked as a guard on the midnight shift at the slime plant at Homestake Mines. In his free time he enjoyed fishing in Spearfish Canyon.

An Introduction

My mother, Eleanore Euphemia Sandelin, was born in Calumet, Michigan, in 1891, to Henry (Henrik) Sandelin and his wife, Albertina, who had migrated from Finland to America in the 1800s, settling in northern Michigan. My grandfather was a Laplander, complete with costume and carved skis. The only memento I have of his is a beautiful little seven-inch-long scrimshaw knife with handle and sheath made of either reindeer antler or bone and depicting a Laplander couple dressed in native costume, among other subjects. It is a lovely ivory color and one of my treasures. Grandfather Sandelin worked in the copper mines in northern Michigan and later for a while in Butte, Montana, before returning to Michigan.

My grandmother Albertina died horribly of cancer of the womb and rectum after failed surgery when my mother was only twelve years old. Her father eventually married Hilda, the hired girl, which offended my mother deeply, so at age nineteen she went with some so-called friends to Deadwood, South Dakota, where they abandoned her.

She had nowhere to turn, and her first week alone in Deadwood, still a wild town, was pretty traumatic. She saw a violent murder at the railroad station when one man shot another dead; a suicide from the roof of her hotel when a man jumped off while she was looking out of her window; and she lived for a week on five cents' worth of cinnamon buns until she found work with a tailor named Taylor, not his real name, where she learned to sew men's clothing expertly, also to dry-clean, iron, and mend.

My mother met my father on a streetcar between Lead and Deadwood, and when he came to call on her, he laid his big, heavy gun on the table, which "scared" her, she told me. Against his family's wishes, as they were "socially prominent" in Fort Wayne and my mother was just a "Finnish working girl," they were married in 1912. My brother, Alfred Brandriff, was born in 1913, and I came along a year and a half later in 1914. It seems I was a very fussy baby and cried all the time until the neighbors complained. My mother told them, "Do you think I enjoy it?" Eventually, of course, I calmed down and became a quite submissive child.

It was rather an adventure to live in Deadwood where, according to my mother, Sioux Indians would come to our back door and ask for "biscuit," their word for bread. My mother always gave them some and whatever else she could spare, even though she was a little frightened, but no harm ever came to her.

When I was three years old, we left Deadwood and went to Indianapolis for a few months where my father tested cars on the Indianapolis Motor

Speedway, which he enjoyed. Then we moved on to Detroit where he worked for Liberty Diesel Engines. World War I was still being fought, but he wasn't drafted as he had a family. From Detroit we went to Cleveland, Ohio, to visit my father's sister Lydia and her husband, my Uncle Arthur Edgerton. They had a little boy, my cousin Alfred Dixon (called "Boydie") who was a year older than me and one of my most favorite people in the world, he was always so sweet and kind to me.

In 1919 after we left Cleveland, we traveled to New Haven, Connecticut, by train as usual, and I loved sleeping in upper berths and at mealtime hearing the delightful tinkle of the ice in the water glasses as we ate. While my mother and Alfred and I were sitting in Grand Central Station in New York waiting for my father who was on some errand or other, a nice-looking young man stopped by and admired my pretty mother and gave us children each a Hershey bar and fifteen cents. My mother turned and whispered to me, "Don't tell your father." Not warning me never to take candy and money from strangers. Who knew, back then?

On to New Haven where we lived for a few summer months in a Yale Professor's house until my father found work at Coe-Stapley in West Haven on beautiful Long Island Sound. I never knew what products they manufactured. I do remember that the office girls admired my handsome father and chased after him until they learned he was married and had two children, whereupon they apologized and desisted.

In West Haven we lived at first in a two-story house not far from Campbell Avenue, which I liked very much. The first Christmas that I can remember was when my mother came upstairs on Christmas morning, put new red flannel slippers on Alfred and me, then took us downstairs to see, to our great astonishment, a glowing tree lit up by real burning candles, and my father standing nearby with a bucket of water. And, oh, the gifts! Dolls, books, and a pair of white kidskin gloves, the latter from my Aunt Lydia, and certainly not warm enough for a Connecticut winter.

From there we moved to a second-story flat on Noble Street a short distance from Noble School where Alfred and I had been entered into first grade. I assume it was because he hadn't had much schooling before, while we were moving from place to place, never settling down for very long. Even though he was a year and a half older than me, he never objected, just accepted what was handed out.

I loved West Haven and finding wild violets, blackberries, and tiny wild strawberries, sweet and warm from the sun. And going to the beach and Savin Rock amusement park, although we were too poor to go on the rides very often. Or eat the soft shell crabs that smelled so delicious while frying in the concession stands all around. We had to share a nickel package of much-too-sweet caramel corn, our only treat.

To help our financial situation, my mother took in sewing and made beautiful clothes for me, also, and for neighbors; also for her best friend Mary Searle and her daughter Lolita who still lived in South Dakota and paid us a visit in West Haven one summer. Mother made us girls modest little black sateen bathing suits with which we wore thin rubber bathing caps. Even though Lolita was only a couple of years older than me, I was in awe of her beauty, her ringlets of curls, and her talent at ballet. We are still friends. She lives in Reno, Nevada, and we correspond often.

On my seventh birthday my mother took some of her sewing earnings and bought me a beautiful scooter I had yearned for, the very best kind, and I was so thrilled that I decided it was a national holiday and I wouldn't have to go to school. I soon found out differently.

Summers in West Haven were hot but still lovely, and we kids ate slivers of ice from the back of the horse-drawn ice wagon, casually brushing off the dirt if they fell in the road. If we couldn't see the dirt, the ice was clean. Bread, milk, fruits, and vegetables were also delivered by horse and wagon, and little dogs would eat the horse manure, much to our horrified amusement. We called it "banure" because we were holding our noses.

Winters there were very cold with lots of ice and deep snow with the air so damp from the Sound, but I enjoyed it even though I suffered often with colds and laryngitis, my eyes clogged with mucous in the mornings when they would have to be opened with a warm, wet washcloth. When coughing would keep me, and the family, awake in the night, my mother would come into my bedroom, all sleepy-eyed, and give me a china cup containing warm water with a teaspoon of paregoric which would put me to sleep immediately, although I hated the taste of the mixture.

When my father came down with scarlet fever and we were quarantined and I couldn't go to school, my mother sprayed our throats with chlorine-based Zonite which I swallowed, doing me no good, but the rest of us didn't get scarlet fever, so it worked. My mother also disinfected my father's old books in the gas oven until their pages turned brown and crisp, which I enjoyed turning down at the corners, breaking them off, while reading.

Our landlady downstairs, Mrs. Benson, treated me one evening to too many hot roasted chestnuts, and I was sick all night, wishing to die, but couldn't as my mother wouldn't let me. Mrs. Benson raised chickens in the backyard, and I would go into the shed and eat some of the finer chicken-feed which I thought was tasty and unusual. I also ate the blackened ends of burnt matches as I liked the salty taste. It's a wonder I survived to a ripe, old age.

Even though my father's relatives looked down on my mother, they would come to visit us in the summer, and my mother was always nice to them, cooking, cleaning, washing, and ironing for them while they sat around visiting with each other and us children. They would also go off in my Uncle Arthur's new Pierce Arrow automobile to see the sights.

My cousin Boydie would save nickels in a baking powder can all year and then treat me to rides on the merry-go-round which played "Three O'clock in the Morning" over and over. It was a wonderful merry-go-round, and I think it was restored and taken to an amusement park in California, in more recent years, Magic Mountain, if I'm not mistaken.

While in West Haven, we experienced an earthquake. My mother was ironing, and the light bulb hanging from the ceiling above her began to sway. She gave me a strange look and said she felt dizzy. Later we learned why.

We also saw a solar eclipse, which we watched through blackened glass, and my father took some pictures which didn't turn out very well. But it was exciting and interesting.

I remember being spanked only twice in my life, and that was in West Haven. One noon on my way home for lunch, while we were still living in the house near Campbell Avenue, I stood for a long time in front of a candy/novelty store, entranced with a miniature violin and a tray of cheap, garish rings, trying to decide which one I wanted, finally arriving home where my mother was searching for me. I ran all around the yard shouting "Don't beat me, don't beat me!" until my poor mother finally caught up with me, furious for being embarrassed in front of the neighbors, and she spanked me within an inch of my life, deservedly so. No doubt she was frantic with worry, also, as even then bad things sometimes happened to little children, although it wasn't publicized in the newspapers as it is now.

The other time I got a spanking was when she looked out the window in our flat on Noble Street and saw me putting snow down a little girl's back. She didn't know that my friend had done it to me first, but when she got me into the house, she spanked me with the cloth-covered ironing cord as I huddled in a corner on the floor. She was sorry afterwards, and I never told my father. He never spanked me but pretended he would if I misbehaved. A stern look from him was enough to keep me in line.

I loved Noble School, especially learning to read, which became a passion for me the rest of my life, along with writing. And when I wore the cute little panty dresses that my mother made and embroidered for me, my teacher would take me around to show me off to the other teachers, which I enjoyed. Fortunately it didn't make the other little girls jealous, or so I thought.

While we lived in West Haven, I took piano lessons in New Haven with a teacher named Mrs. Vivier. I had an old upright piano to practice on. My mother would take me by trolley car. After my lesson, she would treat me to strawberry shortcake while she had a Coca-Cola and an aspirin for her "headache." On the way home, the stale cigar smoke in the trolley would often make me throw up on the floor.

After five years in West Haven, my father got a job in Stamford, Connecticut, where we lived at first in a little house by the Mill River. It was full of sand fleas, and my mother sprayed Flit in all the rooms at night, which we had to breathe while going to sleep. When the fleas were all gone, we moved to an apartment house, second floor, which was covered with tiny pebbles all over the stucco, which we would scrape off onto the porch floor, making it precarious to walk.

Below our apartment was the Feldman family, nice Jewish people who introduced me to matzoh, tasteless but intriguing to me. I still enjoy bland foods because of the memory.

I continued with my piano lessons and was asked to play the school piano for assembly one morning, but something was wrong with it. Pound as I would at the chosen piece, "Under the Double Eagle," no sound came out, much to my terror and embarrassment. I was soundly teased about it later.

I had my very first boyfriend in Stamford, a darling boy my age named Walter Clegg who bought me a Love Nest candy bar and later a box of chocolates at Christmas, which he hid under his coat before shyly giving it to me in front of my family. We would sit on the back fence and talk, although I don't remember about what. Just kid stuff. I was eleven years old. We also went sledding together, and he would put his arms around me while he sat in back of me on the sled and we went flying down the hill, no cars around. What a romantic moment for me!

So I was very disappointed when my father got a job as a mechanical engineer at Spicer Corporation in Plainfield, New Jersey, and we had to leave. My mother loved moving, even the packing and unpacking, so I had to take my cue from her and be resigned even though I hated leaving Stamford and Walter, my first love. And the adventurous life was over for my father. He had a growing family and had to settle down at last.

In Plainfield I attended Evergreen School. "The finest school we've ever seen," was our motto. A teacher decided I was too advanced for sixth grade. I was skipped into seventh grade, which wasn't fair to my brother Alfred, although he never complained. And it wasn't really fair to me, as I had trouble learning to parse sentences in grammar class, all new to me but not to the other students. Somehow I finally learned, but it wasn't easy.

Alfred and I always got along pretty well together, even though he liked to tease me. While we were doing the dishes, he would flick the dish towel at my bare legs at which time I would chase him all around the house. We shared our first dog, Skippy, and our first bicycle, a secondhand girl's bike, in Plainfield, where we lived in a house not far from Plainfield High School. There I "took" typing, shorthand, and Spanish after graduating from Evergreen.

I played field hockey and was devastated when I got my first "period" and my mother wouldn't let me play for several days. I was so embarrassed when she told me what was happening to me, with no advance warning. She sat on the toilet and I sat on the edge of the bathtub and cried, as she told me only the minimum, nothing about sex—never. She was too old-fashioned and shy to talk about it. So, when I was older, I had to learn from books and girl friends: the usual way, I guess, back in those days, for a lot of girls.

Baby-sitting at age eleven became a way for me to earn money for "extras." I remember sitting nervously in a big, cold house staring at an empty fireplace and a goatskin rug after I had put the two Challoner children to bed. I had to stay all night, as the parents wouldn't get home until very late. When I decided it was time for me to go to bed, I would go upstairs, undress, put on my nightie, and huddle under the covers, never hearing them come home. They surely must have been trusting to leave their children with an eleven-year-old child. What could I have done if someone had broken into the house with evil intentions?

When I sat with the two Aitken children—Jimmy and Alfred—they lived upstairs from us, so it was no problem. My parents were downstairs and could have come to my rescue. One night Mrs. Aitken left a big chocolate cake and told me I could have a piece, but I sliced off too big a chunk for me to get down. I had to flush half of it down the toilet, feeling very guilty.

Little Jimmy Aitken and his baby brother loved for me to read to them and tell them made-up stories. When I stayed overnight, in the morning Jimmy would get into bed with me and we would play "king of the mountain" with him perching on my upraised knees and sliding down. I never had enough covers to keep me warm, but I didn't dream of complaining. Mrs. Aitken had some kind of little Oriental rug that had one corner turned up. I was forever trying to smooth it down with my foot until my mother told me it was supposed to be like that.

Eventually I stopped taking piano lessons, as I wasn't very good at it and disliked practicing. My hands were too small to reach an octave comfortably. My brother had been studying the violin until one day he left his violin—borrowed from our Uncle Arthur—under a newspaper on the davenport. During one of our "romps" I sat on it and broke it in half, ending Alfred's career as a violinist, much to his regret in later years. He has always loved good music, just as our father had. My father loved symphonies and opera and Lily Pons. On Sundays he would listen to classical music on the radio until it would play in my head long after.

I never heard my parents use endearments with each other, but often my mother would call Alfred and me "honey." I was "Clara Louise" to her, although the rest of the family, all of the relatives, called me "Sister" or "Sis," as Alfred and my cousin Alfred Edgerton (Boydie) still do.

When Spicer Corporation moved from Plainfield to Toledo, Ohio, in the late 1920s, we went along, living in the Waldorf Hotel until we found a house on Overland Parkway in West Toledo. It was across the street from Lorene Braunschweiger who became a lifelong friend. She became Lorene Taylor after she married Harold Taylor, a pharmacist we both met at the University of Toledo when we were all students. Now in our early eighties, we still correspond.

Alfred and I attended Scott High School on Collingwood Avenue, our first big school. The stone steps leading to the upper floors were well-worn into grooves from the feet of all our predecessors. Again I took shorthand and typing, which stood me in good stead when I entered the University of Toledo at age sixteen (almost seventeen) in 1931.

During an English class at Scott High we were told to choose a book to read and review orally in class. My choice was one of my father's old books *The Sign At Six* by Stewart Edward White, which I thought was interesting. When I finished talking about it in class, however, the principal's daughter, who was also in that class and an intellectual snob and poet, sneered at my choice as being unworthy of notice until a kind young male student, Duane Freese, came to my rescue, saying that Stewart Edward White was "nobody's fool." He earned my everlasting gratitude. In later years, when I read White's *Arizona Nights,* I knew again what Duane was talking about.

In history class one day, a smart-aleck boy sitting next to me turned and smirked and said, "I'll bet you're a virgin." Being such a green, unsophisticated kid, I was not sure what he was talking about. I decided he was accusing me of thinking I was "holy" like the Virgin Mother, so I glared at him and said, "I am not!" I'll never forget the look on his face as he sputtered with laughter until the teacher told him to shut up. Fortunately she did not ask what the laughter was all about.

In the restrooms there was a little toilet paper dispenser near the door, where we were supposed to grab a sheet or two before heading for a stall, and one day when I was desperately trying to take sheet after sheet for my needs, a girl waiting impatiently for her turn snapped at me, "Are you planning to write a book?" Is it still that way at Scott High?

I continued to play field hockey, and I also very much wanted to become a cheerleader, as I was full to the brim with school spirit, but the teacher in charge turned me down as not having a loud enough voice, not even giving me a trial to show that I did. A big disappointment as girls nowadays know, but I got over it. Didn't I?

When I entered the University of Toledo, called T.U. back then, in the fall of 1931 when I was sixteen, going on seventeen in November, the buildings were brand new, the school having moved from smaller quarters elsewhere. It was a small school back then, there was tremendous school spirit, and everyone, it seemed, attended all the games, yelling our heads off. And everyone seemed to know everyone else. The only buildings were the tower building containing the offices, classrooms, laboratories, cafeteria, and library; and the field house. There was a football field and a field for other sports. In the spring of 1935 a Student Union was dedicated. Now there are the Glass Bowl Stadium and dozens of buildings including dormitories serving many thousands of students, and I daresay everyone doesn't know everyone, although I imagine the school spirit has continued undiminished. And I continue to check the newspapers for the scores after the football and basketball games. An article appeared in the Winter 1997 *Alumni Magazine* about me and my adventures in the Southwest after my marriage.

An Introduction

For my first year at the University, we had moved from Overland Parkway to Perth Street so that I could walk to school, but as it proved to be too unhandy for my father to get to his job at Spicer's, we moved back to West Toledo to a nice house on Royalton Road across the street from the Schneiders, a lovely family with two boys, Leo and Robert (Bob for short), with whom we played all kinds of games including horseshoes for which my Dad put up a light in the backyard so that we could play at night in the vacant lot next door.

Leo's parents and brother Bob have passed away, but Leo, in his early eighties, is one of my dearest friends in the whole world, kind and understanding, someone in whom I can confide, and we correspond and talk on the phone frequently. He was writing to me the day he received my letter telling of Monty's murder, and it devastated him so, that he was unable to finish writing beyond a final sentence expressing his grief. He has been a great comfort to me.

From Royalton Road we moved a few short blocks away to Craigwood Road where my parents had had a house built in the mid-1930s and where my brother Alfred lived until he entered a nursing home, a lovely place called Heartland Holly Glen, chosen for him by his kind and caring neighbors Marcia and Peter Benedict when he became unable to take care of himself any more. They have been wonderful friends to both of us, and I am eternally grateful to them for their kindness to Alfred.

During the summer of 1933, the Chicago World's Fair was a fascinating place to go and not too far away for Toledo citizens to attend, so our parents took Alfred and me for a three-day visit when we went to the Planetarium among other interesting things, and I had a sketch done of me in profile wearing a little cap over my curls, made by Mr. Baumgarten of Baumgarten Studio, where he was located in the General Exhibits, Pavilion 2. This picture was framed, under glass, and I still have it, here in my living room, propped in a corner on a shelf, giving me something wonderful to remember, a happy trip with my parents and brother more than sixty-one years ago. Was that really me, looking so young and pretty with smooth, unlined skin? How I have changed! Couldn't be helped.

The early 1930s were the years of the Great Depression, the banks had closed, so to earn my tuition, book, and clothes money, I went to work summers as a vacation stenographer at Spicer Corporation for sixteen dollars a week, first for my father in the Engineering Department, later in

Service and Sales as needed when the regular stenographers went on their vacations for a week or two.

During my four years at T.U., I worked as a secretary for Dean Clair K. Searles, head of the College of Business Administration, with a Service Scholarship to pay for my tuition. I studied hard and made good grades except in my second semester of Accounting when I received a generous C grade. I never did become a "Lady CPA," as my first Accounting professor, Dean Donald Parks, had hoped. It was all too confusing for me, so I turned to Secretarial Management as my major.

One of my favorite teachers was Professor of English Jessie Stafford who inspired me to become a writer. One day she read one of my essays in class, which was a nostalgic piece about my experience living by the Mill River in Stamford, Connecticut. The girl sitting next to me, named Daisy, accused me of plagiarism, saying she had read the story some place else. But Mrs. Stafford stuck up for me and compared my writing to that of Marcel Proust's Remembrance of Things Past. She knew I wasn't capable of cheating. Her faith and trust in me was a real inspiration.

During my first semester, I was invited to join three different sororities after "rushing" parties were over, and I chose Psi Chi Phi as I liked the girls there best, and it wasn't one of the "butterfly" sororities, as we called them when they were involved in mostly social activities. Wilma Liffring, later Wilma Drake when she married classmate Vern Drake, was my "big sister." She really treated me like a sister, and we still correspond or talk on the phone when she calls me on my birthday. We did have parties and dances and other social events, but we also played basketball, field hockey, archery, and softball and went swimming together. We were also good students and kept our grades up. The sororities at T.U. at that time were not "national," nor were the fraternities except for one, Sigma Delta Rho. Belonging to a sorority did me a world of good, bringing me out of my shyness and giving me lots of good friends for life.

During my youth in Toledo, we never depended on the city fathers to provide entertainment for us as young people nowadays often do when they complain that they have "nothing to do" and expect others to find entertainment for them. We had wienie roasts, picnics, and swimming parties. We belonged to church young people's societies and took part in plays; I was "Mary" in a play called "Go Slow, Mary" at the Pilgrim Congregational Church on Sylvania Avenue. We also had fun visiting each other, talking and joking and laughing in our living rooms or on front porches in the summer. We read, listened to the radio, went dancing and ice skating, and played board games, horseshoes, and tennis. We Psi Chi Phi girls attended sorority cottage on different lakes in Michigan, a big event for all of us. We found our own fun. No drinking, no drugs, at least among my friends. Hardly anyone smoked. I dated one boy who smoked and felt sick to my stomach all night. Never again. I also had one blind date with a boy who had been drinking. When I opened the door upon his arrival, he acted astonished that I wasn't ugly. Never saw him again!

After I received my Bachelor in Business Administration degree in June, 1935, I went to work for the DeVilbiss Corporation in Toledo in their Export Department for $13.50 per week, even though I could have earned more at Spicer's (which later became Dana Corporation). I wanted to be on my own.

My boss at DeVilbiss was a Spaniard, a Basque, who told me right off that his previous secretary had belonged to him "body and soul." I didn't take the hint. It was probably a joke. Who knows? After two years there, learning to answer letters from all over the world on my own and also when my boss went to Toledo, Spain, on vacation, I grew bored and quit even though I was offered a raise to keep me there.

I then went to work at Owens-Illinois Glass in downtown Toledo, in the Closure Division, where there were four bosses. My immediate boss was Thad Trotter. The other three were Eugene Hildreth, Stan Delaplane, and Bob Robinson, all very nice men. The other two secretaries were Katherine Mainz and Arlene Judy who were lovely and kind to me.

For a while my desk was by a window where I could watch the Great Lakes freighters and Coast Guard boats coming and going on the Maumee River below, and I would dream of traveling to distant places and having exciting adventures. But after the department was remodeled, my desk was moved away from the window to an area where I had only four walls and the backs of my co-workers to look at. No more dreaming.

I had stopped going to church a few years before, but now, feeling sad and disappointed at the way my life was going, I turned for comfort to a little Episcopalian church, St. Matthew's, on Sylvania Avenue. There was a fine young pastor at St. Matthew's named Charles Stires. As I had not been baptized after I was born, I had him perform that ceremony, and also my confirmation, in March, 1937. The occasion was noted in the 1929 edition of *The Book of Common Prayer and Hymnal* presented to me by my parents "with love" and inscribed, also, "With best wishes for every good thing in life on the day of your confirmation—Your friend and rector, Charles R. Stires." Later he moved away to Oradell, New Jersey, to serve at a church there, and he was greatly missed by his Toledo "flock." Everyone loved and admired him for his sincere and very moving sermons.

I did have two wonderful adventures on two vacations. One was a pre-season cruise on a Canadian steamship, which I believe was called the SS *Thunder Bay* and which carried only 300 passengers. It left from Detroit, went through Lakes Ontario and Erie, down the St. Lawrence River to Toronto, Montreal, and Quebec. I saw Niagara Falls and many lovely islands, and the other passengers and the crew were very friendly and kind. I never felt seasick, but one time I became "landsick" after returning to the ship from a day sightseeing in Montreal. I was given hot milktoast for supper that night, as I had told my waiter it always settled my stomach when I felt sick.

I would have liked to go on sailing forever, and when I returned home to a hot, empty house—no one there to greet me—I sat down and cried.

My other memorable vacation was to Potawatomie Inn on a beautiful lake in Indiana where I made friends with two other girls, and we went swimming and hiking together. We also went dancing at a place across the lake where I met a handsome, sweet young Navy Ensign Bruno Varnagaris, "Varney" for short. After the dance was over, he took me back to the inn and I never saw him again. But when I was visiting my family in December, 1941, I received a Christmas card from Varney, which had a beautiful picture of his ship, the USS *Indianapolis,* a cruiser which took part in the fighting in the Pacific against the Japanese. The postmark on the envelope was December 6, 1941!

For years I wondered if Varney had survived the sinking of the Indianapolis on July 30, 1945, when it was torpedoed by a Japanese submarine on its way from Guam to Leyte and sank in twelve minutes. Survivors weren't discovered until August 2–8, and only 316 men survived out of a total crew of 1,199, according to the Reference Department of the Prescott Library. But they informed me that Bruno Varnagaris wasn't listed among the crew, so my hope is that he was transferred to another ship and survived the war. He would be an old man now, as I am an old woman in my eighties.

Everyone in the office at Owens-Illinois smoked, the men at their desks and the girls in the restroom. The air was thick with smoke from both cigars and cigarettes, and when I went home at night, my lungs, nose and mouth, clothing, and hair and skin were saturated with stale tobacco smoke that eventually made me ill. After a year and a half I had to quit that job, never having made more than eighty dollars a month, a fair day's wages now in the 1990s.

I took the train to Detroit and went to the Henry Ford Hospital for a complete going-over. After many tests and X-rays and conferences, a wonderful doctor, James I. Baltz, M.D., to whom I am forever indebted, told me I should spend the following winter of 1940–41 in either Florida or Arizona to escape the rigors of a raw, cold winter in Toledo.

Naturally, I chose Arizona, as Florida seemed too civilized for my tastes. So, in November, 1940, I headed by train for Phoenix, then a small town of about 40,000 people where it was safe to walk around alone at night. The air was clean and clear, and the people were friendly. I loved it, was happy, and that was where my adventures finally began.

2

The Adventure Begins

I had written to the YWCA at Phoenix, Arizona, for a room reservation for the winter and traveled by train, waking up in the Pullman berth one morning when it was barely light and the train had stopped at a small desert town in New Mexico. I opened the curtain, and there was my first mountain, actually a bare, reddish sandstone hill, not really very big, but to me it loomed as big as the biggest mountain, as I had never seen one before except in South Dakota where I was too young to notice. I felt too deeply moved and excited for any more sleep.

All morning as we rushed along, I drank in the sights of the desert, rejoicing in the view of the vast, lonely, empty stretches, each barren hill, hardly daring to believe in the reality of this peaceful land, not fearing the strangeness. Indeed, I remember wondering how it would feel to get off the train in the middle of the desert and let it go on without me, watch it disappear in the distance, and then stand there all alone, a small speck under the vast, blue bowl of the sky and listen to the silence, the wonderful humming silence I had heard about, and feel something I had never felt before. But what? I didn't know, and I wanted to know. Some day I would know. And I have never forgotten the way I felt that morning.

It was a mild November evening when I arrived in Phoenix. The air was clean and clear, soft and still, as I left the train and took a taxi to the "Y" with its dim courtyard and palm trees outlined against the evening sky. A small pool was surrounded by beautiful young Mexican boys and girls talking, singing, and laughing in the soft dusk, a scene so new and so poignant that I began to feel a little lonely for the first time since leaving home. I was a stranger and didn't belong here yet.

It was a bad moment for me when the bored-looking middle-aged woman at the desk, perhaps fed up with the antics and exuberance of youth, met me as apathetically as though I had come from the next block instead of a city two thousand miles away. Later Mrs. Hanover and I became pretty good friends, but she showed no interest in me that night as she led me up to my tiny room on the second floor, unlocked the door, handed me the key, turned on the light, watched the taxi driver put my suitcases by the dresser, then left without a word.

I had to hunt up the rest room/shower facility by myself, and on my return I saw girls clustered in one of the other rooms, but they didn't make any overtures, perhaps too shy as that was also my failing in a strange, new setting.

And then the light bulb in my room chose that moment to burn out. When I hurried down to the desk to get a new bulb, Mrs. Hanover wearily told me she had no extras, that the housekeeper had them locked up and I would have to wait until morning when she showed up with the keys.

I undressed in the dark, washed at the basin in one corner of the room, crawled into bed, and cried myself to sleep. Thus began the big adventure of the city girl who wanted to live and know hardship!

But the next morning I awoke in my now sunny room with a renewed feeling of excitement, the blues of the previous night dispelled. My first day in Arizona. I still remember how it felt, the same amazed and grateful wonder, the famous Arizona sun shining out of that marvelous deep blue sky as I stepped out into the clean, pleasant city of Phoenix with its surrounding desert and hills waiting to be explored. How lucky I felt!

At first I ate my meals frugally at a drugstore counter before discovering a cafeteria not far away, also one at the nearby YMCA. After I met the other residents and the employees at the "Y," I learned that there was a small kitchen with a refrigerator and hot plate where I could cook simple foods, soups, and even a small steak occasionally when one of the girls showed me how. There were also set tubs where we could wash clothes before hanging them on the roof clotheslines where they dried in no time in the hot sun.

Luckily the "Y" charged only five dollars a week rent for a room, and groceries were cheap back then, so I didn't have to ask my parents for money very often, but they were always generous. I wanted to be as free and independent as possible.

After I met the other girls, some of whom had office jobs or were attending business college, it gave me the fun of dormitory life, visiting in each other's rooms, something I hadn't known before, having lived at home while attending college. There were also a couple of older women in residence, spending the winter away from the bitterly cold weather back East where their homes were. So I had a good variety of companionship to choose from, although I was also happy to go about alone exploring, on the well-known theory that "he travels fastest who travels alone," although my happy ramblings couldn't be described as a form of rapid travel.

Two or three weeks after my arrival, a lovely Jewish girl from New York City moved into a room down the hall, and we soon became great friends. Florence Junger was suffering from asthma and hoping that the dry desert air would give her some relief so her days were as free as mine, and before long we were going everywhere together as we seemed to have pretty much in common. She was a college graduate, a dietitian, from Hunter College. She shared my interest in the desert, enjoyed music, reading, sunbathing on the roof of the "Y," and she laughed at my jokes.

Together Florence and I started a weekly bulletin board "newspaper" called "Y's Cracks" edited by the "Two Y's Babies." The other residents pounced on each issue to see what lies we had cooked up about them each week. When we had no other news, we made some up: "All the News Unfit to Print." We also made up tasty little jokes, our version of the weather report, and rhymes about the other residents. One wistful bit of verse was inspired by the approaching marriage of one of our members:

> TO MAGGIE
> When you march on up the aisle
> Dressed in gold with matching smile
> And promise you will always be
> Full of love and loyalty,
> Then you leave for your new life
> As your William's brand new wife,
> Don't forget to heave a sigh
> For us poor spinsters at the "Y."

We did miss having boyfriends, and one day a young man from a nearby shop followed me to the "Y" after I had been out for a walk, and he came into the building and asked Mrs. Hanover who I was, but she refused to play cupid. She told me about him later, and I never saw him again.

Our greatest pleasure was our trips to the desert. Sometimes we went by bus which never took us far enough, other times resident Alice Drought (later Dr. Alice Drought) drove us around in her car. Best of all were the Dons' Club trips on Sundays. In those days the Dons' trips were not as heavily attended as they are now, so different members would provide free transportation for us poor souls without cars. Those trips were a delight, taking us far afield to ghost towns, old mines, and on up to Wickenburg, so we came to know parts of Arizona we might not have seen otherwise.

On one trip to the ghost mining town of Congress, author Oren Arnold placed his big cowboy hat on my head, gave me his rifle to hold, and posed me beside the door of a tumbledown adobe house, told me to look as though I were gunning for an outlaw named Curly Bill, and took a picture, which he sent to me later. Dressed in my linen slack suit and saddle shoes, I looked much too civilized for the part, but it was a lot of fun for a city girl.

The big Dons' trip of the winter was to the Superstitions where we hiked, pretended to prospect and find gold, ate and drank, and at dusk enjoyed the traditional "firefall" down a cliff, a marvelous end to a perfect day.

By that time Florence and the other girls and I had decided to go horseback riding which I had approached with mixed feelings, for, to me, horses were an unknown quantity, large animals of uncertain disposition. I had been on a horse only once before, at sorority cottage in Michigan, riding around a lake while wearing shorts and ending up with severe saddle sores. Now I pictured myself being bucked off into the cactus. But I bought myself a pair of Levi's and joined the party. And that is when we found Red Star Stable and Bill.

I'll never forget the way my future husband Bill (Wilfred) Parks looked when I first saw him. We took the bus down South Central Avenue toward South Mountain to the stable out on the desert amid the sahuaros, other cactus, greasewood bushes, and mesquite and ironwood trees. The stable was owned by Phoenix lawyer Dick Brumbach and his wife, and Bill was running it for them.

Bill had been camped in the desert, before applying for the job, when he had seen and reported a young woman rider abusing her horse which she had rented from Mr. Brumbach that Sunday. There was no one he had been able to hire for the job at the low "Depression" wages of fifteen dollars a month, plus duck eggs from the resident flock of ducks. As Mr.

Brumbach had only one arm, it made it very difficult for him to handle the horses. Mrs. Brumbach was an invalid.

A slender good-looking, dark-haired man about five feet eight inches in height and weighing around 150 pounds, Bill was wearing old blue-and-white striped bib overalls, a long-sleeved un-ironed blue work shirt, brown work shoes, and a marvelous big cowboy hat with the Montana "beaver slide" crease down the front. Clean-shaven, with clean hands and face, he had such an air of complete confidence and self-assurance, we were very much impressed. And we soon knew that he was a gentle-man, as well as a gentle man.

Bill was living in a tiny one-room shack not far from the stables, with no plumbing, just an outhouse nearby and an outside water hydrant. A single light bulb hung in the shack where there was just room enough for his 48"-wide metal folding cot, his card table, a folding chair, and a tiny wood-burning stove for heat in the chilly desert winter nights. Most of his belongings were stored inside his old black two-door 1928 Chevy sedan. He had no way to wash clothes except in a big galvanized metal bucket. A white enamel basin was used for sponge baths and for shaving.

He cooked his meals on a gasoline two-burner campstove, usually a pot of beans or potato and onion soup, sometimes rice and prunes, eaten with plain white bread, no butter, That was all he could afford. Supplemented by the duck eggs, of course.

For his meager wage of fifteen dollars a month and the eggs, he kept the barn and corrals clean; fed, watered, shod, curried, brushed, and saddled the twenty horses; and rented them out to the "dudes," including us girls who came to ride. Almost broke, he needed the job, and he loved it as he loved horses, having been with horses since he was born on a farm near Iuka, Kansas, and fell off his first pony at the age of two. In other words, he looked like a happy man.

He had always been an outdoor person since his farm days, living and working on ranches and farms all over the West except when he enlisted and served in the Army during World War I in France, returning home after the Armistice without having been wounded and with stories of having visited Paris and Monaco while on leave.

After we girls had made two or three visits to the stable, I learned that Bill was a writer, using his experiences as material, including having worked as a crane operator at Boulder Dam (now Hoover Dam); driving a street car in Los Angeles in 1928 and 1929, also selling real estate there briefly; and working as a guide for Riddle at Las Vegas and Death Valley;

and as a guide at Grand Canyon in the summer of 1935. He told me that he had done everything but "shine shoes and herd sheep."

He had also been working on some short stories which he sent to his friend and mentor, author Rupert Hughes in Los Angeles, for criticism which Mr. Hughes generously gave along with high praise for Bill's writing ability, telling him he would become a famous name in American letters. After Bill died, while I was sorting through his papers, I found many wonderful letters that Mr. Hughes had written to Bill. He had tried many times to market Bill's stories but without success.

Bill was also working on a novel about old Arizona, which he tentatively called "Happy Land of Hell" but later titled it *The Mestizo*, which he dedicated "To my friend Rupert Hughes" and which Macmillan published in 1955, McDonald of London, England, published in 1956, and which appeared in paperback in England, put out by Foursquare Paperbacks. Mr. Hughes wrote that he was "very flattered" to have the book dedicated to him, and that "it has had such a picturesque history I am sure it is a splendid work." Bill sent him a copy of the book and received a letter from Mr. Hughes's brother Felix to the effect that "my brother has not been well for the last two years, otherwise he would have written to you before this. Rupert wishes me to thank you for your book and hopes to be able to write to you about it one of these days." And that was the last that Bill heard from either man, sad to say. That was in April, 1955.

To get back to my story. When Bill showed me an article he had written about the Grand Canyon for a blind girl and which had been published in *Desert Magazine*, that's when I fell in love with him. I knew that he was "special."

The first time I rode at Red Star, Bill put me on a gentle horse to start out with, a pretty little buckskin named Diane, and assured me that I would do fine. Later he told me I was a "natural-born rider" which made me feel better, and I graduated to more spirited horses as time went on. I still remember the names of some of the Red Star horses: Duke, Brumbach's own horse; Fox, Mrs. B.'s horse which would rear up at a signal as Bill demonstrated for us so that we could take pictures, much to our delight; Paddy, Tony, Queen, Princess, Bay Cricket; Gray Cricket for children if they promised to treat him right as he was old; Dan, Teddy, Bally who had to be killed later when a girl ran him into a car while galloping heedlessly down a wash into the road; and Chapo, Bill's favorite which "rode like a rocking chair."

Bill would use Chapo to chase after troublesome riders, searching them out after he climbed up an the bale stack and looked around over the desert where they were riding. Prospective riders would promise to behave, but they didn't always keep their promises, giving Bill extra trouble and work which he didn't need. Arguments and near-fights would ensue, but most riders were pretty nice.

In March we girls from the "Y" went with Bill on an evening ride and campfire cookout in a lovely, clean sandwash surrounded by mesquite trees and greasewood bushes, and when I handed Bill a box of Fig Newtons for dessert, his hand took hold of mine, our eyes met for a long moment in the firelight, and I took that as a sign that he also cared for me.

And he did. After a while, when we went out to the stable to ride, I stayed behind sometimes to visit with Bill while he worked on his car engine, as he was planning to leave for the Grand Canyon in April. We decided that I would go along with a girl friend, Florence Junger if she agreed, as chaperone. To see if I liked his way of life, camping out, cooking on a campfire or campstove, living in a tent or under the stars when the weather was nice, then get married and head for Idaho to work in the sugar beet fields.

Thrilled and excited about the coming adventure, I had no misgivings, sure that I would love his kind of life, and I had trouble sleeping until the day we three would take off. And Florence loved the idea, sharing my excitement.

I had been writing faithfully to my parents and brother two or three times a week on my little portable Underwood typewriter, but when they received my letter about our plans and my intention to get married, no matter what, they were shocked. My father wrote me a beautiful, tender letter asking me to consider carefully what I was going to do but expressing faith in my judgment, and my mother begged me to wait, to come home for a visit first and get married in the fall if I was still sure that that was what I wanted to do. Or if I wanted to stay in Phoenix for the summer, they would support me financially. I learned much later that my mother phoned my Aunt Lydia in Cleveland and cried over the phone while telling her my plans. I think my father rather envied me my impending adventure, and, as I refused to give in, he gave me his blessing, so my mother relented in spite of her doubts and worries. Another thing that bothered them at the time was that my brother Alfred had just been inducted into the Army. Two blows at one time.

The only real "date" Bill and I had was to meet his beloved Aunt Florence Hayes of Phoenix, in Encanto Park to see the wood duck, a lovely visit, although she didn't know about our plans. We didn't tell her, just in case things didn't work out. But after we were married and wrote her the news from Idaho, she sent us a note which said "Bless you, my children" at the beginning of her loving message. Bill's mother, Nellie Knapp Parks, was Aunt Florence's sister who had died in childbirth when Bill was six years old, so Aunt Florence became like a mother to both of us and a best friend for me in spite of her being thirty-four years older.

Bill's father, John Parks, was still alive and living in Bend, Oregon, with Bill's younger brother Herschel.

There were three older brothers, Lloyd, Harry, and Russell, and a sister, Lucile, younger than the boys. Years after we were married I did get to meet Lloyd and Herschel, also Lucile, but not Bill's father or Harry and Russell. And after both Bill's father and mine had died, I learned that they had both been born in Ft. Wayne, Indiana, but it was too late to learn if their families had been acquainted. A disappointment to me, and our fathers would have been so interested in the coincidence, I'm sure.

On the seventh of April, dressed in our blue jeans, western shirts, hats, and scarves, Florence and I loaded our suitcases and my typewriter into Bill's car, the "Horizon Hunter," which was already pretty much over-loaded, inside and on the running boards, fenders, and bumpers, with all he owned—big canteens, food boxes, a metal chuck box, a small trunk containing his manuscripts and writing materials, typewriter, suitcases, bedding, tent, metal cot, shovel, axe, tool box, and a gas can for white gas to use in the campstove.

A tight squeeze.

Wedged in the front seat beside Bill, Florence and I made it more than a load, but the poor old car never groaned. We were on our way.

As we had had a rather late start, we decided to make "dry camp" the first night on the desert north of Wickenburg at the foot of Yarnell Hill in a Joshua tree forest. We heated some canned food over a campfire, ate hungrily of the simple fare, rinsed our dishes with water from one of the three big canteens, relieved ourselves in the dark in back of bushes away from camp, brushed our teeth; then, still dressed, settled ourselves to sleep on blankets and tarp, under and over us, on the hard sand.

The desert night air was cold, the ground getting harder as the night progressed, but the coyotes sang, the stars were bright, I was lying next to the man I loved, and I was happy. We didn't sleep much, especially

Florence whose asthma kept her awake, but she was a good sport, using her inhaler without complaint.

Early the next morning after a leisurely campfire breakfast of coffee, boiled eggs, and toast, we broke camp, packed the car, and headed for the mountains. Now I was to learn for the first time what it was like to pray an old car, too heavily loaded, up a steep grade.

Halfway up Yarnell Hill, far above the desert with its tiny ribbons of road and thinly scattered bits of buildings, one of our tires went flat, our first mishap of the trip. Cars whooshed past and huge semi-trailer trucks ground slowly by on the narrow two-lane road while Florence and I stood guard up and down the road, ready to warn Bill if danger threatened, while he calmly changed the tire on the edge of the near-precipice. His wonderful strength, just what my wretched nerves needed. How could I worry about anything if he didn't? He knew what he was doing and how to do it. He had done it all before.

It was dark and cold when we finally reached the Grand Canyon public campground, but Bill knew through previous experience just where the best campsites were, protected from the wind, yet handy to water and restrooms.

Expertly he pitched his small five-by-seven "car tent," set up the cot and bedding, and made camp while Florence and I struggled to fix supper by the flickering light of a campfire built from wood Bill gathered from the ground nearby. It was so cold that we had to sleep in our jeans, shirts, and jackets as we had the night before, piling on all available blankets, Bill in the front seat of the car, we girls on the cot inside the tent.

Next morning our bones ached from both the cold and the unyielding link springs of the cot, which we could feel plainly through the layers of canvas, cot pad, and quilt which constituted our mattress. Florence's asthma was worse; although she bravely tried to hide it, I could see that she was suffering. I felt sorry for her, but as soon as the stiffness wore out of my bones, I couldn't help feeling wonderfully alive and happy. The air was cold and crisp and fragrant with the smell of pine and juniper, I was wildly hungry for the first time in months, and I had Bill to smile at as I began my first real lesson in campfire cookery.

Bill was tolerant of my ignorance and mistakes, seeing my eagerness to learn, my love for his wilderness country, my willingness to make the best of an uncomfortable situation. We three spent that first morning getting our first views of Bill's beloved Grand Canyon, which made us gasp in awe and amazement at the incredible sight spread out before us. Florence admitted it was all well worth her suffering.

In the afternoon while Florence tried to get some much needed rest, Bill and I hiked down the Bright Angel trail, turned off on a deer trail, and sat together on a rock ledge, away from passing hikers, sheltered from the wind, feasting our eyes on the beauty stretched out in the near and far distance before us. Bill had hiked hundreds of miles on Canyon trails, and he told me quietly of the things he had seen and learned, while I listened eagerly as the magnificent spectacle became more friendly and intimate as seen through his eyes.

It was then that we decided we would make our life together. We had no doubts as we kissed, a tender romantic moment. I was never happier.

We stayed on at the Canyon two more days, the weather becoming colder, and then one morning we awoke to a snow storm. Poor Florence! Poor us, too. I felt frozen through as I tried to fix our meals with my gloves on, while Bill had come down with a bad cold from having slept in the car without sufficient covers. We could have rented a cabin, but we didn't want to spare the money, so we decided that as the Canyon was now fogged-in, we might as well leave, take Florence to Williams where she could catch the bus to Phoenix as planned, while we headed for Kingman where we would be married before we continued with our journey north.

By now, Florence was pretty much fed up with the rigors of camping, and I could see that the romance of the life was no longer apparent to her when we parted in the cafe in Williams where we ate lunch. In her eyes instead was a look that plainly said, "I hope you know what you're doing," and she wept as she kissed me good-bye.

And then Bill and I were off into a future as hazy as the snowstorm into which we were heading, but I felt no fear, only a calm, sure happiness that I was doing the right thing, for beside me was the man I loved and trusted taking me into a life that promised, not financial security perhaps, but security of the spirit, a life that would be full of love and beauty and adventure, with possible hardship as the price I was only too willing to pay. That feeling I had had back in Phoenix wasn't false, it was real and deep, and it had finally, unerringly, led me to this moment.

3

Married in Blue Jeans

After we left Williams, the swirling snow became thicker, making the trip through the mountains hazardous, but luck was with us. There were few other cars on the road, and we made it over the steep grades and around the curves without mishap, although we had to go so slowly that it was night by the time we reached Seligman where we stopped for hamburgers and coffee before going on, in both our minds the thought that we hadn't made it to Kingman in time to be married that day.

Bill's cold was much worse, he was feverish and miserable, the car was drafty and chilly as it had no heater, and then in the lower country the snow turned to a cold rain. When we reached Peach Springs, we saw an auto camp and knew that we must stay there for the night, convention be hanged. Bill needed nursing care, our funds were limited, we could afford only one cabin which we rented as "man and wife." We certainly looked married with all that luggage and camping equipment, and we already felt married in our hearts. What a cozy home that warm cabin was after the cold, wet night we had just come through.

Bill wasn't any better in the morning after a restless night, even with my arm around him for comfort. We knew that he had 'flu and not just a cold, but we decided to go on. After a nourishing breakfast of hot Cream of Wheat, eggs, coffee, and vanilla wafers, prepared and eaten in the tiny kitchenette, we loaded up the car and were in Kingman by noon.

It was April 12th, 1941, a date that would live in our minds and hearts for fifty-four years.

Bill asked the marriage license clerk if there was any place on the license where you had to state that the bridegroom had a cold. And then we were married, Bill in his hiking clothes, me in my flannel shirt, blue jeans, and peasant scarf but feeling no less married for that. Dear Judge Wishon who married us never looked at our clothes, he looked at our faces and seemed satisfied with what he saw shining out of our eyes, and he kissed me.

By mistake (?) Bill kissed me twice during the ceremony, once when he placed the plain gold band I had chosen on my finger, and again when we were pronounced husband and wife. It was a lovely wedding even if the bride did wear overalls instead of white satin and lace as my mother and aunts had hoped for.

After lunch we drove west from Kingman into the hills where Bill suddenly stopped the car, got out, and walked off into the desert where he picked my wedding bouquet, a lovely bunch of large, deep purple asters, my favorite flower from that day on.

We stopped briefly at Boulder Dam where Bill had worked when it was being built, first stamping concrete, later as a crane operator until the carbon monoxide made him too ill to work. By the time we reached Las Vegas, Bill's chills and fever got the best of him, so we stopped at the Old Ranch Auto Court on the outskirts of town under some big cotton-woods. Mr. and Mrs. Ed Gates were old friends of Bill's and were the owners and operators of Old Ranch. They gave me some equipment I needed for nursing Bill back to health.

Bill undressed to his long johns and staggered into bed, and I took over, first placing my precious bouquet in a jar of water. We were in what was called a "summer cabin," having screens and canvas flaps instead of windows, but a small wood stove kept us comfortable in the chilly desert night so long as I stoked it with the wood provided, off and on when needed. And it came in useful for cooking our meals.

For supper I prepared a pot of thick, nourishing potato soup, adding a can of oysters, which was our favorite camping dish which Bill had taught me to fix, I hadn't eaten potato soup before meeting Bill, but this dish tasted like food for the gods, with my new outdoor appetite.

Next morning after breakfast, I cleared away the dishes, then attended to Bill's needs, making him as comfortable as possible, then walked in to Vegas to shop for groceries and medicine, which I decided should be a thick T-bone steak, butter, bananas, and other strengthening foods. With my arms loaded, I wandered in and out of the small gambling places, watching with curiosity and fascination the great variety of gamblers, in-cluding housewives, throwing their money down the different fancy "rat holes" the town offered. But I wasn't tempted to follow their example. I knew that Bill had only about ten dollars left after paying for gas, oil, food, and cabin rent, while I had around thirty dollars in my purse (I accused Bill of marrying me for my money), and if we had car trouble or other emergencies, our funds could disappear rapidly. I guess I was too dumb or naive to worry about our financial status. As soon as he was well, we would start camping again and our expenses would be at a minimum, and I knew that everything was going to work out all right. I never doubted it for a moment. My faith never wavered.

In a few days Bill was well again although still pretty shaky, so we left Las Vegas and drove north to an old campsite of Bill's on the desert near Glendale, Nevada. We called it the Camp of the Old Mormon Water Wheel as there was an ancient creaking water wheel making trickling music not far off.

This was also the Camp of the Can Opener Skunk. One night we heard something rustling around in one of our grub boxes, which was sitting on the ground near the car, and Bill said drowsily that he bet it was a skunk, and I said, "Well, he'll have to have a can opener to get anything to eat in there."

As we planned to stay at this camp for several days, we set up the tent just for privacy while taking sponge baths and changing clothes, but the cot was under the stars as the weather was mild and clear. Once again I heard the thrilling howl and yap of the coyote echo through the hills and breathed the fresh sweet desert air, waking in the night to see the stars on their timeless journey through the heavens.

And, at last, I heard the wonderful humming silence of the desert and the peace it brings to one's whole being. Now I felt part of the desert and one of its creatures. Homeless, almost without funds, only an old car for transportation, the future uncertain, I was completely happy with Bill and his companionship and love and faith in our future.

Although we had the campstove and enough white gas for it, I preferred the continuing novelty and fun of cooking over a campfire, bringing sticks of wood back with me from my walks, and before long I became quite handy at building fires and cooking over coals. I enjoyed it so much that I wouldn't let Bill help me any more, which didn't displease him one bit.

Our meals were simple, potato/oyster stew, or beans; hot cereal for breakfast along with eggs boiled in the coffee water and bread toasted over coals. Everything tasted far better than anything I had eaten in the most expensive restaurants. Boiled coffee, cowboy style, was pretty strong, but it hit the spot after a night in the open.

Our evenings spent talking in front of the glowing campfire coals were much finer entertainment than any stage plays, movies, or dances I had ever attended. Bill's tales about the West and its history and legends were of great interest to me, as well as his stories about himself and the people he had met during his adventures and the different jobs he had held, including cotton picker, lettuce trimmer, fruit tramp, beet thinner, wheat harvesting, working with horses at farms and ranches, the crane operator job at Boulder Dam, and the street car stint in Los Angeles. Also as a guide in Death Valley and the Grand Canyon. What a wealth of experience to use in his writing! It was all so new and strange to me, so different from anything I had ever known or heard about in my sheltered life. Bill told me also that he hadn't gone any farther than eighth grade in school, for, when he and his brother Herschel had gone from the farm to the high school in town, the students made fun of them, so the two brothers rebelled, went home, and never went back. Bill was self-taught through much time spent in libraries and the books he acquired. His interests were varied and wide: astronomy, geology, botany, biology, animals, birds, butterflies, people; name it, he studied it.

One thing important that Bill didn't have to teach me was to leave Nature's parks and gardens out in the wild as unspoiled and lovely as I found them. We buried everything (trash, garbage, and "bathroom business," as Bill called it) burned all papers, and kept our camp and surrounding area as neat and clean as we had found it.

4

The Hard Work Begins

After a few lazy days loafing in the sun and studying the birds and desert plants and insects, prospecting for gold and silver without success, Bill had his strength back, so we broke camp and started north again. When we drove up on the bench above the Virgin River, we caught glimpses of the Valley of Fire which Bill promised to show me some day. So many places to see, so many things to do, would we live long enough? Now I wanted to live forever.

And then we had our first argument. We stayed for two nights with Otto Fife and his family, old friends of Bill's in Cedar City, Utah, as Otto wanted to drive us out to see his lead mine. That first morning when we went to make the bed, Bill insisted that the bedspread belonged a certain way while I insisted just as positively that it should be the other way, that he had it wrong side out. He settled it by calling in Otto's wife who said I was right, whereupon we laughed and kissed and I forgave him, for how was he to know any better when his usual bedspread was a piece of canvas?

After traveling and camping out in Utah for several days, we finally reached Filer, Idaho, where Bill planned to work in the beet fields, so now I began to know the other, more sober side of his life—hard work. And how hard he did have to work to earn his fun and adventures and freedom!

We moved into a tiny one-room shack on the Hawkins farm, for which we paid one dollar a week rent plus fifty cents a month for light, one bare bulb hanging from the ceiling. Water was free—if you walked a hundred feet with a bucket or canteen and pumped it out of the ground. And, of course, there was the usual outhouse not too far away, to use in good weather or bad.

30

After cleaning out the cabin with a shovel and stub of broom and some water, and covering the holes in the walls with newspaper tacked up, we carried in our cot, bedding, card table, folding chair, and grub boxes. The campstove sat on a low shelf in one corner and under it went our food and dish boxes. A straight wooden chair and a small trash burner for heat came with the shack which was now so crowded that if one of us wanted to walk around, the other had to sit on the bed. Home, sweet home! Not.

Bill didn't like it, and neither did I. We much preferred living out-of-doors, but there was no place to camp. We were surrounded by farms, so we accepted the inevitable and made the best of it. We could have rented a better cabin, in Filer, but we had to save enough money for our trip south in the fall; we had no desire to be caught in an Idaho winter. A few months in the desert were well worth any temporary discomfort, and from now on, wherever Bill was, that was home. I had no need for luxuries.

Our first night in the shack, however, was what we called ever after "one night of horror." After the light was out, we discovered that we had guests: mice, dozens of them. Even though I am not afraid of mice, I object to their jumping up onto my pillow and tugging at my hair to get nesting materials just as I am about to drop off to sleep. Next day Bill plugged all the holes and cracks, and a small "trapline" finished off those in residence.

As it was still too early in the spring for the sugar beet thinning, Bill worked at odd jobs for one of the nearby farmers for a few days until finally he gathered together a crew of beet-thinners, migrant field workers; contracted for fields with several farmers; and the work began. After watching for a while, I begged to help. It didn't look all that hard. So Bill bought a short-handled hoe for me and showed me how to chop out the tiny beet plants every fourteen or sixteen inches with my right hand, while the left hand grabbed up any extras snuggled too close to the single beet that would become the mature one to be harvested in the fall. All this was done, of course, in either a backbreaking crouch, moving along as rapidly as possible, passing one foot in front of the other, known as the "Filipino Over-Step"; or pulling yourself along on one knee, the "Mexican Crawl," either method slow murder to muscles. Not "all that hard"? Tell me about it.

I chose the "Filipino Over-Step" as being easier on my one lone pair of jeans, and before long I was taking pride in the fact that I could thin beets as fast, and often more cleanly, than any "fruit tramp," although I couldn't work very long at a time. And, oh, getting out of bed in the morning! I could hardly move and went about my breakfast chores in a half-crouch until I limbered up.

But I loved going to the fields and working with Bill, keeping him company, and we made jokes about how long the rows were and would think up our own definitions of beet-thinner's terms, such as, a "row" is a strip of ground which is twice as long from the middle to the end as it is from the beginning to the middle. "Tangled-up doubles" were a device of the devil to make us earn our magnificent wage of eight dollars an acre, while the "devil" was whichever farmer we were working for at the moment, usually referred to as "the old devil" when he started down a row peering at one's work to make sure you hadn't left any "doubles." They seemed surprised that they didn't have to complain about the work of Bill's "city girl wife," even if she wasn't much of a "hand."

I realized, of course, that I was quite a curiosity to the farm folk around there who had known Bill from his previous bachelor existence. What could Bill have been thinking of, they must have wondered, marrying a girl who wasn't much of a hand in the fields, acted afraid of cattle, couldn't mend his clothes worth a darn (pun intended) and spent her spare time wandering idly in country lanes or sitting on a fence watching sunsets or the chickens and cows eat? Even one big bull, alone in his small pasture, expressed loud displeasure at my bright blue jacket and threatened to charge through the fence at me as Bill and I wandered by one Sunday afternoon.

And I made mistakes which the neighbors knew nothing about. There must be a special angel watching over young brides to protect them from the consequences of their ignorance. One day a farmer's wife, Mrs. Holman, gave me a quart jar of her home-canned string beans. As we had no ice box, I kept the opened jar on a shelf for three days, using some beans each day until they were gone, Why we didn't become victims of deadly botulism, I'll never know.

Our life on that farm, although simple, was different from anything I had ever known. No plumbing, no bathroom, any bathing had to be done as sponge baths using an enamel wash basin of water heated over the campstove. No washing machine nor set tubs, just a big galvanized metal bucket to wash and then rinse our clothes. Taking pity on me, Bill decided that washing would "wear out" his overalls, so I didn't have to struggle with them. When they became ragged and dirty, he bought new ones. Same with my jeans. But it was clean, country dirt I would console myself and try to ignore it. We wore our clothes un-ironed, of course. Our "best clothes," Bill's hiking breeches and my linen slack suit, were rarely worn so needed neither washing nor ironing, as we had no social life, nor wanted one.

Knowing little about mending or sewing, I had a hard time patching Bill's overalls and mending his socks, but I did my best. But when he teased me about the square white patches in his pants and referred to them as "windows," I threatened to embroider lace curtains with faces looking out, so, pretending alarm, he desisted.

Outside of watching the beautiful flaming sunsets and taking walks, we had no recreation or entertainment, not even a radio. Not wanting to spend our hard-earned money for a daily newspaper, we would stroll over to the nearest gas station in the evening to read theirs as Bill was very much concerned about the war in Europe. Sometimes we would spare a nickel for a cup of sherbet or a candy bar, our only luxuries. We were saving toward something we wanted more, a winter in Arizona on the desert. It was worth any sacrifice, and doing without luxuries was an intriguing experience, an adventure to me, getting down to the basic essentials in life. I discovered that a person could be happy with a roof to keep the rain off and walls to keep out the cold, simple food, one outfit of clothes at a time, and even a hard bed to sleep on, if he has one other ingredient: a loving, congenial companion. No matter how doubtful the future, no one could feel insecure or deprived under such circumstances.

Curious about our expenses, I kept a list for one month of all the money we spent. It came to $29.44, including rent, lights, gas and oil, and food for two hard-working people. I could hardly believe it. Of course, we purchased our milk at half-price at the farmhouse and received an occasional gift of home-churned butter, eggs, cornbread, and home-canned fruits and vegetables, but not enough to make much difference.

And to save money, I learned to cut Bill's hair, our first barber shop under an apple tree by a straw stack. Not a very good job, but I improved in time and became Bill's barber for the fifty-four years we were together.

I was quite interested in the other migrant workers and enjoyed talking to them in the field during lunch. Two of the men, "Big Red" and Ike, who didn't seem to fit in with the rest yet worked very well in the field, revealed rather sinister pasts during their talks with us and with each other. The younger man, Ike, wore a nice-looking snap brim felt hat and looked almost handsome until he took his hat off and you could see how the strange shape of his head gave him a rather menacing aspect. But he was quiet-spoken with Bill and me, proved to be one of Bill's best workers, and never gave any trouble. I think we got along so well with him because Bill praised his work and treated him as a fellow human being in spite of the man's shady past.

After beet-thinning was over, we were able to straighten up at last, for now came the weeding of the beet fields with long-handled hoes. For this work, no crew was needed, and Bill and I hired out alone to do certain fields, Bill doing most of the work, of course.

When the weeding was over, a nearby farmer asked Bill to help with haying. Bill was reluctant to work for this man as he had been a hard person to deal with and wouldn't pay much, but finally, as there was no other work right then, Bill consented, to his later sorrow.

As Bill had expected, the farmer drove him too hard, the hay dust irritated his sinuses, and it was such a hot day that by noon Bill had had two nose bleeds. Then, in the early afternoon, came catastrophe. Some rotten equipment gave way and Bill fell, hitting the base of his spine on a two-by-eight. He was in such agony at first that he could hardly move and could no longer work. Finally he staggered home by himself and dropped face down onto the bed, his nerves shot by the pain.

That night the farmer stopped by, talked uneasily for a few minutes, carefully avoiding the subject of Bill's accident and the extent of his injury, then gave Bill fifty cents for his "half-day's work." Bill was so stunned by such treatment, he couldn't think, but after the farmer had left, he said he should have thrown the money in the miserly old wretch's face. And for several years Bill continued to have some trouble with his back as a result of that accident.

For days he was in such misery he couldn't work or even sleep, and finally he went in to Twin Falls to consult a doctor, but instead of helping Bill, the fool doctor punched and prodded him and told him he had a bad appendix which should come out! As for the spine, Bill mustn't work for six weeks. Five dollars, please. Five whole dollars, for what?

Desperate, Bill found another doctor, this one informing him that he could get him into the Veterans' hospital in Boise for treatment, as Bill had told him that he had served in the Army in France during World War I. A hospital room? Four walls? No birds or trees or sunsets or mountains to look at, just a ceiling and four walls, and no telling what they might do to him. Appalled, Bill decided to let his old friend Mother Nature do the healing.

After a conference, consulting our finances, we decided to leave Idaho temporarily for a camping trip into the mountains of central Nevada. Not knowing exactly where we were headed or what we would find, we loaded the Horizon Hunter once more with all of our belongings and pointed her south, glad to be on the road again.

5

Vacation in Paradise

Bill was in a lot of pain and very nervous as we drove through Wells, Nevada, that first evening when suddenly a car careened out of a side street and almost hit us which upset Bill so much that he became violently ill, so after driving a few miles farther, we turned off on a dirt road leading to the hills, parked the car, and decided to spend the night sitting up. Bill was just too sick and miserable to help me make camp.

Propping pillows at our backs, we slept in fits and starts, waking often to hear coyotes yapping after jackrabbits in the nearby hills. I twisted and turned, stiff and cramped, trying to get comfortable, tempted to spread a tarp and blanket on the ground and stretch out, but not wanting to risk unknown territory alone nor disturb Bill, I stayed put.

After what seemed years, it was dawn, and while Bill was deep in exhausted sleep, I heard a weird roaring noise moving toward us down the canyon, unlike anything I had ever heard before. Frightened and nervous after a wretched night, I sat and shivered, hating to awaken Bill, but finally in desperation I did, just before the source of the terrible noise came into sight, a huge, ill-tempered, old curly-haired bull who wandered by our car bellowing, without a glance at us.

I laughed hysterically in relief, and even Bill was amused in spite of his misery. As it was now daylight and further sleep impossible, I suggested that we get out the campstove and grub box and I would fix breakfast. It was such a beautiful, quiet morning there in our secluded nook that we couldn't help but enjoy ourselves and begin to feel better as we ate our leisurely meal at our card table, then lounged aimlessly in the warm sunshine before packing up our equipment and supplies.

When we reached Ely, Nevada, we filled our big canteens with water and bought the supplies we knew we would need for the next six weeks: flour, sugar, lard, salt, coffee, rice, potatoes and onions, canned milk, canned oysters, beans and prunes, baking powder, and eggs.

Then, headed away from civilization into the mountains, we planned to camp at the best place we could find near water. On and on we drove over the rough dirt roads, hitting washboard stretches that threatened to shake our outfit to pieces, passing small isolated settlements, until finally we reached the mountains. Would our heavily loaded car make the steep, winding grades? That question was always foremost in our minds, for not to do so could mean disaster.

"They never made a better motor than they put in these '28 Chevys," Bill would remark encouragingly as we strained forward as if to help the stout little car in its earnest efforts to top each hill.

Wondering if we would find a good campsite before darkness fell, suddenly we rounded a curve and there before us was the prettiest little canyon in all of God's country, with lush green fields and orchards and a rushing mountain stream of clean, clear water at the bottom of the canyon, while pines and junipers, cactus and sage covered the slopes of the hills. This was it! And we had arrived without disaster. Bill began to feel better as we drove slowly along the narrow dirt road, exclaiming over the beauty of the place. Who could have guessed such a charming spot could be hidden in these mountains which looked so barren from the highway? When we stopped at a small fruit ranch half-way up the canyon to get information about possible camping, we learned that this was Adaven—Nevada spelled backwards—and we met the rancher and his wife, Ralph and Peggy Huber, two of the nicest and most hospitable people we could ever hope to know. They immediately invited us to camp in their orchard where we would have ready access to good water in the stream nearby, dry wood in nearby hills for campfires, and also all the fruit we wanted as soon as it ripened! Apples, peaches, pears, and cherries. Paradise!

Incredulous at our good fortune, we drove down into the orchard and set up our bed under an apple tree and the tent nearby for privacy while bathing and changing clothes.

This was the medicine Bill needed. Each morning he awoke feeling refreshed and stronger, resting most of the time at first during the day. But after a while we began to take short hikes together, prospecting for gold; hunting for Indian ruins and caves and searching for artifacts; studying the flowers, plants, and birds; and stalking the deer for the sheer joy of seeing the beautiful wild creatures. On one walk an angry falcon hawk swooped down at our heads, shrieking at us as we came too close to his nest. He could have inflicted real damage to our eyes if we hadn't dodged and hurried on. During long evenings we sat by our campfire and talked, or visited at the house with Ralph and Peggy.

I did all my cooking over a campfire at a rock fireplace Bill constructed just outside the orchard but close enough to our camp for carrying supplies and utensils. I made bread in our Dutch oven, the first time I had used it. My initial effort was an extravagant, egg-rich Sally Lunn suggested by my only cookbook, but as I didn't know how to "regulate" the temperature of my oven, how many or how few coals to pile under and over it, nor how long to bake the bread, we opened the lid to a blackened, smoking mess. My next effort was a plain, sober biscuit dough, no eggs, and profiting by the previous experience, this loaf, although quite brown, was pronounced a success. In fact, our outdoor appetites called it fit for a king. Eaten with applesauce made from the early apples that fell on our bed, and butter purchased at half-price from the Hubers, Dutch oven bread made a wonderfully satisfying meal.

To augment our diet, Ralph would sometimes present us with a round steak, luscious deep red meat, from his underground cellar. He called it "beef," and we asked no questions. Other times Bill would take our .22 rifle and get us a cottontail rabbit to stew or fry.

One day a Los Angeles dentist and his young son visited the ranch, and they went out into the hills with a gun. After a while we heard a shot, and eventually the two returned empty-handed. Bill overheard the man telling Ralph that he had wounded a doe but couldn't find her. Hungry for fresh meat and feeling pity for the wounded animal, Bill offered to track her in return for a share of the meat.

The visitor scoffed at the idea of Bill's tracking the doe in the thick brush, and at first he refused to describe where he had shot her. But Ralph talked him into it, and Bill went off on foot with Ralph's rifle while I waited back in camp, full of confidence in Bill who could track like an Indian.

Sure enough, in about an hour, here came Bill with the news that he had tracked the deer by continually "cutting for sign," following bits of broken brush when he could see no more blood, and he finally found her lying wounded in the brush, whereupon he shot her in the head to end her suffering.

Instead of being grateful, the city man bawled Bill out for killing the deer so that she couldn't be bled properly. And Ralph Huber, gentleman that he was, kept out of the argument, brought out his horse, and went after the carcass. That night we dined luxuriously on young deer liver, than which there surely is no better meat.

Next day, with the meat butchered out and safely stored in the cellar, the head, hide, and hooves buried deep in the ground away from coyotes, who should come along but the game warden and his wife! What if they had arrived the day before? Dreadful thought—a fine and/or jail? We couldn't afford it. Although the game warden was said to be lenient with locals protecting their crops from deer, he would have liked nothing better than to pin something illegal on an outsider.

Evidently he suspected nothing. He pitched his tent in the orchard not far from our camp, then borrowed Ralph's horse to ride off into the mountains to a mining camp, leaving his wife at the ranch to visit with Peggy.

Meanwhile, that morning Peggy had given us a mouthwatering package of T-bone steaks which we decided we had better have for lunch while the warden was away. The delectable smell of the frying meat must have permeated the air for miles around, for it not only attracted hundreds of flies, forcing us to eat behind the mosquito bar of our tent, but also brought the game warden's wife who came wandering casually through the orchard, peering at the nearly opaque curtain of the mosquito bar which hid us from her view.

We were not surprised that evening when the warden himself walked into our camp and glanced at our supper preparations while he chatted, but all that met his roving eye was a lovely, innocuous batch of golden brown pancakes. Shortly, unrewarded, he returned to his own campfire and bothered us no more. In the morning he and his wife were gone, and once again the tantalizing, illegal fragrance of frying venison enticed the entire fly population of the surrounding hills.

Each day Mother Nature was working her magic, and Bill was feeling more like his old self all the time, although he still felt some pain in his back. But now he could hike for a whole day in the hills, and we were confident that when we returned to Idaho for the beet harvest, the two of us working hard could make our winter stake.

The week before we left, Ralph and Peggy took us on a trip in their pickup truck over the mountains to a silver mining camp where Bill and I were charmed with the arrangements in the miners' roomy shack, the metal-covered work table big enough for cutting up a whole side of beef, the handy shelves and cupboards for dishes, utensils, and food supplies, the big wood-burning range, and all kinds of space to work in, while outside were the mountains and desert for a front yard, a valuable mine to provide them with a more than adequate living, and wonderful peace and privacy. In spite of the isolation, we couldn't help wishing that this spread could have been ours. Here were freedom and adventure and a whole world of mountains and desert to feast our eyes on.

In spite of the fruits and vegetables, milk and butter, and occasional meat given to us, within six weeks our own supplies of other foods ran low, and we regretfully realized it was time to leave. Bill had his health and strength back, the beet harvest was approaching, and we knew we must return to Idaho.

Once more it was that inevitable moment when we had to part with good friends. We had lost our hearts to the Hubers, and were sad to leave, for we knew that we might return only in memory, no matter what extravagant promises we made to the contrary.

Loaded down with gifts of fruit and sweet corn, we slowly made our way out of the ranch yard, waving our hands until we were out of sight, then headed the Horizon Hunter up the canyon, having decided to go out the other way, over the "divide," and down into Railroad Valley.

6

Back to Work

Once again our over-loaded outfit barely made it in low gear over a steep mountain grade, and we breathed a deep sigh of relief as we started down into the valley. As usual, we traveled slowly, and it was late afternoon when Bill sighted a likely looking gold prospect in the hills to the east. We turned off onto a little-used dirt road and drove for a few miles until we came to a small mining camp. Our best prospecting always turned out to be on someone else's claim, hence worthless to us.

The miner, named Steele, a lonely middle-aged man with only a small dog for company, cordially invited us to camp with him for the night, which we were only too glad to do. It was always a treat for us to talk to lone prospectors, miners, and ranchers off in the hills, in mining camps, and ghost towns, and they invariably welcomed our company. They could see, not only by our old car and camping gear, but by our manner that we were "one of them." Proud I was not to be classed with the city dude.

In return for this miner's hospitality, I dug into our meager supplies and prepared a good supper for all of us, serving most of our sweet corn and slicing up a big bowl of fresh peaches, both of which were a rare treat for this man of the hills. Moths fluttered around the oil lamp and danced along the edges of our plates as we ate and talked and laughed, Steele telling us stories of his life and confiding some of his secrets to us as we became good friends.

We were interested to learn that our host had run a hundred-mile trap line with his old truck, trapping coyotes whose bounty helped pay for his mining supplies. He had also "skunked" some rich city dudes by salting a gold mine and selling it to them. They thought they were "skunking" him in return by getting the mine for almost nothing.

To cap the evening, Steele presented us with a silver mine on top of a mountain, but he warned us that it was too steep up there for using a burro to pack supplies in and silver out—one slip on the pine needles and zip! You were down off the mountain with the seat of your pants gone. We didn't investigate our gift, holding it in reserve until we owned more then one pair of pants to invest in it, and to our regret, we never returned. But we thought often of our friend and hoped he was still there, for men like that were the ones who made our West.

We set our cot up on the porch and had a good night's rest, and the next morning after a hearty pancake breakfast, Bill decided we could stay another day so that he could hike back into the hills and do some prospecting. I stayed at camp to "keep house" for a change—wash dishes, sweep the floor, and wash some clothes.

After I was finished and had nothing more to do, Steele suggested that I take his fishing pole and a can of worms and catch some fish for supper, at the little creek that ran above his place. I had no license, so I hesitated, not knowing what to say, until he grinned slyly and mentioned that the game warden was away on the other side of the mountain, so off I went to "bend" the law.

So long as I floundered in the thick brush along the stream and let the fish see and hear me, I caught nothing but a mess of scratches on my hands, arms, and face, but finally when I sat down quietly in the shade by a little pool, I managed to hook five small fish which I somehow cleaned by myself and proudly cooked for our supper.

That poor lonely man, he hated to see us leave the next morning, for he didn't like to cook for himself and seemed to enjoy my efforts, which I had to admit were getting better all the time, slated to an outdoor person's tastes. But we had to go. We thanked him for his hospitality; he had shared with us the best he had. Once again we were on the road and headed north.

As we drove along through the vast stretches of barren Railroad Valley, I amused myself by figuring up our expenses for the previous six weeks. Taking into account gas and oil already used and some yet to be purchased, our total costs including food and minor car repairs came to less than thirty-five dollars. Bill couldn't believe it until I went over the figures with him at our desert camp that night, and they showed that I was correct. And we had lived like kings!

Our second night on the road after leaving Steele's camp, we turned off toward Duck Creek not far from Wells, Nevada. The canyon was overgrown with brush and aspens and the ground covered with dried "cheat grass," so we dared not have a campfire and had to use our camp-stove to prepare supper.

After we had eaten, and food and supplies were packed away out of reach of animals and insects, we pulled up handfuls of the dry grass, piled it on the ground for our bed, and over it spread a tarp, cot pad, and quilt for our mattress, adding the rest of our blankets to lay over us, plus a piece of canvas as a spread to keep out the dampness arising from the creek. Bill always knew what we should do for our comfort, and it made a marvelous bed, I have never slept so well on any high-priced inner-spring mattress. I could never get enough of sleeping under the stars with all the sweet fresh air in the world to breathe.

Next morning after breakfast we wandered up the canyon among the lovely slender aspens, storing up another unforgettable memory to take away with us.

People who drive the speed limit in fast modern cars will never know the real fun of traveling. In our little old car we saw so many interesting things as we went along at a speed of thirty-five to forty miles an hour on paved roads, fifteen to twenty-five miles our speed on dirt roads. We could stop to explore, climb a hill, or prospect for gold and silver when-ever we had the urge and saw a likely prospect. Hence, we were still on the road back to Filer a third night when most people would have reached such a destination in a day and a half at the most.

To compensate for having to return to work, we decided to give our-selves a real treat and drive up into the mountains of Minidoka National Forest of southern Idaho. As expected, the scenery was magnificent, although the dirt road was rough, narrow, and one-track much of the way, with infrequent turn-outs which you had to back up to if you met another car coming down, and it was hundreds of feet to the canyon floor below. Fortunately we met no other cars as the Horizon Hunter labored slowly, in low gear as usual, up the steep grades, but we were beginning to regret our decision to go up there when suddenly we caught our first glimpse of the strange and wonderful forest that is Minidoka. By some freak of Nature, huge full-grown trees grew in groves in between which there was nothing but sage and grass, no scrub or second-growth timber at all that we could see. Is it still like that fifty-six years later?

There were many rather tame deer along the road, we counted twenty-four, and the park-like groves of tall evergreens continued until we reached the top of the mountain where the Fathers and Sons Campground was situated. Here we stopped and got out of the car, no one else around.

The air was deliciously scented with pine and fir, but it was rapidly turning quite chilly. The sun had set beyond the mountains, and we had no choice but to spend the night there, for it was out of the question to risk the drive down to the valley in the dark.

Bill quickly gathered dead wood and made a campfire in one of the fireplaces provided, and we managed a warm and satisfying supper, but we soon realized it was going to be too cold to sleep out at that high altitude. Resigning ourselves stoically to one more of those endless nights sitting up in the front seat of the car, we arranged our pillows and blankets as best we could and settled down for whatever snatches of sleep might come our way. Bright moonlight filtered restlessly through the trees as they swayed in the wind, and in spite of my discomfort, I was captivated by the ageless magic of a wilderness night.

Morning finally came as it somehow always did in spite of our feelings to the contrary during the wee small hours, and after one of our usual hearty campfire breakfasts of hot cereal, eggs, coffee, toast, fruit, and cookies, we decided once again that it had been worth all our trouble just to be there.

We broke camp leisurely as we enjoyed the beauty of the sunlit forest and listened to the calls of birds as they flitted like tiny shadows through the trees. And, of course, we went down the mountain in low gear, so by afternoon we were happy to realize that we still weren't at Filer. As our canteens were full of Minidoka water, we saw no harm in a further night of camping, this on the dry, flat high desert not far from Oakley.

It was another lovely moonlight night, and mild enough at the lower altitude for sleeping out in the open, so after supper we set up our cot and enjoyed a wonderful rest, waking occasionally to listen to the shrill music of the coyotes and acknowledge the moon's journey to the West.

In the morning after the dishes and pans were washed and packed, I wandered over to investigate a small abandoned fruit orchard which still boasted a few scraggly apple trees which gave mute testimony to someone's failure to make a living in this lonely spot. As I stood there idly, thinking about nothing and gazing out at the cheerful, sun-warmed desert, I suddenly looked above me, and there on the bottom branch of the tree under which I stood was a huge old porcupine lying motionless and staring down at me with dark, unblinking eyes. So someone was making a living there after all!

Moving slightly out of the way, just in case my new friend should lose his balance, I addressed him by name and asked him how he was doing. But, as I didn't know porcupine language and he didn't savvy Horizon Hunter talk, we were sadly unable to communicate. When I called Bill over from where he was breaking camp, he was interested but unable to interpret. So we bid our new lonely friend good-bye, finished loading the car, and reluctantly headed for Filer and work.

After all those nights in the open, was it any wonder we felt stifled sleeping in the narrow confines of the tiny one-room shack again? The late summer heat and closeness were almost more than we could bear, but we knew we had to get used to it. That was one place we could never think of as a home, it was so unprepossessing. The camp at Duck Creek was far more of a real home to us, as all our camps were, for it was beautifully furnished, with the sky for a roof, the hospitable ground for a bed, the trees for both protection from the wind and as decoration, and a little running stream provided water and music, a lullaby all through the night.

It was now time for the bean harvest, too early for the beet topping, and as the field dust bothered Bill's sinuses, he bought a mask with dust filters for protection and hired out to work, while I was "lucky" enough to land a job at a local "bean factory," sitting in front of a moving belt carrying seed beans and peas while workers hand-picked weed seeds, dirt, and "dead ones" out of the mass of good seed as the belt sped along. My wages were $2.40 per day plus a possible sixteen cents' bonus for doing more then the quota, of which I never made more then four cents, but at least I usually made the quota so that I wasn't fired.

Sitting at that seed conveyor on a hard straight chair was almost as tough on the back as beet-thinning, for my back ached and burned nearly all day from holding my hands out in front of me, no matter how I twisted, turned, and stretched and tried to relax. When I asked one of the older girls who had worked there off and on for five years if she ever got used to the work, she flatly replied, "Never." Chair legs were sawed off part way, pillows were used, and still the girls suffered, me along with them.

Well, I decided, it wouldn't last forever. I could stand it when I knew I would be leaving in a few weeks, and just think of all that extra money, far more than I had earned in the beet-thinning. It made me feel useful, and, also, I was interested in trying a different kind of work and learning how much discomfort I could stand. A new kind of adventure, I guess, but not much fun.

After Bill was through with the bean threshing, he began to work in the sugar beet harvest. Mechanical diggers brought the big beets out of the ground while the workers went down the rows with huge, wicked-looking knives with a hook on the end to pull the beets up to the workers' hands. Chopping off the stems and leaves, they then tossed the beets into piles to be loaded later into the truck.

It was no job for a woman, although Bill said that some of the Japanese women in Colorado worked in the beet-topping. I had visions of myself chopping off a hand or foot and had no wish to join this type of work even if Bill had let me, but it was interesting to watch. Tough as it was, I preferred the seed factory. And now our good thinning job paid off, for the nice clean fields produced a lot of huge beets, which meant good money for the workers.

And so our autumn work went on. We labored diligently and stored away our treasure for the winter, even as the ants and squirrels and chipmunks.

7

Back to the Desert

Harvest was finished, it was early November, most of the birds had
flown South, and it was time for us to leave also, as threatening gray
clouds promised winter storms. So, with "snow on our tail feathers" and
our entire outfit loaded once more into our Chevy, we struck out for the
low deserts and warm sunshine.

Once again we decided that we had earned a vacation, for, in spite of
our six weeks' layoff in Nevada, we had far more than the hundred-
dollar goal we had set ourselves for our winter stake. Bill had worked
long and hard at the beet topping, and I knew that my work at the seed
factory had been a big help, also. Not only that, Bill had been promised
the job at Red Star Stable again that coming winter.

So we must celebrate. Where should we go? As we drove along, we
happily discussed the possibilities. At one time Bill had been a guide in
Death Valley, and as he described for me its wonders and remarked that
it would be comfortably warm for sleeping out this time of year, I eagerly
fell in with his suggestion that we spend a few days there, camping, resting, and exploring the country.

But first we must get there. We drove steadily along until we arrived
at Ely, Nevada, by nightfall. As we were worn out with the long day of
continuous travel, Bill decided that we might spend the night in an auto
court, but when we learned that the price of a cabin would be three-and-
a-half dollars, then figured mentally how long it had taken us to earn
that amount in beet field or seed factory, we unanimously voted to sleep
out. So after hamburgers and coffee, we left Ely and headed to Ward
Mountain where we parked in a juniper grove and "slept" sitting up for
the rest of the night.

Ward Mountain's frosting of early snow shone coldly in the moonlight, and no matter how we huddled under our blankets, we couldn't keep warm, so Bill got out of the car and started a fire of dry juniper branches nearby. After a while, dead for sleep, he returned to the front seat and we tried to pretend that the fire was warming us and not all outdoors.

Finally, not satisfied with the mere illusion of warmth, I crawled stiffly out of the car and decided that to stay alive, I had better spend the rest of the night moving around gathering wood and keeping the fire going, for I could sleep in the morning while Bill was driving.

Now I know how sentries must feel, waiting out the night alone, glancing again and again toward the East, imagining they see dawn light, realizing it is false, over and over, until finally a faint gray light creeps over the rim of the world to herald the coming of the sun.

Once more revived by hot coffee and a good breakfast eaten by a cheerful campfire, we congratulated ourselves that we were still alive and healthy and had saved the magnificent sum of three-and-a-half dollars by not giving in to the temporary lure of a warm room and soft bed. Why, that much money would buy us three or four days of camping grub in Death Valley, and some left over.

Determined to reach Death Valley for a good rest that night, we made an early start from our camp at Ward Mountain and drove steadily all day on the road that goes through Tonopah and Goldfield, stopping briefly to have a quick lunch, ignoring good-looking gold prospects, until we reached Beatty, then Rhyolite, in the late afternoon, where we stretched our legs, went to the "brush," and looked around us at these famous old mining towns, reluctant to pass by with only a glance.

So it was night by the time we reached "Daylight Pass" that led down into Death Valley from an elevation of 4,300 feet, and although we were exhausted and Bill had a bad headache from lack of sleep and the long day's drive, we made up our minds to sleep in the Valley that night.

There was a strange moonlight mist on the hills as we started down the winding grade, and as Bill was unfamiliar with this road, he didn't realize how steep the descent was so hadn't shifted into low gear. Pretty soon our brakes began to smell, and as these old cars had no emergency brake to speak of, in order to get traction on the curves, Bill had to step on the gas, which catapulted us downward and downward, faster and faster. Not daring to speak, I sat tensely, gripping my hands together. Were we about to make Death Valley live up to its name once more?

To our great relief, we finally reached a more level stretch where Bill was able to shift into low, and we continued at a more reasonable pace, after a long time reaching the foot of the mountain, lucky once again that we hadn't met any other cars on a steep road. Soon we were at the campground near Furnace Creek, exhausted in mind, nerves, and body, too worn out even to think of eating.

As the night was warm, rattlers would be on the move, so we dared not spread our bed on the ground. Tired as he was, Bill had to untie the different parts of the steel camp cot from the fenders and bumpers of the car, set them up, then haul out the bedding which we both spread out. It was well worth the trouble. We slept like the dead. And in the morning, there it was, Death Valley, spread out before us, vast and silent and mysterious, reaching to the Panamints to the South and Southwest, with 12,000-foot Telescope Peak looming starkly in the West, and the Funeral Mountains at our back.

All around our camp were dune-like pastel-colored marls, remnants of an ancient lake bottom which had been overlaid by other alluvial materials, lavas, and so forth, which had eventually eroded away. In the bed of the valley stretched the mesquite thickets to which the Panamint Indians had been unjustly banished by the white men who took the oasis and its water for themselves and their palm groves.

Eager to explore, I hurried through breakfast and camp chores, after which Bill set a pot of beans on the campstove to cook, lay down on the cot in the shade of a mesquite tree, and announced that he would stay at camp and rest and watch the beans so that I could go off on a hike.

Wearing my hat, for the sun was hot, I eagerly headed for a pastel-striped mesa north of the campground. It was tough climbing, but when I reached the top, I found a wonderful view of the Valley and the huge, barren but colorful mountains hovering like menacing giants along its rim. The prospectors who explored those hills were a hardy group indeed!

As it was my birthday, for a uniquely welcome gift Bill negotiated with another party of visitors who were staying at Furnace Creek, to take us in their car on the following day on the steep drive up to Dante's View, far too tough a climb for the faithful Horizon Hunter.

It was unforgettable. Like standing on the edge of the world and gazing into some strange never-never land on a different planet. Far below us lay the basement of our country, Bad Water, at an altitude of 279 feet below sea level. Stretched out before us was the country where men had suffered and died in their struggle to reach the gold fields of California. But not, as so many believe, dying of thirst; for, in spite of its aridness, there is plenty of water to be found in Death Valley in springs and wells. They died from starvation, from fighting with Indians and with each other, from hate and greed and fear. And the mark of their dying still hangs like a strange, invisible cloud, obscuring the beauty and promise of the Valley from all but the most discerning, those who love, respect, and accept the desert for what it is.

The hot November sun makes one realize what the summer can be like, yet a few hardy dried-out souls, mainly storekeepers and prospectors, do manage to stay on and survive a heat that sometimes reaches 137 degrees in the shade, with vicious mesquite gnats to add to the torment of not only the white men but the poor remaining Indians living down in the mesquite flats.

Not far from our campsite was a beautiful little ditch of sparkling water, the loveliest sight in any desert, rushing down from springs in the mountains to the north and heading for the oasis at Furnace Creek. Gently enticing us and exciting our thirst, we followed it one hot morning down to the store and soda fountain where we indulged in luscious, cool, satisfying chocolate milkshakes. Nothing in our lives ever tasted better. Having earned this trip to Death Valley and this treat through hard work, I enjoyed both to the depths of my being.

After five lovely days of loafing in the sun and nights of sleeping under the stars, we decided to take the road east to Death Valley Junction, thereby eliminating the steep grades of Daylight Pass. After we reached the Reno/Las Vegas highway, on an impulse we struck south on the rough desert road to the ghost mining town of Johnnie, Nevada.

Although there were still a few scattered inhabitants at Johnnie, strangely enough the place didn't appear hospitable, so we drove on back to some mine buildings we had noticed tucked between the hills, hoping to find shelter for the night as the sky looked stormy. Finding the place apparently deserted, we explored a couple of the vacant cabins and chose the likeliest one for our lodging. It was pretty tumbledown, but it had two single steel cots with link springs where we could spread our bedding, and there was even a lamp with some oil still in it, so we moved in and I started to prepare an early supper.

While we were eating, we heard footsteps outside in the gravel. Upon investigating, we saw a man approaching slowly in the dusk, heading for the next cabin over. Bill called to him, but before answering, the man entered the cabin and lit his lamp which he brought to the doorway to shine on Bill. Afterwards he told us he had done this, as he had recently been shot at through the window of his cabin, and he wanted to make sure who we were before talking to us. Also, we noticed that he had a gun handy in his cabin.

We invited him to join us at supper, but he declined, saying he had food already fixed that had to be eaten before it spoiled, so that evening after dishes were done, we went over to his cabin to visit with him.

The man's name was Kloth, and he turned out to be the caretaker for the mine while the owners were away, and he proved to be a wonderful human being, friendly and kind, delighted to have someone to talk to. He was a prospector and placer miner, of German descent, about eighty years old, and he spoke with such a thick accent and was so deaf that he and Bill had a hard time communicating, although the old gentleman had less trouble understanding my higher-pitched voice.

Unconsciously, Bill assumed Mr. Kloth's accent and way of speaking in an effort to make him understand, but this made it all the harder for both of them. By the time we left there two days later, I could hardly make out what Bill was saying myself. I wonder what would have happened if we had stayed there two weeks.

Mr. Kloth had a small dog for company, and when we asked what his pet's name was, he merely said with a twinkle, "Askim." Which we did, but he wouldn't tell us. Cute.

Eager as always to do some prospecting (who knew on what untouched hill we might strike it rich?) and interested in information the old man had generously given him about the mining in the district and likely silver prospects, Bill decided we should stay there for a day so that he could hike in the nearby hills.

I was all too ready to agree, so after Kloth went off to his placer diggings and Bill headed up the nearest wash, I spent the day wandering alone around the camp, fascinated with the haphazard arrangement of the sunburned old buildings, dreaming about the things that must have taken place there in earlier days, dimly remembering my former city life as something remote and unreal. Only this was real, this feeling of complete peace in the silence of the desert. As I rested in the pleasantly hot fall sunshine, I felt deeply grateful once more that this wonderful, friendly desert country was now my home.

After we left Johnnie we prospected our way through the hills and desert on to Las Vegas and through Boulder Dam, then turned off on the road below the Dam to camp for the night at Willow Beach. The air was so chilly and damp from the roaring Colorado River that we decided we would be warmer sleeping on the ground, but the sand also proved to be a cold, and hard, bed. Frequently we woke in the night to turn over and stretch our cramped and stiffened muscles and listen to the fearsome braying of the fighting bands of wild burros, known to old-time prospectors as "desert nightingales," which roamed in the canyon along the river.

However, our campfire breakfast took the kinks out of our bodies and spirits, and, as always, the scenery made the cold night worth the discomfort. Camping out can have its disadvantages, but, for us, they are usually outweighed by the advantages. We try to protect ourselves from storm, cold, and wind, and then make the best of each situation, for we know that even the worst conditions don't last forever, and if we didn't like it where we were, we were free to move on and hope to find a better place.

After a brief exploration of the canyon, we decided to drive that day to the abandoned silver mining town of White Hills, Arizona. On the way we saw a number of huge tarantulas crossing the road every fifty or a hundred yards, all headed in the same direction. A strange migration. What if their path had crossed our camp of the night before? No doubt it had been too cold for them to be on the move.

White Hills was a real ghost town, dreaming placidly in the sun of prosperous days gone by. Extensive ore dumps spread out from the hills, and it is said that several million dollars in silver were taken from the mines.

Two miners, who were living in a couple of newer cabins apart from the ghost town, made us welcome and recommended the old barber shop as the most comfortable building to bunk in if we cared to "muck it out" with a broom.

Apart from a loose screen door, some broken floor boards, old newspapers, and yellowed pulp "thrillers," all overlaid with a coating of ancient dust, the barber shop was fine, as it had a large brass bed with a spring as a base where we could spread our tarp and blankets.

After cleaning the place out a little, we brought in our campstove, folding card table and chairs, our bedding, and cooking equipment with supplies, after which I peeled some potatoes and onions and fixed a light but nourishing supper of potato soup, toast, and prunes. We didn't know where the water supply might be, but we had our two-gallon and three-gallon canteens full, as we always carried plenty of water in case we had to make "dry camp." This made dishwashing rather sketchy, also bathing, but we managed well enough. We didn't use tin dishes but had crockery cups, enamelware bowls, and pretty blue dime store plates as they held the heat better than tin and made the food more appetizing.

Potato soup, traveling, and fresh air always put me in a stupor, so shortly after rinsing out the dishes and putting things in the metal grub box out of reach of rodents, I was ready for bed. Bill sat up for a while and read ancient murder mystery magazines by the light of our kerosene lantern.

It was a mild night, the door was open, and I have never felt so cozy as when I lay there and listened to the rusty chains of the ore buckets clanking gently in the wind, heard the kangaroo mice scampering in and out of the sagging screen door, and watched the soft glow of the lantern shine through the cobwebs of that dusty little room. Drowsy and contented, I thought of the time when that same room had once been noisy with the arguments and discussions of men getting their Saturday night shearing, then fell asleep, half waking when Bill came to bed, after which I slept soundly until morning.

While I was fixing breakfast and Bill was packing our bedding into the car, he mentioned, oh so casually, that the kangaroo mice had jumped up on the bed and raced around my pillow, while he was still up. I laughed, for the desert mice are cunning and clean and not at all objectionable, and I was grateful that they hadn't coveted any of my hair for nest-building and kept me awake, as the mice had that first dreadful night in the shack at Filer.

After wandering around White Hills, looking at the interesting old tumbledown buildings and taking pictures, exploring and prospecting, we met an old-timer who told us stories of the early days of the town and about the mining in the district.

As we drove slowly on to Kingman, we stopped occasionally for more prospecting, so it was evening when we started up the steep, winding mountain road to Goldroad. For its length, that road beat any other we had been on, for curves, and it was so narrow that no passing was allowed for long stretches, making drivers who came up behind us quite impatient with our slow-moving vehicle. By the time we reached the pass, I was impossibly tired and nervous, so we stopped at the viewpoint turn-out, set up our cot, and spent the night. Oddly enough, the warmer air of the desert poured up the mountainside around us, and we had a much more comfortable night than at the lower elevation of Willow Beach.

Next morning we dressed just in time to avoid being seen by the first tourists who stopped to cool their engines and enjoy the view. "Viewpoint doesn't include us," we muttered to ourselves, as we went ahead and fixed breakfast over our campstove, sitting on the edge of our cot to eat it under the curious, sidelong glances of various travelers.

Back in those days we could camp near main roads without feeling fearful of intruders or being attacked; it was all so much different and safer. But not any more. Too many bad things are happening to tourists, sometimes in established campgrounds. Bill and I had the best of it in those early years, and thinking back, we were grateful.

Comforted by a good night's rest and a full stomach, I was ready for the steep, curving road down the mountains, but I was never sure we would make it. Eventually I became more relaxed and trusting that our guardian angels would take care of us, although I knew that even they couldn't guarantee that a '28 Chevy would last forever, no matter how well it had been made or what good care Bill gave it.

We drove south through the Mojave desert which, with its black lava rocks and sparse vegetation, was my least favorite desert; then we crossed back into Arizona at Parker.

That night we camped on the desert between Aguila and Congress Junction where Bill gave me the nickname of "Coyote Clara," for here it was that I howled at the coyotes, and they answered, one big old boy getting so excited that his voice acquired special trills and quavers as he loped across the desert toward our camp. Evidently getting wind and sight of us, he suddenly stopped calling, but the following morning several coyotes answered me again when Bill told me to howl. I was thrilled with my new accomplishment and not at all offended with my new western nickname.

We planned to spend that night in a deserted cabin at the foot of famed Rich Hill where in the early days prospectors, cowboys, and sheepherders had found a half million dollars in gold nuggets under the boulders at the top of the hill and in the rock slides below. Every rock on that hill has been turned over hundreds of times, especially after heavy rains.

That morning, while I stayed at the shack to look after our belongings, Bill climbed the hill to look around, although he had little hope or expectation of finding any gold. To my dismay, a short while after he left, some cowboys drove a large herd of bawling cattle with sharp, curving horns through the cabin yard to the water troughs nearby, and I worried how Bill would get through to me when he returned, for I was completely surrounded, and I had no way of knowing how long the cattle might be there.

A woman who was helping work the cattle rode up to the shack and bluntly informed me that this was her place, and she didn't want strangers stopping there. I could understand her attitude, for she was probably afraid campers would burn the place down, but even so, she made me feel like some kind of an undesirable tramp, and my face burned as I informed her that I couldn't leave until my husband returned, whereupon she muttered something hostile, turned her horse, and rode off.

As Bill had seen from the hill what had happened and guessed what was up, he hurried down to rejoin me. By that time the cattle had been watered and driven away, so we were able to load the car and glad to leave, although we were disappointed at not being able to spend another night there. But it was really time for him to report for work at Red Star Stable as the season for winter visitors on the desert was upon us and the horses had to be brought up from summer pasture sixty miles from Phoenix. So we turned the Horizon Hunter toward the riding stable after the most exciting and rewarding journey I had ever taken, and in less than a year's time. It was still 1941.

8

Red Star Stable and Beyond

From Rich Hill we drove directly to the riding stable, and once again were crowded into a tiny shack, this one even smaller than the one at Filer. It had a dirt floor and no windows, just screens and canvas flaps, in one corner the tiny trash burner for heat. As crowded as we were, I enjoyed living there, for the clean desert air poured in, and outside was the whole wonderful desert with cactus, greasewood bushes, and palo verde, mesquite and ironwood trees for our garden, with the cheerful, friendly Salt River Mountains and the Estrella range with its noble Montezuma Peak as our "south wall."

Bill spread clean white granite sand from a nearby wash onto our floor, and with the flaps up so that we could see the desert, I had a feeling that we were still camping out. In back of the shack, Bill fixed me a retreat, or patio, with a clean sand floor, among the palo verde and ironwood trees, where I would be out of sight of horseback riders and could read and write or just sit and look at the mountains and desert and listen to the birds of which there were a great number: the chattering, bustling cactus wrens, the friendly canyon wrens with their lilting song, the fierce-looking Palmer thrasher whose lovely voice belied his looks, and the brilliant darting Arizona cardinal which is a bit larger than his eastern cousin.

Many migratory birds also came through, attracted by the grain the horses spilled, and the water troughs. We were also surrounded by domestic birds, a large flock of chickens, and some ducks who heralded the approach of prospective riders as well as any watch dog. We also had an Airedale dog named Buster and a young tom cat named Tom to keep us company, although their main job was to catch the mice around the stable in the hay and grain, at which occupation Buster was more energetic than

Tom. Bill was still receiving only fifteen dollars a month plus duck eggs, Depression wages, which didn't bother us, as we still had most of our winter stake left and were able to manage fine with our expenses so modest, mostly for food.

I enjoyed wandering around in the corrals, getting to know the horses and soon learned all their names and characteristics. One of my favorite diversions was putting a neck rope on Gray Cricket, the twenty-six-year-old Grandpa horse, and leading him up the road to the irrigation canal bank to eat grass, as his digestion was poor. He was quite deaf, and when he was suddenly startled by approaching cars, he would jump against me and nearly knock me down, but I forgave him as he was almost at the end of a long and busy life. We let small children ride "Grandpa" on Sunday, but they knew that if they didn't ride nicely and take good care of him, they would never get to ride him again.

Sometimes I stayed at the stable and watched over things while Bill rode Chapo, his favorite horse, after riders he had misgivings about, to make sure that they weren't abusing their mounts. There is a lot of grief at times in the riding stable business, and the worst is watching how supposedly intelligent people can mistreat the horses, sometimes thoughtlessly, sometimes intentionally, trying to see how much they can get out of their dollar's worth of riding, it seems. On the other hand was the rider who would let the horse boss him. Afraid, or not knowing how to make the animal behave, he would ruin the horse for subsequent riders unless Bill immediately took the animal out for some gentle but firm disciplining.

As for Chapo, he just wasn't a riding stable type of horse as few people could handle him. He was full of fear and suspicion as to what riders might do to him, but he and Bill understood each other, and Bill had no trouble making Chapo do anything he wanted him to. Bill rode as though he were part of the horse, a wonderful sight to see. The following year we bought Chapo, and later I got up enough courage to ride him, although Bill assured me that I needn't worry, that Chapo always acted as though he were taking care of me. Which suited me fine.

I had promised my parents that I would spend Christmas with them in 1941, so in early December I took the train to Toledo. My brother Alfred was in the army by then, as it was the tragic December of Pearl Harbor and the beginning of America's involvement in the war. Although Bill was in the draft, he had served in France during World War I, so he wasn't called to serve, but he was ready to go if he was needed. And this visit was when I received the Christmas card with the picture of the USS *Indianapolis* from Bruno Varnagaris, "Varney," with the tell-tale postmark of December 6, 1941, causing me to wonder ever after if he had survived the war. I still have his card, here in front of me.

Although I was happy to be with my parents again, I missed Bill, and it wasn't long before I was fed up with the raw, gray days, dirty snow and slush, and the confinement and sameness of city life. I hated to disappoint my mother and father who had always been so good to me, but they couldn't help seeing that I was longing for Bill and our life together in the out-of-doors. It wasn't the kind of life they would have chosen, but they could see that it had been good for me and that I was happy, so that was what counted.

After my visit was over, they let me go without a word of reproach, paid for my railroad ticket, and gave me a new warm tweed winter coat, some useful cooking utensils for camping out, three cookbooks, a fine portable Philco radio, and two one-hundred-dollar war bonds that we could save or use in an emergency, bless their generous hearts! I left behind all of my dresses, dress shoes, hats, and spring coat, except the suit and hat I wore while traveling. I knew that when I reached Arizona, I would once again live in jeans and slacks, shirts, and flat heels, with no further need for "city clothes."

I had insisted on traveling by day coach to save my father's money, as I didn't mind sleeping sitting up. It was old stuff to me by now. Bill and Aunt Florence met me at the railroad station in Phoenix. It was a joyful reunion, and I promptly gave Aunt Florence my city hat. That night I slept once more in Bill's arms in the cool fragrant desert air that poured through our shack, and next morning there were the desert and mountains waiting in the warm winter sunshine to welcome me home, while I rejoiced in the sight of the giant sahuaro cactus which assured me that I was indeed in my beloved Arizona once more.

I was sorry when April came and it was time for the horses to be driven to pasture, a long hard ride for Bill, for, as I have mentioned, the summer pasture was sixty miles away. Mr. Brumbach went along in his car, and they spent one uncomfortable night sleeping on the ground at a stable along the way where Brumbach had made the usual arrangements for the horses to be penned, fed, and watered.

After discussing plans for the summer, including a possible return to Filer, we finally decided to drive to Paonia, Colorado, to visit Shyrl Knight, a former cowboy friend of Bill's who had a fruit ranch near there, and if we liked it, we might settle down and grow fruit and garden produce to help out in the war effort.

In order to avoid going up steep Yarnell Hill with its heavy traffic, and to look at some different scenery, we traveled by way of the old Black Canyon road. On the way we camped for one night at Cherry, Arizona, a gold-mining district, and fell in love with the way the sun shone through the manzanita bushes, oaks, pines, junipers, and huge old walnut trees, a beautiful, wild park-like place that appealed to us for its very isolation and peace. But we went on.

Another night we spread our bed on the red sand of Oak Creek Canyon and were rewarded with a breakfast view of the sunlight gilding the red and cream cliffs and pinnacles which, with the tender greens of spring foliage, created an unforgettable picture. Again, we went on.

We were making pretty good time until on a barren, lonely stretch northeast of Holbrook, one of our tires went flat. This was bad, as none of our tires was much good, nor were the spares. Bill quickly changed the tire, and we drove on as rapidly as possible in the growing dusk, trying to find a suitable place to camp for the night, when right on the edge of the Painted Desert, bam! another rotten tire betrayed us, and there we were with no place to get off the road.

And it was our first wedding anniversary, April 12th.

I can't pretend that I enjoyed such incidents, and neither did Bill. We didn't try to fool ourselves. It was tough going sometimes, but we usually tried to laugh off our troubles even though the laugh often ended in a groan. And I couldn't pretend that the previous year had been one of total bliss. Bill and I had had some disagreements; sometimes I was in the wrong, sometimes he was. He objected to what he thought were my attempts to change his ways. Perhaps unconsciously I was guilty of this, but I didn't mean to be. I was too happy to be following his way of life to want to change him. And in spite of occasional discomforts, I never regretted my decision to be Bill's partner for life. It was everything I had longed for, the adventure, the traveling, even the hardship which I found gave me strength, knowing how much I could take.

The beauty of the Painted Desert was hidden in the black, overcast night, the air cold and raw, and Bill felt too tired to cope with another tire. So, after a cold supper eaten in the dark, we resigned ourselves to the inevitable night of sitting up in the car, worrying meanwhile about our tire situation, for tire rationing was being enforced, and we certainly weren't "essential" to anybody but ourselves until we found productive work to do.

It turned out to be the longest, coldest night we had yet known, and grateful we were to see the red, black, gray, and green formations of the Painted Desert gradually appear in the first faint light of dawn. As usual, the sight before us in the sunrise more then compensated for our night's hardship, and while Bill struggled with the tire, I wandered out into the desert, walking up and down the rough, barren knolls as though I had all the energy in the world.

There was no place around there where I could fix breakfast, so we drove on, and soon we were so hungry that we stopped at a small cafe and had a good breakfast, an unusual and desperate action for us in those days. Pay a dollar for two breakfasts? We could eat for a whole day on less than a dollar!

That night we must surely get a good rest. We were in a daze, and Bill had to stop once and nap in the car so that he wouldn't fall asleep while driving. Then, of course, we had another flat which made our situation even more precarious. Would we ever make it to Colorado? Or even to the next town?

After a fruitless effort to secure a new or good used tire at Gallup, New Mexico, we started north through the Navajo country. Much of the land through which we now traveled was empty and lonely and looked almost desolate in the bleak gray light from the cloudy sky. Long before dark we began to look for a campsite, and by great good luck we found a wonderful place to turn off the road near a beautiful huge rock formation which we called "Organ Rock" from the way the wind sounded as it blew over and around it in the night. But we had no need for a lullaby. It would have taken a dynamite blast under our cot to awaken us.

Next morning as we drove along, a big handsome Navajo man tried to thumb a ride with us, but as soon as he got a closer look at our load, he grinned, shook his head, and stepped back, and we smiled and waved at him, looked at each other and laughed, wishing we had the good sense to travel as lightly as he did, even though it wasn't possible.

Whenever we saw a carload of migrant workers taking off down the road with what looked like a few blankets, a sack of potatoes, and not much else, we would consider our load, shake our heads, and wonder. But our car was all the home we had, and with our equipment and supplies, we were self-sufficient no matter if we broke down in the most desolate spot, as we had at times.

At Shiprock a young Navajo woman in the back of a truck gave me a beautiful smile which warmed my heart as we drove on into Colorado under a stormy sky. It began to rain, so we decided to stay at an inexpensive auto court in Cortez for the night. By morning a light skiff of snow had fallen, the air was cold and raw, and after we had driven only a short distance, another tire died. Desperately Bill changed it using one of our wretched spares, and at Monticello, Utah, he had a "boot" put into one tire, improving our situation slightly.

That night we parked our car near a man-made cave in a red sandstone cliff near the LaSal Mountains, and after a discouraging rain-swept night sitting up, we envied that "cave man" his cozy home, although we didn't get to meet him.

After the weather cleared that morning, we drove on to Moab where Bill perjured himself to get a new tire, obtaining the necessary rationing certificate stating that we were entitled to this essential piece of new rubber. But we consoled ourselves that we weren't hampering the war effort by our subterfuge, for it turned out that tires our size were actually obsolete, although still available.

Bill rearranged our one new and three of the best of our five old tires to the greatest advantage which took up a good part of our day, so we didn't get much mileage behind us that afternoon before we decided we'd better look for a place to spend the night. The sky was thick with lowering storm clouds. A night out would be miserable, and as we had no wish for another session of sitting up in the front seat, we decided to hunt for a cabin.

Our spirits drooping as we drove on and on, finding no auto courts, until finally after dark we saw ahead the light of a gas station. We stopped to get gas and information and were told that they had some cabins vacant, but we'd have to supply our own bedding. No problem.

After a glance at our old car and camping gear, the unshaven, middle-aged man in charge told us it would be seventy-five cents for the night. Misinterpreting our look at each other, he lowered the rent to fifty cents and said we could have the cabin that leaked over the stove.

Jubilantly we moved in. Soon the room was warm, and a pot of thick potato soup simmered on the wood range, and in a reckless moment I opened and dumped a can of oysters into the stew, opened a can of pears and a box of sugar cookies. A feast!

After we were in bed with the light from cracks in the stove flickering against the ceiling as the dying fire snapped cozily, the rain started, and we lay there and listened to it hitting the roof and splashing on the ground outside, drops of water from the leaking roof hissing on the hot stove, while we congratulated ourselves on our wonderful luck. A home for the night.

As usual, the next morning, after the rain had quit, Bill met an old prospector. I believe he would have met a prospector if he was drifting on a raft in the middle of the Pacific Ocean, and they would promptly go off to look for a mine on the nearest island. Anyway, Bill went off with this particular prospector to look over a vanadium prospect, while I spent the day alone at the cabin, having a grand time resting, washing some clothes, and then wandering over the nearby hills. High desert country, it was different from any we had been in before, with its rolling hills covered with rocks, dried grass, and a few junipers, but it was interesting and restful to the eyes even though I didn't care to live there.

In back of the service station and cabins was a barn around which a few chickens scratched, so in the afternoon I decided to see if I could buy some fresh eggs. The proprietor, who still hadn't shaved, was alone in the station (customers were few that time of year) and although he didn't have any eggs on hand, he said we could go down to the barn and search for some.

When we entered the barn, the man hesitated, looked at me rather strangely, then asked me if I wanted to go up into the hay to look for eggs. Suddenly I felt uneasy. I glanced up at the hay stack, then back at the man's face, my heart starting to beat faster. It was so quiet there in the dusty barn with only the sounds of chickens rustling in the straw and no cars going by on the highway, and there we were, apparently the only people for miles around, Bill off somewhere in the hills. Not knowing what to think, but knowing what not to do, I looked at him calmly with no visible fear or animosity and said firmly but in a friendly voice, "No, I don't think I want to," edging toward the open door which was nearest to me.

Without another word, he turned and went to search for the eggs which he gave me as a gift, refusing any payment. After I thanked him, he returned to his station, and I headed back to the cabin to start supper.

Next morning as we were about to leave, the can of eggs held carefully in my lap, the proprietor came out to say goodbye, his face now cleanly shaven, his thin hair wet and neatly combed, and he wore a clean blue shirt.

As usual, the prospect Bill had looked at was good but belonged to someone else. Well, he had had the fun of prospecting without the responsibilities of working the mine with the possible danger of going broke. Mining is not a poor man's game, Bill told me, unless you are lucky enough to find a ledge full of gold and silver near the surface of the ground and can pick out the pure ore and cart it away forthwith. He said that more money has gone into the ground than ever came out of it. Still, it's fun looking.

That morning we crossed into Colorado and drove along without mishap until we reached Paonia where we broke our rear axle while crossing a bridge near town. After we had a new axle installed, we continued on until we reached the ranch home of Bill's friend Shyrl Knight and his family, his wife, Esther, and two fine children, Hobart and Shirley. After a warm welcome, we were treated to a delicious country-style chicken supper with all the trimmings, and although they had no spare room for us to bunk in, we were invited to put our cot and spread out our belongings in their spacious attic, which we did.

For several days Bill and I hiked in the hills, looking over the possibilities for a place of our own, but somehow we couldn't feel the same way about Colorado as we did our beloved Arizona. The mountains were gorgeous but not as friendly as our Arizona mountains. They were too big, too majestic and overpowering with their aloofly gleaming expanses of snow. And even the nearby hills covered with sage and juniper didn't appeal to us. They made us feel hemmed-in, and the sagebrush was the home of the sheep tick whose bite could cause the dreaded Rocky Mountain spotted fever.

After every hike, we had to examine ourselves all over for ticks, shuddering when we found one embedded in our skin, carefully using different methods to make it loosen its grip without leaving its head behind. And if we couldn't feel free to hike in this country without that risk, how could we make a home here? Impossible.

How about Cherry, back in Arizona? The gently rounded hills of Cherry, the lovely parks of oaks, walnut trees and alligator junipers, manzanita and pines, the soul-expanding views of friendly mountains and the desert? We could go there, do some prospecting, and if we spotted a likely claim, settle there, do our location work, plant a garden, grow produce to sell in Prescott, and later on build a cabin and develop our mine. Excitedly we made our plans, told the Knights good-bye, never to forget their generous hospitality, and we were on our way.

9

We Return to Arizona

As we had entered Colorado from Utah, we decided to return to Arizona by a different route in order to see new country, cross new horizons, which meant taking the "Million Dollar Highway" over Red Mountain Pass and on down into New Mexico.

Up and up we drove through the thickly forested mountains, the air becoming thinner and colder, a gray spring sky threatening storm, until we were at Ouray, Colorado, at an elevation nearly 8,000 feet. There was snow on the lower slopes, and now in the late afternoon, snow flurries began to hit our windshield. To cross the pass in the night in the face of a snowstorm was out of the question, and there was no place to camp out of the weather, no old abandoned cabin or ghost town. We must, therefore, spend some of our hard-earned dwindling funds for a cabin in an auto court.

The first place we tried had gas heat, which always gave Bill a headache, ever since he was poisoned by carbon monoxide when he worked at Boulder Dam. Although we had paid for our cabin and moved in, we weren't satisfied, so Bill drove off across town to see if he could find a place with a wood stove, while I stayed behind with our things.

To kill time, I dug out some supplies and pans and began to mix filling for two pumpkin pies, Bill's favorite food. It was partly mixed when Bill returned with the good news that he had found a place with a wood heater and also had been able to get our money refunded on this cabin. So, with a big bowl of pumpkin filling in my lap, we drove carefully to the new place where luckily the stove had a small oven, and I was able to finish my pies. I so seldom had an oven that I couldn't resist using one when I had the chance. And did those pies taste good! It was lucky we hadn't attempted the mountain road in the night, for a blizzard piled snow several inches deep on the highway. And as the storm continued all that day, by the second morning our car was almost obliterated by more than a foot of snow.

When the weather cleared, the snow plows were right at work along with the warm April sun, and we began to inquire in the town as to when it would be safe to proceed over the mountain. We began to hear wild tales of what spring snow slides and "mud slips" could do in those mountains, sweeping cars off the highway at times, through concussion caused by an avalanche, thousands of feet into the canyons below.

Uneasily Bill and I discussed the pros and cons of our situation, but as time and money were in short supply, we decided we must continue on the route we had chosen, no matter what the risk.

Our third and last evening at the auto court we spent visiting with the family who owned and operated it. The man was an old-timer in the region, and also had spent several years in the Canadian wilds. He told us a hair-raising yarn of a forced nighttime hike he had taken in the Canadian forest which abounded with wolves and wolverines when he had smoked one cigarette after another, he said, so that the glowing coal would keep the wild beasts from attacking him.

He also warned us of the danger from snow slides but agreed that we could probably make it through all right after the snow plows had cleared the way.

It was a beautiful, clean, sparkling morning when we slowly ground our way up the mountain road toward this new and dangerous horizon. I was very afraid for the first mile on the narrow, one-track road, but the scenery was so magnificent that I began to relax and drank in the beauty of majestic forests and the unbroken expanses of snow stretching far above timberline.

On and on we drove, usually in low gear, hardly daring to speak of our hopes and fears, talking only of the scene around us, although we were tense with trying to will our over-worked old vehicle up the steep grades. Luckily, we met only two cars and those at convenient turn-outs, and occasionally we took a breather, got out of the car and looked far below and above and all around at a sight that awed and touched us to the depths of our beings despite the danger it spelled to our enterprise.

Why the vibration of our car and the noise of its engine combined with the effects of the warm sun didn't precipitate a slide onto us was a miracle. But on we went, laboring slowly upward, and nothing happened, although I ached all over with the effort of "helping" the Horizon Hunter over the mountain. Bill's outward calmness and self-assurance were all that kept me from going to pieces. I wondered, why couldn't I just sit back and relax and let the car do the work? But somehow I felt that if I didn't put all the force of my will behind our venture, we might not make it, for if our old car no longer felt me helping her and willing her to make the grade, she might give up, which could mean the end of us.

Finally we were there, at Red Mountain Pass, 11,000 feet altitude, at the top of the world it seemed, and we could breathe once more, feeling blessed at our good fortune. We were now at timberline, and gleaming unbroken snowdrifts lay spread over the Rockies before us, a sight worth all the dangers we had passed through.

But how pleasant it was to be heading downward again. Finally we reached the odd little mining town of Silverton with its sunburned frame buildings perched on sunny rocky slopes, where we stopped and stretched our legs while looking around before continuing on to Durango, which in our happy relief seemed to be one of the prettiest little cities we had ever seen.

After window-shopping and buying some groceries, we headed for New Mexico where we rested for the night in an auto court at Aztec, driving on the next day through pretty farming country dressed in delicate, lovely spring greens until we reached Shiprock when we turned south in the late afternoon and started for our "Organ Rock" campsite where we planned to spend the night.

On our way from Shiprock a rattletrap car looking worse than ours passed us going in the opposite direction, loaded with a gang of tough-looking white men who would, we felt sure, be unpleasant to encounter in a wild, lonely place.

It was deep dusk when we turned off onto the old road leading to the Navajo well near Organ Rock where we had camped on our trip north, and it was dark by the time we had our bed set up out in the open. I was about to start a campfire and prepare supper when an old car rattled by on the highway, slowed, stopped, and backed up, then turned off on our road and drove to within a hundred yards of our camp. Who was it? Surely they hadn't seen us? Was it the gang of toughs we had seen earlier? We waited tensely, not talking, just listening and watching.

The car doors opened, then banged shut, and three dim shadowy figures approached in the starlight.

"Hello!" Bill called, walking toward them a few feet.

No reply. On they marched.

"Hello!" from Bill.

Still no answer as they headed straight for us.

We had no weapon handy. Our .22 rifle was packed in the car and unloaded. What should we do? I didn't feel frightened for some strange reason. I felt blank, waiting for whatever might happen.

"Hello!" Bill spoke a third time. The three "menacing" figures were only twenty feet away.

"Hello," came a soft voice. They walked up closer and stopped a few feet away. "We are looking for the well," said the same voice, a quiet gentle Navajo voice, that of a young man. They carried a bucket and needed water for the radiator of their car, they told us.

Smiling with relief, we got out our flashlight, careful not to offend them by shining it in their faces, then Bill showed them where the well was. After they had dipped up some water, thanked us, and left, we laughed softly, grateful that our visitors had been only gentle Navajos and not a party of white bandits.

We've always felt safe in Indian country, and although I realized how helpless we were, sound asleep out in the open, I slept very well that night, lulled once again by the "music" the wind played on the huge rock formation near our camp.

In the morning while we were sitting on our cot eating breakfast, the Navajo whose hogan was situated nearest the well, came to call on us. Very politely he sat on the dike of rock back of our camp, carefully gazing off across country and not staring at us, until we invited him down and gave him an apple and part of a box of graham crackers. He could see by our outfit that we weren't rich, and he neither asked for nor expected anything, but politely accepted the small token of our hospitality.

As we talked quietly together, he told us in broken English where his home lay and that he had seven children, two horses, and many sheep. When Bill brought out his powerful little French binoculars and let the Navajo look through them at his sheep, he turned them also toward the snow-capped mountains in the distance, exclaiming "Whee!" when he saw how close they came in the glasses.

After our friend left, a singing Navajo man drove by with a horse and wagon and waved gaily to us, continuing to chant his joy in the beauty of the morning until he was out of sight down the long straight road.

And it was a beautiful morning, we agreed joyfully. Would that we also could chant our pleasure to be in the strange and marvelous country of the Navajo.

It is a land of vast distances where time means little. Red and cream-colored sandstone buttes and mesas are carved out of the landscape, into which the Navajo hogan of mud and cedars blends as no white man's dwelling of artificial materials ever would. Small bands of sheep move slowly over the sparse grazing land, tended by the colorful wind-blown figures of women and children in their velvets and satins and gay blankets, and an occasional lone horseman with tall-crowned hat trots leisurely across this high desert country, perhaps on a simple errand or visit which may take him a hundred miles.

We were in Gallup before noon, and as it was Saturday, we did some necessary shopping, then sat in the car and watched the colorful crowds of Navajos wandering along the streets going in and out of the stores and lining up at the movie house for the Saturday afternoon matinee. What impressed us most was that all of their faces wore such happy, pleasant expressions, so unlike the sour looks of some of the whites.

When we crossed the line from New Mexico to Arizona early that afternoon, we were so happy to be home again that we celebrated by stopping at a Navajo hogan where a family was at work weaving and carding wool, and spent fifty cents for a tiny blanket a little girl had made, her first attempt. Encouraged by their friendliness, we stood there for a little while and watched them work. How pleasing to us the beautiful, child-like smiles of the Navajos!

The little blanket we bought from the child became a symbol for us. Wherever we hung it was our home.

Driving steadily and without mishap all that day, we were near Canyon Diablo not far from Flagstaff when night fell. Seeing a nice little dirt road leading into the junipers, we turned off and followed it, for there was nothing we liked better than to camp in a juniper grove. We were not only hidden from the highway and protected from the night wind, but there was usually a plentiful supply of dead wood for our campfire.

After a light supper, we spread our tarp and other bedding on the soft springy ground under a thick bushy juniper and were soon deep in exhausted sleep. We should have been warned by the still, mild air and the overcast sky, for around midnight we were suddenly awakened by drops of rain falling through the tree branches onto our faces.

We staggered blindly up in the pitch blackness, picked up armloads of bedding, bumping into each other as we groped for the car, finally stuffing the blankets and pillows every which way into the car. Then we crawled in for another interminable session of sleeping sitting up. And it turned out that that was the end of the rain.

By dawn, after a few cat naps and much turning and twisting, stretching and groaning, we decided it wasn't going to rain any more after all, but by that time it was too late to sleep outside on the ground, so we had a good campfire breakfast and got an early start in order to reach Cherry by afternoon. Today we would be in our new "home"!

10

Pickpocket Mine

So it was that on an afternoon in the last week of April we drove once more into the pretty hills of the Cherry mining country. Upon inquiring at the lone store and gas station, we learned that we might be able to rent a cabin at a mine a few miles away. The road was rough and steep in places, but we made it and were able to rent a small cabin at the mine owned by the Tuckers.

Mr. Tucker told us of several likely gold prospects about two miles from his place, which we could find by following an old road until we came to a wide sandy wash wherein lay a beautiful park of big oaks, alligator junipers, and manzanita bushes. There was also a lot of oak brush, catclaw, manzanita, and squaw bush on the hills, which made the going very difficult, almost impossible unless you followed wash, trail, or road.

To save gas money and also keep from abusing the Horizon Hunter any more than we had to, we hiked over and back each day, a four-mile round trip which didn't include the ground we covered while prospecting, until Bill staked out our claim and started the necessary location work with pick and shovel.

In front of me as I write is the notice from the Assay Office of the Shattuck Denn Mining Corporation, Iron King Branch, for the Pickpocket Mine, telling us that our ore assayed at $6.65 a ton at the surface, and signed by Geo. L. Diehl. This was enough to encourage us to think of this place as our future home, so after a couple of weeks we agreed it would save rent, time, and effort to camp by our claim. We moved out of the cabin and pitched our small five-by-seven tent below our No. 1 claim which I had named the Pickpocket Mine as gold often comes in pockets in that district.

Bill staked out a second claim which took in a pretty little spring, but as it was about a half mile above us in the wash, we hauled our drinking and cooking water from Cherry two miles away when we drove in for mail and groceries.

The weather was lovely and mild after an earlier cold spell, and we loved being able to camp in one place which we could fix up the way we wanted. Our tent was set up under some young oaks, and near it Bill fixed a screened apple box cupboard to keep food safe from insects and animals. He found an old wooden table to supplement our rickety card table, and built a fireplace below us in the bank of the wash where it would be protected from wind. Situated under a manzanita bush, at night the glowing campfire lit up the glossy leaves and shiny red bark like a cathedral window. I did all of my cooking over campfire coals as I preferred it, and that way we could save on gasoline.

It was all too necessary that we save. We had less than a hundred dollars left, but our living costs were low, just for food, besides gas and oil for trips to Cherry and an occasional trip to Prescott thirty miles west of us; also we spent a small amount for garden seeds and some tools.

Our first move after locating our mine and setting up our camp, was to clear a piece of ground in the brush, a very hard job kibitzed by some neighboring miners who kept telling us to get a bulldozer. After which we planted a garden, our new neighbors assuring us it would be watered by the summer rains due in June.

In order to conserve on moisture and labor, we dug our garden in small round basins in each of which we planted a few seeds, similar to the Zuni Indians' method, only their basins were square, making a waffle design.

At the mine where we had stayed the first couple of weeks, there had been water only a few feet below the surface of the wash, and as water was our big problem, Bill began to dig a well in our wash where he had been assured there would be water, not very far down. After digging nearly twenty feet down, using a crude handmade ladder for ascent and descent, Bill found nothing but dry sand, so he started a new well farther up the wash where he was told there would positively be water.

Bill did the well-digging in spare moments, as the garden was taking a great deal of our time. After we had our hundreds of basins dug and the seeds planted, we had to water them to get the seed germinating. As the garden couldn't wait for the well, instead of further digging, we had to get water elsewhere. There was a flooded, abandoned mine on the hill above our camp, about two hundred yards away, and if we hiked up there, we could go down into the shaft and dip out water for our garden, using three buckets and a big canteen we had found.

The mine water was full of slime and wiggletails and unsuitable for cooking or drinking, but I strained and heated it for bathing and washing dishes and clothes, lessening the amount we had to haul from Cherry. We would dip out a can full of the mine water for each basin as we walked down the rows, returning time after time to the mine shaft until all basins had been watered.

One day when we were up at the mine on one of our daily trips for water, Bill had just started down the runway when I noticed an ugly dark head flick out from under some rocks at a point right above Bill's head. Quietly but firmly I said, "Bill. Come right up out of there."

Without question, he turned and walked slowly, carefully to the top of the shaft, whereupon I showed him what I had seen. A big, black rock rattler, the first rattlesnake I had ever seen in the wild. What if it had struck Bill in the head! Disaster! But it hadn't, and now our problem was to kill the snake before he fell into the mine where our precious garden water supply was.

We each took a long stick and maneuvered him out of his protective rocks. Then Bill heaved a big flat rock onto the snake's head and finished him off. My western education had taken a big leap forward.

In spite of all our hard work, we were pleased and excited by our beautiful new home. At night we sat by our campfire talking over our plans and listening to the elf owls and the coyotes. One night we heard the distinctive (to Bill) cry of a mountain lion as he headed up the wash toward the mountains. Sometimes during the day we would stop work and take a short hike up one of the hills from which we would get a soul-satisfying view of friendly Baker Butte in the far distance and lovely little Onion Hill nearby to the South.

On one of his hikes Bill brought me a gift, a blooming century plant stem which we placed in a bucket of water in the patio under the oak trees where we ate our meals. Tiny hummingbirds, flashing their bright colors, would fly fearlessly to the orange-red blossoms to eat the nectar and the ants which climbed around the flowers.

It was a wonderful place for birds, and I had my mother send me their Mexican string hammock which they had no use for, and I lay in it under the walnut trees and watched the grosbeaks, flycatchers and warblers, band-tailed pigeons, flickers and woodpeckers, tanagers, gnatcatchers, vireos and orioles, towhees, and many other birds as they went about their business. From my observation of these and the birds I had met on the desert, I composed the following little verses:

THE ARIZONA BIRD, SEEN AND ALSO HEARD

From flower to flower flits the hummer.
His jewel-like colors brighten the summer.

Into the birds' morning symphony
The phainopepla slips a brief melody.

The Gambel quail gather in the mesquite
To chatter and rest and gossip and eat.

Across the wash the roadrunner goes.
Could you run as fast? Nobody knows.

The cactus wren's tune is both short and catchy,
But his voice is hoarse, so we call him Mr. Scratchy.

Up above the clouds the golden eagle has flown.
He's tired of earth and wants to be alone.

The canyon wren's song is bright and sweet.
In the Grand Canyon it's a wonderful treat.

There are too many gnats for the little gnatcatcher,
But he does his best and tries to fly faster.

The gila woodpecker's home in the giant sahuaro
Is cozy and warm and truly safe from sorrow.

The tiny mother verdin screams, "Don't you touch my nest!"
As she tries to look big by puffing up her breast.

In the twilight's gloom the elf owl's call
Sounds like the bouncing of a ping pong ball.

Horizon Hunters

The whippoorwill, seeking bugs at night,
Hunts with swift and noiseless flight.

The Palmer thrasher looks fierce with his long, curved bill,
But his sweet song heard in a sandwash gives you a thrill.

Scratching with both feet in the sand,
The towhee leaves his little brand.

Perched on a flowering century plant,
The oriole eats honey and the little black ant.

The crested jay in the tall yellow pine
Shrieks, "What's yours is mine, and what's mine is mine!"

Searching for worms in the walnut tree's shade,
The tanager sings a shy sweet serenade.

Hopping up and down the trunk of a tree,
The wood peewee asks for your sympathy.

The grosbeak's bill is short and thick
For crushing seeds with one sharp click.

The falcon hawk warns, "Don't come too close,
Or I'll swoop down and pluck off your nose!"

The vermilion flycatcher, bright in the setting sun,
Seeks "just one more fly" before his day is done.

The only all red bird with a crest,
The cardinal is a favorite bird guest.

Watch out for your chickens when Swainson's hawk's above;
There's nothing he likes better than "chicken-in-the-rough."

You know for sure that summer's here
When the white-winged doves appear.

Sweet and cheerful all day long
Is the desert sparrow's "sewing machine song."

The buzzard is as ugly as anything we've seen,
But we must admit we need him to keep the desert clean.

There are still people who think that the Arizona desert and hills are arid and devoid of life, but nothing could be further from the truth. They are alive with all kinds of birds, animals, insects, and vegetation.

We had numerous animal visitors at the Pickpocket Mine, so on one of our trips to Prescott we invested in some poultry wire and barbed wire for a fence to protect our garden from range cattle, rabbits, squirrels and chipmunks, and also the pack rats. For this Bill had to secure permission from the forest ranger to cut down a few small trees for posts, after which there were post holes to dig and wire to stretch and staple, with which work I helped him the best I could.

Our little Paradise was the home of a great many different kinds of insects including gorgeous butterflies as well as pesky flies, some mosquitoes, vicious buffalo gnats, and a species of long-legged, gauzy-winged creature whose special delight was to land in our soup. We named these the "flying miserables."

As the days turned warmer, a new creature came to torment us, a tiny, almost invisible insect called the "no-see-'em" gnat which appeared to breakfast on us as soon as the sun rose each mild spring morning. He was no special problem to the miners with their screened cabins, but to people living and working out-of-doors he was a constant misery. In spite of the hot days, we had to cook, eat, and work in long-sleeved shirts, gloves, and "burnooses" to protect our heads and necks, as well as mosquito-bar veils, all of which the little devils managed somehow to penetrate, while we prayed for the coming of the rains which our neighbors assured us would prove the end of our tormentors.

In spite of our troubles and primitive methods of gardening, we managed pretty well and soon had a fine big garden coming along: 165 basins of potatoes, good-sized patches of peas, string beans, tomatoes, squash, melons, pumpkins, beets, carrots, onions, two kinds of corn, some watermelons, and a large patch of navy beans.

We walked in that garden so many times with our buckets and dip cans that we could still remember after many years which part of the garden had which kind of produce growing. It was a gratifying sight, all those tender young growing things which were to be marketed eventually at the rate of "a thousand pounds a week" and bring us all kinds of money at the Prescott markets.

With the money we would receive, we planned to develop our mine, build a cabin, and surely dig a successful water well which Bill hadn't yet been able to do after three dry-as-dust holes. But surely, we reasoned, there had to be water down there some place with a flooded mine just over the hill. And if we had gone down with our mine, we might have been flooded out with water where we didn't want it!

We never worked harder in our lives than we did trying to make a go of that place at Cherry. With the war on and gasoline and tires rationed, we knew we had to have a home for the duration. We drove ourselves to the limit from sun-up to dusk, falling into bed exhausted each night. In spite of it all, and our simple diet forced by dwindling funds, we felt well and didn't consider ourselves ill-used, for we were working for ourselves.

But finally we had to admit defeat. Hot winds roared up out of the low desert through the hills and canyons drying the ground as fast as we could water it. Ants nipped off the tiny beet and carrot sprouts. Pack rats feasted on the tomato plants. Baby rabbits squeezed through the poultry wire and nibbled the young corn. Ground squirrels climbed the unprotected fence posts and cleaned up what the others left. And no summer rains. It was the first year of drought.

Gold mining went out about then; it was the spring of 1942. Mining was "never a poor man's game," and that was what we were, not only poor but darned near broke. But I can't remember our being afraid for the future. We were as optimistic as ever, for we still had our health and strength, the Horizon Hunter was still serving us as faithfully as ever, and we were in Arizona! Everything would be all right, for there was no place for us to go but up! Failure wasn't in our vocabulary.

On the advice of a local miner, Roy Cornett, we decided to make our fresh start at Bellemont where an ordnance depot was being built. I have never forgotten our last morning at Cherry. I was up and dressed before sunrise, and, taking the loaded .22 rifle, went forth in the sweet mild dawn to shoot a rabbit for breakfast. When I reached the foot of the hill leading to the flooded mine, I glanced up to see a coyote sitting at the top gazing down at me. I raised the rifle and sighted, waited for a long moment, but found I could not shoot.

The coyote had as much right there as I did. Usually I thought of the coyote as a mean and sneaky animal, although thrilling to hear in the night, but that morning I felt that all animals were our brothers and sisters, and I almost envied him, for he had his freedom and his living there in those hills, while we must leave and go into servitude once more to other people.

As I lowered my gun, the coyote stood up, turned, and trotted gracefully off into the brush. When I reached the top of the hill, I saw that in return for my sparing his life, he had left me his breakfast, for near the mine was a nice, fat cottontail rabbit hopping along, oblivious to my presence, and our hoped-for breakfast disappeared into the bushes.

I walked back to the crest of the hill and looked off toward the horizon and said my farewells to the hills of Cherry, gilded now by the rising sun, after which I returned to camp to fix a breakfast of flapjacks to give us strength for packing up our equipment and loading the car.

So we abandoned the Pickpocket Mine which had lived up to its name, but not as we had hoped.

11

Our Forest Camp
at Bellemont

Upon reaching Bellemont and taking stock of our liquid assets, we found that our cash on hand was a rock bottom thirty-five cents. But we did have some cans of food and a half sack of potatoes to last us until Bill's new job would bring in a pay check. Upon applying at the personnel office, he had been hired as a guard at the ordnance depot.

As we had no place to stay our first night there, we drove back to Parks where there was a little picnic grounds among the huge Ponderosa pines, and there we spread our bedding on the hard rocky ground as it was late, and we were too tired to assemble the cot. And I remember it as one of the best rests I had ever had. I had become tough.

Next day we found a private camp about a mile from town where for two dollars a week we were given a place to park our car and pitch our tent. We weren't allowed to camp out in the forest as we would have preferred, but the camp did supply water and rest rooms. Too late, however, we learned that the water was bad, and we soon became miserably ill with dysentery along with most of the rest of that camp's residents and all the surrounding camps. When I boiled and strained the water, green scum and tiny red bugs discolored the straining cloth. The water had been hauled from an uncovered, contaminated spring. The saddest part was that children and tiny babies were also suffering, but nothing was done about the water; it was up to all of us to boil and strain it.

The rest rooms, small wooden outhouses, were a disgrace, seldom cared for unless there was a protest, and it was always a trial to use them.

Around us were some trailer houses, and only one other tent, near ours, a large wall tent housing a varied assortment of adults, children, dogs, and chickens, a "grapes of wrath" kind of family who stayed aloof from the rest of the people. As the sides of their tent were kept rolled up during the heat of the day, we couldn't help seeing what went on. They lived fairly quietly and harmoniously in spite of their crowded quarters, never seeming to mind the dust that settled in their food, clothes, and bedding whenever the wind blew; ignoring the chickens roosting on iron bedsteads and wooden chair backs; contented with a life in which regular pay checks brought, in generous amounts, the beans and salt pork, greens, biscuits and gravy, which made up their diet, one which didn't appeal to us. I bought all our food at a store in Bellemont.

The impartial wind also blew dust into our tent, but we didn't feel like paying forty dollars a month for one of the crude, unfurnished one-room frame shacks that boasted no modern conveniences beyond a bare light bulb hanging from the ceiling. We had to save our money, as our plans did not include staying on at Bellemont for the winter, one of the coldest inhabited spots in Arizona.

When the Army took over the guard work, Bill was hired as a time-keeper with the construction company, working out in the field with Navajo labor crews. He liked this job, as he enjoyed being with the Indians, some of whom were "long hairs" who knew few words of English. Bill was fair with them and got along fine.

As there was no job for me, and my housekeeping duties were at a bare minimum, my days were pretty lazy, unusual for me after our hard work at Cherry. After I recovered from the effects of the bad water, Bill had a relapse and also caught a bad cold. We had no medicines, and I decided he needed paregoric for relief from abdominal pain, and we also needed an alarm clock, so one morning, leaving Bill in bed, I decided to hitch a ride to Flagstaff.

A youngish man in an old black car stopped on the highway for me, and after a close look at his face which appeared harmless enough, I got into the car. He talked pleasantly for awhile, then mentioned that another woman, from Texas, whom he had picked up, made advances toward him, but when he responded, she pulled a knife on him, so he had had to stop and let her out.

I didn't know what to think, but after a moment, keeping a straight face, I opened my purse, reached in, groped for my small pocket knife, and hid it in my hand the rest of the way to Flagstaff. But nothing happened. In fact, my benefactor gallantly offered to take me back to Belle-mont after I had finished my errands. I accepted, not knowing what else to do but somehow confident that I could take care of myself. Crediting my friendly, interested but impersonal attitude with protecting me, I arrived back at Bellemont later that afternoon unscathed, mission completed.

A far more dangerous ride I took later on was with the family of another worker whose trailer was parked a short distance from our tent. After we reached Flagstaff, he promised his wife he wouldn't go near a bar and that he would meet us at a certain time and place, but he showed up two hours late and drunk. I sat up in front with the man and his wife who held their baby girl in her arms, their three-year-old boy stretched out on the back seat for a nap. Back over the mountain roads we went, tearing along at high speed, passing other cars on hill curves, while the woman's nagging made the man act more outrageously than ever, and all the time I chattered on in a shaking voice, trying to ease the situation, my hands gripping each other to stop their trembling. We reached camp, but I'll never know why. I never went in to town again with anyone but safe, steady Bill.

When the summer rains finally arrived, very late in the year, I had to cook our meals over the campstove set on the ground inside the door of the tent. I had to sit on the cot to stir soup or flip pancakes, and we sat there to eat, with our plates balanced on our laps.

With the coming of the rain, we discovered that the tent leaked, so we had to buy a new tarp to spread over the top, and when the weather turned colder, we bought an extra blanket and a new quilted cot pad which made us feel quite luxurious with the added comfort. Food supplies, utensils, and everything else had to be stowed in the car when we weren't using them, which meant daily packing and repacking, arranging and rearranging, so that first things needed were first up wherever possible. A few things were kept under the bed.

Between showers I enjoyed hiking in the cool, damp forest, watching birds and small animals, once happening upon a small herd of antelope, another time catching sight of a large porcupine resting on the branch of a Ponderosa pine. And one day I found an ancient Indian cave back in the rocks. It appeared to be a perfect hide-out for a mountain lion, but I couldn't resist a closer look, ready at any moment for speedy retreat. The cave turned out to be rather shallow and sheltered only a large pack rat nest from whose tangle of twigs, dried grasses, and pine cones came an occasional rustling of tiny feet, and now and then a pair of bright dark eyes would peer out at me as I poked around the cave, looking for artifacts, finding broken bits of arrowheads and pottery, charred wood, dried corn cobs, and animal bones.

Sometimes Bill and I would walk to my cave early in the evening, build a small campfire, and pretend that we were living alone out in the hills once more with peace and privacy. These excursions helped us to endure the noise, dirt, and lack of privacy of the construction camp.

As Bellemont is high in the mountains of northern Arizona, by the middle of September it was too cold for us to camp out. As no houses were available, we felt justified in following our plan to return to the desert and its warm sunshine even though we had no prospects for work.

12

Spur Cross Ranch

How good it felt to be on the road again. As we were less than a hundred miles from Grand Canyon, we decided to go there before we left for the desert. With light hearts we turned north at the junction near Williams, and after two hours we were once more at Grand Canyon village where we rented a cabin in the auto court. Because of the war, the village was almost deserted; the Canyon was ours and ours alone as we wandered along the rim, hiked down the Bright Angel and Kaibab Trails part way, and feasted our eyes and spirits on the ever-changing beauty of the world's first natural wonder, the only sound the sighing of the wind in the pines and junipers.

After three days we left and drove on down to the desert choosing a roundabout way and taking side trips as we went. We drove up through the Date Creek Mountains to Hillside to see what that was like as a possible future home, then returned to the main highway and drove down to Wickenburg. Instead of continuing south, we turned west toward the dome of the Harquahala Mountains which we wanted to see at closer range, but before we reached the turn-off at Salome, there was an enticing dirt road north from Wenden into the Harcuvars, toward which mountains we headed to camp for the night.

It was one of the loveliest camps we ever made. Tall graceful ocotillos, giant sahuaros, fragrant greasewood, mesquites and palo verdes, and a cheerful granite sand wash gave us the kind of desert camp we liked the best. As we lay on our cot out in the open, we saw the stars appearing in the mountain pass, above us a brilliant display, the sky a black velvet backdrop for its thousands of precious gems.

Next morning we drove over the pass, unable to resist seeing the desert beyond, before we turned back to Wenden and continued west to Salome, then headed southeast on the dirt road past the majestic Harquahalas, the rugged Big Horn Mountains, and the jagged, barren Eagle Tails, a daunting place for old-time prospectors. We drove slowly, talking about the Harquahalas as a possible future home, for we had heard that there were springs and oak trees at the top of the mountain, and one prospector was said to be making a fair living from a little "stringer" of gold.

If he had a spring, he could have a garden, and even if he was isolated, he could still hike to Salome for supplies he needed and manage all right. Wouldn't it be nice, we thought, if we had a deal like that?

We continued on past the Saddle Mountains and on to Arlington near which town Chapo and the other horses were still on summer pasture. After renewing our acquaintance with them, luring them with carrots as they were rather wild after their summer of freedom, we drove to Phoenix and then to the desert south of town where we pitched our tent in the citrus orchard at the riding stable, although it wasn't being reopened because of the war.

We decided we would try to find jobs at a ranch in the hills and help raise beef for the war effort, so, putting the horse before the ranch, we bought Bill's beloved Chapo. When we rented a horse trailer and drove to the pasture to get him, however, he fought wildly against being loaded, banging his head against a fence post in his desperate effort to escape, which unfortunately resulted in partial deafness.

The ranch owner insisted he could get Chapo into the trailer, but we called it quits, and Bill drove me back to Red Star, returned the trailer, got a lift out to the ranch, and rode Chapo the sixty long miles to the stable, both of them arriving worn out, in the early hours of the morning.

They quickly recovered, and in his joy at having his own horse, Bill decided that I should have a horse, also. After looking around, we bought a beautiful, half-broke chestnut filly whom we named Bonnie. Then we had to buy saddles, bridles, and blankets which took a substantial bite out of our remaining funds.

While waiting for a response to our newspaper ad for work, we went to pick cotton, interesting to me as a new kind of work but much too hard for me to continue at it. And my pay was far from enough to make it worthwhile. I could eat up for lunch more than I had made during the morning.

We received two replies to our ad, and after investigating both offers, we decided on a small dude and cattle ranch called Spur Cross where they needed a couple to run it, the woman to act as cook and hostess, the man as cowhand and dude wrangler. I hadn't really considered the dude business, and what did I know about cooking for guests? Sure, I knew enough to satisfy Bill and me with good plain food, but what business did I—who had learned to cook over a campfire-have cooking for paying guests? Bill said, "It's up to you." He thought I was a wonderful cook and gave me all kinds of praise and encouragement to boost my confidence.

Well, what else could we do? We had to have a job, we had a "family" to feed now, two hungry horses, with hay and grain pretty expensive. No matter how I felt about it, I would have to bluff my way through and do my best. Spur Cross Ranch, located five miles from Cave Creek, wasn't ready for business yet, so I would be required to cook for only Bill and a hired man and myself. I could study my cookbooks and experiment and work into the job gradually. So we took the job.

Now the problem was to move our outfit to the ranch, a distance of thirty-five miles. We hadn't moved with horses before, and as we couldn't haul Chapo in a trailer, there was no point in moving Bonnie that way. We wanted to do the job all in one day, and as I couldn't drive and was too inexperienced to bring the horses through Phoenix traffic, Bill drove me out into the desert to teach me how to drive, and the day before we were to leave for the ranch, Bill rode Chapo and led Bonnie clear across Phoenix and paid a riding stable to keep them overnight, then he returned to the stable and me by bus.

Next morning, loaded to the ceiling, running boards, and bumpers with saddles, bridles, blankets, and everything else we owned, we set out for the stable on the edge of the desert. Bill had me drive the car down the road a few miles while he brought the horses. I sat there for a long time until finally they showed up, and Bill had me drive on again for a couple more miles. And so on.

After about fifteen miles of this, we had lunch while the horses ate grain. Then Bill had me mount Chapo and lead Bonnie while he took the car. Slowly, slowly, the miles went by, the mountains seemingly as far away as ever, as the horses plodded along. I began to realize what pioneer women must have felt, traveling across the desert in the early days with the covered wagons.

We had had the horses given distemper shots, and they were still feeling the effects of the serum, so they were more tired than they should have been. When I wearied of prodding them onward, Bill would take over once more, walking and leading them much of the time, while I drove the car. The country was becoming more rolling, but I was doing all right so far, and at last I turned in at the driveway of the Black Mountain Store and gas station at Cave Creek, five miles from Spur Cross Ranch.

The air had turned cold, and I shivered from nervousness and fatigue as I walked around to stretch my legs and wait for Bill and the horses. Finally they appeared over the last little hill, and when Bill rode up with the tired, reluctant horses, he asked me, "Which would you rather do, drive the car or ride the horses the rest of the way?" Neither, I wanted to yell, neither.

"I'll take the car," I said.

But I hadn't had enough experience for mountain driving, I didn't know the road, which was rough, narrow, and winding, the grades short and steep, so I would go around a curve, then down into a wash, forget what to do next, and stall the engine. Bill would ride up, dismount, and patiently start the motor, and I would grit my teeth and drive in low gear out of the wash, go around another curve, down into another wash, and stall again. Luckily, I didn't meet another car nor crash into anyone else, nor drive off the edge of a cliff or wreck the motor. My guardian angel was looking after me.

Night fell when we were still a couple of miles from the ranch, so Bill said he would take the horses on the rest of the way, then walk back and bring me on in with the car. I felt foolish not to be more help. I should have taken the horses while Bill drove the car, but I didn't know the country, and by now the tired horses needed a firm hand which I certainly didn't have.

We finally got there and were met by the couple whose place we were taking. As the horses were already in a corral and fed, we needed some food ourselves. Supper was over, and all that was left were some potatoes and string beans which we ate with a glass of milk each and went to bed, more dead than alive.

Next morning before we were up, the other couple had left, and we were in charge. Just like that. I was now a ranch woman, willy nilly. The place was a mess, and I had my hands full cleaning up the main ranch house the first few days. Fred, our boss, had explained to us how my predecessor had spent her time crocheting and reading comic books, and I soon saw that it must have been true. I made a clean sweep of everything and went on from there.

None of the guest cabins was ready for occupancy; they still required some plumbing, carpentry work, and painting. Fred and the hired man, a frail farmer from North Dakota who had asthma, helped Bill, although Bill had little say as to how things should be done, so results were pretty haphazard with cheap materials and insufficient tools to work with. It soon appeared that all Fred wanted was to get things done somehow, anyhow, and be ready for business and make money as soon as possible.

As each cabin was finished, I arranged the nondescript secondhand furniture, cheap curtains, and linens as best I could. When I was through, everything was neat and clean but not what you would call attractive. But the rates charged were to be the lowest of any guest ranch in the area, so it would probably do. We would have to make up the deficiencies in other ways.

I began to practice up on my cooking, reading all my cookbooks; but there again, I had little to work with. I had to use my own kitchen equipment to supplement the ranch's skimpy supply, and only an ancient three-burner kerosene stove with portable stove-top oven, and a temperamental elephant of a wood and coal range which took forever to heat and used an enormous quantity of fuel. This latter stove was supposed to operate the water heater, also, but that was a myth, so I heated water on the kerosene stove in a tea kettle and buckets. Nice going.

Food supplies were meager until guests were expected. For our first Thanksgiving dinner at Spur Cross, Bill and I feasted on scrambled eggs and sardines. The hired man went in to town to eat with friends.

Fred was very disappointed with the first lunch I served him. Not having much to offer, I chose a new recipe from a chain store magazine, called Savory Salmon and Corn, which turned out to be a nice, thick potato soup with corn and salmon added, a really swell camping dish, but not what our boss had in mind for the guest business. The next time he came for lunch, he brought some fresh meat and other goodies, so I turned out a nice meal with all the trimmings, and he seemed pleased.

Besides plumbing, painting, and carpentering, Bill was involved in a number of other chores: he had to dig and repair cesspools; feed, care for, and shoe eight horses; feed and milk two cows; and take care of four young pigs and some chickens. All this in addition to riding the range to look for cattle and doctor them when necessary; and when the water holes dried out, he had to dig them deeper. A busy man.

Bill discovered right at the start that some fences were down, and he had to ride out and bring in what cattle he could find that bore the ranch brand. Those he couldn't find were chalked up to modern-day "black market" beef rustlers. Bill had to repair the fences and water gaps wherever they were torn out, and later had to move a half-mile of fence that was encroaching on a neighbor's range. Did I say he was busy?

In his spare time, he repaired corrals and the barn roof, built a separate corral for Bonnie, and overhauled the light plant. At night after supper he fought with the temperamental old gasoline engine which pumped water from the well up to the tank on the hill above the house. Later he helped put up a windmill to supplement the engine and save on gasoline.

In the morning after milking the two cows before breakfast, Bill chopped and sawed wood for the kitchen stove and living room heater and tried to get a supply ahead for the heaters in the two small one-room cabins. The three-room cabin, which had two bathrooms, was heated by a fuel-oil stove.

Besides working on the cabins and cleaning the main house with its huge living room and dining room, sun porch bedroom (to be used later for a hired girl), the bathroom with shower, and one guest room besides our tiny, stuffy bedroom next to the kitchen, I had other things to fill my days. There were large rugs to clean with only a broom and carpet sweeper, no vacuum cleaner. I washed clothes and bedding in a small secondhand electric washing machine. I wrote letters to prospective guests, cooked and served meals to Fred and his family and friends on their weekend trips to the ranch, then cleaned up after them when they left. I also helped Bill at the corrals or on the range when he needed an extra hand. I was busy too.

In our "spare time" we took care of six cats and two dogs, and also pulled cactus thorns out of them when needed. And occasionally drove into Cave Creek for supplies.

All this before we had guests. And we were doing it for a total cash wage of fifty dollars a month for the two of us, plus room and board such as it was, and the joy of working on a ranch in the hills; also feed for our two horses which we used in the ranch work. With the expressed agreement that later on we would receive five percent of gross income when we had paying guests. Later, Fred tried to deny that he had promised this, but finally we made him remember when we had a place full of guests and he needed us. When we left the ranch a year and a half later, our last and largest check came to a grand total of $120.00, our base pay having been raised finally to $80.00 a month.

We were so busy that we had no time to visit with the neighbors, and

Fred reported to us that the villagers had complained that we weren't sociable. One night soon after our arrival at the ranch, some of the local men drove up the dark winding road from the village saloon and paid us a visit. They walked into the house loudly demanding refreshments, and they were drunk. We had nothing to offer them, so one hulking "gentleman" in a pony skin vest ordered me to serve him some raw onions, bread, and ketchup. After I gave him what he wanted, he sat munching on the food at the kitchen table while some of his tipsy cronies snickered as they watched him, and in the living room Bill was prevailing upon one of the more sober men to talk his friends into leaving, which he did when he realized how upset I felt.

Later we became good friends with some of our close neighbors who were ranchers and mine owners, old timers in the district, particularly Theodore and Catherine Jones of the Cahava Ranch, but we never did fit in with the "saloon set" whose frequent pastime was throwing bottles and getting into fights at village dances. It used to be a pretty wild community. I have no idea what Cave Creek is like now.

After we had been at Spur Cross a few weeks, Fred brought some carrier pigeons for us to feed, care for, and help train, to be a "mail service" between the ranch and his mansion in town, but it didn't work out. We couldn't believe our eyes the day we saw Fred, exasperated, start spanking those pigeons with a small board as he stood hunched over in their coop in the back yard on the bank of the sand wash.

A few months later when the female pigeons began to sit on their nests, a red racer slipped in and swiped some of the eggs. We saw him, but he moved too swiftly for us to stop him. When a few eggs finally hatched, the snake killed the baby birds. The one-inch poultry wire of the pen wasn't fine enough to keep him out, as a red racer is very slender.

As my kitchen was on the north side of the house with an adjoining back porch, it was very gloomy, especially as the walls and ceiling were painted a dark brown. It was a small room, so I decided I would paint it myself and was supplied with some cheap whitewash, which did a poor job but made the room brighter.

One forenoon as I was enameling the woodwork around the unhandy set-tub type kitchen sink, Fred's station wagon swung around the house, and as I went to the living room window to look, paint brush in hand, the car doors opened and out stepped Fred, his young son Jimmy, and a new hired hand named Paul to take the place of the ex-farmer who had quit, and lastly a woman and two girls, one aged ten and the other a three-year-old.

Spotted with paint, tired, hot, and messy, I greeted the party and was informed that I was to prepare lunch for everyone and take on the mother and children as guests for a few weeks. We weren't ready! We didn't even have enough dishes or table ware, just some chipped and cracked odds and ends and a miscellaneous collection of tin knives, forks, and spoons, although I had asked for suitable items several times. But I didn't dream of backing down on this assignment, as I liked the looks of this family.

"See that you don't get any paint into the lunch," teased Paul, the new hired hand, a youngish ex-newspaperman from Ohio, whose ranching knowledge turned out to be strictly limited to one boyhood experience at milking a cow.

He didn't know how to saddle a horse, chop wood, or feed stock, work cattle, carpenter, plumb, build fence, shoe horses, or dig cesspools; but he was hired and willing to learn, and it was up to Bill to train him. We showed him his quarters, a small room in the building with the light plant, a noisy place when someone got up in the middle of the night and turned on a light, which automatically started the engine. But Paul was willing to put up with it to get the job. He wanted the experience of living and working on a ranch.

I was tired of trying to "make do" with cheap, secondhand junk, and even our employer's young son Jimmy confided to us that anything the family didn't want in their house in town, they brought out to the ranch. This came as no surprise to us. I asked Fred how he expected me to take care of guests without decent dishes and table ware. Acting surprised, he promised to do something immediately, and after a few days he showed up with some heavy, restaurant-type equipment and an assortment of stainless steel knives, forks, and spoons, not all matching, but serviceable.

I was pleased that we had let Mrs. King and her two little girls, Dorothy and Mary, stay in spite of all the extra work, for the woman turned out to be a good friend to me, uncomplaining about the obvious defects of the ranch. And Bill and I fell in love with the beautiful children, who were sweet, polite, and intelligent. Dorothy had an adult sense of humor that was very entertaining to me, and she became quite a companion for me while I went about my work, offering to help me, but as she was a paying guest, I wouldn't permit it.

Before long two more guests joined our party, and Bill was given a second hired hand for a short time so that he could get caught up on the work. I was still struggling with my cooking but managed to turn out successful meals through sheer doggedness, even baking two apple pies, the first I had ever tried since I was eleven years old and had baked one under my mother's tutelage. Everyone pronounced them perfect, and I agreed.

The work was getting to be too much for me, so Fred showed up one evening with a hired girl, an Arizona ranch girl who said she was sixteen but later we learned that she was only fifteen. However, Betty was a good kid, cheerful and friendly, although inexperienced at housework, but she was paid only $35.00 per month so was the best we could get. Fred went on the theory that "all kinds of people are willing to work for almost nothing for the joy of being on a desert ranch." They call it "psychic income." Be that as it may, because of the low cash wage, we had trouble getting the hired help to forego any of their psychic wage. They preferred riding on the range to helping at the stove, and I had to let my hired girl have every afternoon off if I expected her to do the supper dishes. She was of some help in the mornings with other chores if I worked along with her.

Having some spare time after breakfast was out of the way, occasionally I would go along with Bill when he took guests for their morning ride. Bill loved riding along desert mountain trails on Chapo with sweet little Mary on the saddle in front of him, and Chapo behaved like a lamb. One day Mrs. King remarked that her horse wasn't minding her, and Mary piped up very authoritatively, "If you can't ride the horse, you'll have to get off." Bill had to laugh. Mrs. King and her little girls were as dear to me as any family could have been, and I felt a deep sense of loss when they left after a few weeks due to the illness of Mr. King back home in Milwaukee. They were the kind of people who made the ranch job bearable for Bill and me.

Sometimes I helped work cattle on my horse Bonnie, and due to Bill's training, she soon had plenty of savvy for the work and was very smart in the rocks, keeping out of cactus, also. One day, on spring round-up, she and I worked a cactus-covered mesa all by ourselves. We called it the "Devil's Garden," and we gathered fourteen head of cattle and brought them in to the home corrals. Bill had watched me from the top of a hill and was surprised and pleased at my and Bonnie's progress.

Occasionally I rode Chapo who was full of life and fun to ride. Once a wild mustang, he had been "creased," shot by a wild horse hunter, and there was still a "crease mark" visible on the back of his neck near the end of his mane. So you didn't dare fire a gun near him, which Bill discovered the day he rode out to finish off an old sick cow who was bogged down near one of the springs. Bill had to walk home several miles, arriving disgusted and tired to find Chapo wet and trembling at the back gate of the corral.

For entertainment for us and the guests, we sometimes staged "hold-ups" for new guests. The hired girl and I, dressed in overalls and men's felt hats pulled down over our eyes with our hair shoved up out of sight, took unloaded rifles down to the creek crossing, hid in the mesquite flat, and jumped out at the car bearing new guests when it came into view, which startled but pleased the guests with their ranch initiation.

The first time we tried a "hold-up," Bill was bringing a guest out in the ranch truck and knew nothing about our plan. He almost turned and ran into me, he said later, I looked so disreputable in his old clothes! Other times we and the hired help would pull the stunt on our boss and his guests, which Fred loved and which thrilled the guests. Cheap entertainment.

Then one spring night Bill drove from town with a truck load of hay and grain and three suitcases. We had no guests at the time as it was late in the season, but Bill announced that a new guest would arrive in the morning and this was some of his luggage. While we were all eating a late supper, Betty let out a shrill scream, pointed at the dining room window, and began to yell about the horrible face she had seen peering in at her. No one else had seen anything, but Bill and Paul got up and went out to investigate while I stayed behind to try to quiet the hysterical girl. Then I happened to think, what was Bill thinking of, going out there unarmed to face some menacing stranger? I ran into our bedroom, grabbed the ranch shotgun, and went outside, Betty tagging along, afraid to be left alone.

There under the window beyond Bill was a crouching figure hiding in the shadow. "Come on out of there," Bill demanded.

"Come out, fellow," said Paul bravely.

Slowly the figure arose, getting taller and taller until he towered over Bill.

"What's this all about?" I asked. Bill turned and saw me with the shotgun which I held at the ready but pointed at the ground.

"Is that gun loaded?" Bill asked quickly.

I didn't reply. I didn't know nor care. What difference did it make? The sight of it should discourage any bandit, I thought. Let him think it's loaded, whether it was or not.

Bill began to laugh strangely. I stared at him, wondering what was ailing him. "You'd better come out here into the light," he told the stranger, "and I'll perform the introductions."

It was the new guest, performing a "hold-up" in reverse, Bill's idea of a good joke until I showed up with the shotgun which did turn out to be unloaded. But what if it hadn't been? We laughed, then shuddered over what could have happened. We never played a practical joke again.

A big problem I had was trying to cook under rationing, as we weren't given special tickets by the ration board and had to collect stamps from our guests. This placed me under a handicap unless generous guests would give me some extra stamps, usually for sugar. But I never knew what to count on. Sometimes Fred would butcher a young steer or one of the pigs, for which he had to get special permission, but he kept the best cuts of meat for his family and entertaining in town, and he collected our stamps for whatever he brought out to the ranch. I managed pretty well, although I had trouble cooking the tougher, frozen cuts of meat he brought me. And one afternoon while I was struggling to fix Swiss steaks, Fred sat in the kitchen and began to criticize my way of doing things and complain about the prices we paid for food, until I felt like heaving a slab of the meat in his face and heading down the road.

I did become proficient at making nice salads, potato and other vegetable dishes, and filling desserts, with plenty of good bread, ranch butter, coffee, and milk to top off the meals. When male guests complained that they weren't getting enough meat, their wives would always take my side. They knew what I had to put up with and gave me wonderful moral support.

Fred's personal friends from town were permitted to take horses out without supervision from Bill, and on one occasion a male rider, in a fit of temper over what he thought was the disobedience of the gelding named Sinbad, whipped it with a thorny mesquite switch. And Bill found thorns in the poor animal's hide as evidence of the tale brought to him by other members of the riding party who were disgusted by the exhibition. As a result, Sinbad turned into a bucker and was no longer safe for women and children who weren't expert riders, although Bill had done his best to tame the horse down.

Aside from guide trips in the desert and mountains, we let the guests shift pretty much for themselves and provide their own entertainment, which most of them preferred to do, such as bridge and other card games, reading, and talking during long evenings and on rainy days.

Bill's stories at mealtimes were a big hit when he told about his adventures and experiences or those of other people he had met. I never tired of hearing the same tales over and over, watching the interest and delight of each new set of guests listening enthralled with Bill's knowledge of birds and animals, plants and geology, and almost any topic that might come up. If Bill had to be on the range at lunch time, I felt inadequate at having to take his place as spokesman although I did my best as it was part of my job as hostess.

Sometimes Bill would plan special horseback picnic trips for guests and even have them help with the cattle, which they loved to do. One day I went along, and after lunch Bill proposed that we try a new way back with which he was unfamiliar but which would give us some different scenery. We all agreed and then got lost, so while Bill went on alone to scout the way, we stayed behind on our horses, perched on the side of a hill. A couple of the guests began to complain, but most thought it a great adventure to tell about when they returned home. Bill soon found the way out, as it is very hard to lose him out in the wilds as I knew from experience, and although the new trail was steep and rough, we made it back to the ranch safely, although Chapo tried to buck with me when we reached the creek bottom. He was hungry. So was I. But it had been a wonderful outing, a welcome change from the kitchen range!

At times heavy rains brought floods down all the washes and the creek, so outgoing guests would have to cross the raging torrent on horseback to reach Fred's station wagon on the other side, but they thought it was thrilling, especially the children who were transported safely in back of Bill's saddle.

We loved the children of the guests, and Bill taught them to ride the gentler horses, such as old Star, or he let them ride with him if they were too small to ride alone. They also enjoyed making friends with the cats, dogs, horses, calves, burro, and pet pigeon, and a great favorite was our pet fox "Little Hiawatha," named after a cartoon character.

Bill found "Hi" out on the range in a cave one day when he was working with another rancher fixing fence, and the other man had shot the mother fox, leaving two babies alone in the cave. So after the rancher killed one baby, Bill took the second one home inside his shirt. When he was back at the ranch, he spent an hour trying to get Peppy, the mother dog who had just had puppies four days before, to accept the tiny stranger. Peppy snapped at the fox pup at first, but Bill was patient, and after he smeared some of Peppy's milk on the little fox, she permitted him to nurse, giving Bill a reproachful look before she turned her head away. Later "Hi" became her favorite as he didn't pester her all the time the way her bumbling pups did.

After Bill was finished at the barn with introducing the baby fox to Peppy, he came up to the house and told us that Peppy had had another pup. We scoffed that that wasn't possible, but he insisted, so we ran down to look. Sure enough, there was this other pup, although it sure looked strange, almost like a little rat. A runt, we decided, and we apologized to Bill for not believing him. He laughed at us the rest of the day before he finally told us the truth. We forgave him and spent every free moment we could handling and petting the new addition to our animal family.

After "Hi" was a year old, he became restless, so Bill turned him loose in the wash below the barn where he had seen another desert fox not long before. And one day a thoughtless male guest took a rifle out and shot a fox, proudly displaying it to me when he marched through the kitchen, which made me so angry that I found it hard to be civil to him from then on. To make it worse, when he tried to skin the fox as a souvenir fur to show people back east, he broke the tail off and threw the whole thing away. We resolved then never to have another wild pet. That fox could have been Little Hiawatha, we felt sure.

We had names for most of the animals on the ranch, even some of the range cattle. The dogs were Peppy and her two sons Spot and Buttons. The cats were Beauty, Cutie, Dawn, Midnight, Little Midnight, and Sourpuss, with Snowball and Cloudy added later. The only pigeon that had a name was Ikey, who was wild, but we tamed him where he would fly up into our hands to eat corn.

The names of some of the horses I remember were Punkin, Frying Pan, Patches, Sinbad, Sylvia, Joan, Blue, Star, and Dusty, as well as our Bonnie and Chapo. The burro's name was Red as he was pinkish in color, and the milk cows were Sierra Sue and Swiss Miss. Five of the steers were named Rusty, Curly, Bashful, Pat, and Mike, and five calves were Sally, Niño Diablo, Redwing, Smiley Burnette, and Cry Baby. The children found all this naming very interesting and meaningful.

Other favorite guests who visited Spur Cross were: Dr. Cutler who gave Bill a beautiful bird book when he learned of Bill's abiding interest in and love for birds; a nice young serviceman from the Army who came to ride for a few days; and Mrs. Dorothy (Doss) Taylor and her darling little girl Leslie Ann who stayed friends of ours long after we all were gone from Spur Cross. Mrs. Taylor, whom we were invited to call

"Doss," visited us at our home place on the desert at Cave Creek, which we had built a few years later, and brought us a huge carton of boxes of soap powder to use for washing diapers for our new baby, Monty Edward, who was born on August 18, 1947, at Grand Canyon. She also sent us a beautiful table lamp made from a Kachina doll. It is now fifty years old and has a place of honor on a small table in my living room. We learned later that grown-up Leslie Ann married Bill Stewart, a big handsome cowboy from Castle Hot Springs. We have been out of touch for many years, but they all still live in my memory as good friends during a difficult time.

We killed twenty-two rattlesnakes during our year and a half at Spur Cross, Bill having to crawl under the ranch house with a rake to drag some out to kill them so that they wouldn't be underfoot in the night when we had to be outside. I had to shine a mirror reflecting sunlight under the house to reveal the snake before Bill could find it and not be struck. This kind of entertainment was not usually provided the guests, as the snakes didn't appear until the weather warmed up after the season was over. We always took a flashlight with us when we went outside at night.

One day while I was riding for the milk cows on Bonnie, she suddenly stopped and stared, for up ahead in the wash a rattler was stalking a ground squirrel who sat there paralyzed with fear or fascination. When I dismounted, the spell was broken, the squirrel ran up the bank and disappeared. I tossed rocks on the snake's head while it kept moving out from under them in the soft sand, so I took a stick and beat on its head until it was dead.

Bonnie was snorting with fear and plunging, but she let me get back into the saddle before she tore down the wash for home, and I let Bill ride for the milk cows that day. I didn't feel like fighting with Bonnie to get past the dead snake.

We had to be on the watch for other deadly enemies besides snakes: black widow spiders, scorpions, centipedes, tarantulas, and an occasional tiny coral snake, although tarantulas aren't all that bad and never aggressive. But if a place is lived in long enough, the poisonous animal population is kept at a fairly safe minimum. You do have to shake out your shoes and clothes in the morning before getting dressed, just to be on the safe side.

One annoying insect is the "Hualapai Tiger," or "kissing bug," a flat, dull black beetle with a red marking on its back. It injects an anesthetic of some kind into your skin, before sucking your blood, leaving several bites which soon itch intensely and last for days.

The desert can be cruel to people and animals who come into contact with cactus thorns, and it requires pliers and tweezers to do the painful job of removing them. But for those who love the desert, its peace and beauty far outweigh its dangers and discomforts. The deep blue sky, pretty white sandwashes, the friendly hills, magnificent flaming sunsets and sunrises, star-filled nights, mornings when the sun warms the fresh clean air and you hear the cheerful calls of Gambel quail, cactus wrens, cardinals, and other birds in every wash and canyon, and best of all the desert in bloom in the spring, a magical thing when the soft colors of the cactus blossoms, peach mallow, poppies, brittle bush, lupines, and Indian paintbrush cover the hills and valleys; it is almost worth the vicious summer heat to experience a desert spring. But when July comes and even the wood furniture feels hot at temperatures that can reach 118 degrees, and you don't have air conditioning, which we didn't have at Spur Cross, just an electric fan, living and working and even sleeping in the heat can become tough to bear. We drank gallons of lemonade and iced tea, rested in the middle of the day, took frequent cool showers, and tried to make the best of it just to survive.

After another winter at the ranch, putting up with the same situations and conditions as before, Bill and I were fed up and quit. Fred told the remaining guests that he had fired us, but they knew better. One of the men drove down to the Black Mountain Store at Cave Creek, bought bacon, eggs, bread, and other things, came to see us at the cabin where we were staying rent-free, and asked me to fix all of us a bacon and egg lunch, which I did, while he told us that things at Spur Cross had gone down hill since we had left. We had given Fred a one-week notice so that he could find another couple to take our place, and he had brought out a big red-faced man named "Tex" and his wife, and things just weren't working out. Our visitor, named Burns Watling, gave Bill a beautiful hunting knife as a good-bye gift and said he and his wife were returning to Chicago.

Years later we learned that the ranch had been sold and the buildings torn down as they were deteriorating and the taxes were too high, and I can't help wondering how all the animals had fared. The cattle and horses could be sold off, of course, but how about the little ones, the cats and dogs?

13

Sickness and Health

While at Spur Cross Ranch we learned that a Cave Creek man named George Smith had a piece of desert land that he wanted to sell for a hundred dollars, four-and-a-half acres with a good well, a bargain, but he needed the money so was willing to part with it at a loss. After looking the parcel over, we were more than willing to take it over.

We planned to camp there, but our friend Catherine Jones at Cahava Ranch told us of a two-room cabin, owned by Dan Moore who worked as a guard at the prison at Florence, and she was sure she could get it for us rent-free just for taking care of it. It had a corral for Bonnie and Chapo. What more could we ask, even though the cabin had no plumbing or electricity. And it was right across the wash from our place.

While Bill fenced in our piece of palo verde desert, I rested, explored the desert, or rode horseback when I wasn't leading the horses down to a big wash nearby to eat grass in the mesquite thicket, or taking them over to our well to water them. As the Moore cabin had only an open well which had to be cleaned out, we hauled all our water from our own well, a distance of several hundred yards. We didn't mind. We were free, on our own again. We had a home place at last. We had nobody to answer to but ourselves. When Aunt Florence drove out from Phoenix for a visit, she rejoiced with us at our good fortune.

In May I fell ill, had a high fever, couldn't eat, and lost a lot of weight. My liver swelled up and felt like an inflated football, and then I turned yellow. It was infectious hepatitis, and we had no doctor closer than Phoenix, thirty miles away, but Bill took care of me, and eventually I was feeling some better and able to eat a little, although my skin began to itch unbearably in the early heat of the desert.

"We'll go north and camp in the cool pines," Bill decided. "You'll feel better there." And I agreed.

Then we saw an ad in the paper asking for a couple as caretaker for a desert ranch in the mountains near Castle Hot Springs. Just what we wanted. "Let's see if they'll hold the job for us until fall," Bill said. We were told that they would hold it open until August. Surely I would feel well enough by then, so we took the job.

Bill put Bonnie and Chapo on pasture near Phoenix and drove me and our belongings to the forest at Granite Basin Lake near Prescott to camp, and we bought me a fishing license.

I wandered around the pretty little lake, fishing and enjoying the cool pine-scented air, admiring the beauty of Granite Mountain with its huge tumbled boulders, trying to forget my misery. Gradually I began to feel better and was able to eat all I wanted, which was mainly starches.

Although we were bothered by flies and mosquitoes at this camp, it was a lovely spot. In the cool nights deer would come close to our bed, smell us, and snort wildly before bounding off into the forest. Coyotes would howl and yap, so bold that sometimes we would see them in the daytime around the edge of the lake eating dead fish that had floated to the shore. One afternoon a big old coyote trotted by our camp, stopped and sniffed at an apple core we had thrown into the road for the birds, turned his head and gave us a dirty look, then picked up the core and made off with it.

As the season of summer thunderstorms approached, we decided we'd be better off camped away from the tall pines, so after three weeks at Granite Lake, we moved our camp to Indian Creek south of Prescott where there was good drinking water and a beautiful place to set our tent under some gnarled old oak trees. There were also picnic tables, rest rooms, and fireplaces. Perfect.

I began to feel better as I hiked, rested, breathed the good fresh air, ate well, and began to feel and look almost human again, losing most of the yellow color in my skin and eyes. There were other campers but not too close to intrude on our privacy.

For a few days our closest neighbor was a hobo who slept on the pine needles with all of his things, including his food supply, next to him under his blanket. He told Bill that one night he could feel coyotes tugging at his cover, trying to get at his bacon supply. All I ever saw him cook was macaroni which he ate out of the pan without sauce.

When the rains came, he took out down the road, probably hunting shelter in a cave, and that was the last we saw of him.

One morning I hiked across the road to the ski ground where there was a hollow tree fallen across the creek, and four black-and-white kittens living inside, abandoned by someone to fend for themselves, no doubt eating mice and birds and whatever picnickers might leave for them. They were very wild and suspicious of me, but when I took them food, the prettiest kitten soon made up to me, chirping happily whenever I showed up. Bill and I liked cats, so we voted to adopt this one.

I took a big heavy paper shopping bag layered with pine needles and leaves in the bottom, topped with bits of canned Spam, air holes punched in the sides of the bag and set forth to capture our cat. I had no trouble picking him up and putting him into the bag, but after he finished eating the Spam, he began to struggle until he broke open the bag at the air holes, lay quietly in my arms, and purred loudly all the way back to camp. One smart cat.

We named him Spooky, and he proved to be a wise and affectionate companion, staying close by our camp, never venturing into the wilderness, happily playing any games we might offer with string or stick, yet never forcing himself on us when we were busy with camp chores. He was so clean, neat, and beautiful with his glossy black coat, white vest, socks, and whiskers, we had no objection to his sleeping with us on the top of our canvas bedspread at night, where he settled himself with gentle little turnings and twistings, subsiding finally with a soft thump, then turning on his motor to tell us of his contentment.

Whenever Spooky heard baby porcupines whining and barking in the nearby trees at night, he would leap onto Bill's stomach, crouch there in the dark, and listen quietly, sure he was in the safest possible place. If we went outside with a flashlight to look at the porcupines, Spooky would stay worriedly behind in the tent, greeting us with a happy little chirp when we returned to bed. He was a talker.

A couple of old fellows would call on us occasionally, one of them usually arriving at mealtime. As our money was getting dangerously low, we didn't dare to invite him to join us, for that would have become too much of a good thing, for him. I hated to sit there and eat while he sat aside, pretending not to watch as he talked away, but our supplies were getting low, and we had little to offer others.

In August the rains came, thunder striking fiercely in the tall pines, and some of the other campers left. One afternoon after a shower, while Bill was on a short hike, a little girl came running along the wet deserted road across the creek from our camp, crying desperately. When I called to her, she stopped crying and stared over at me, then ran across the little bridge to our camp. She was soaked through and shivering with cold and fright. I bundled her up in a warm blanket and tried to get her to eat some hot Spanish rice I had just fixed, but she was too wrought-up to eat anything. Finally she managed to tell me she was from a girls' camp a few miles away and had become lost from her friends while on a hike in the forest. The old story. Luckily she had had enough common sense to stay on the road she had come across, for there is too much forest south of Prescott for one little girl to cope with.

As soon as Bill returned, he drove her back to her camp, and the grateful camp director reimbursed Bill for the precious rationed gasoline he had used, with some extra for good measure. We needed every ounce of our gas to get to our new job.

Two weeks later it was time to leave. On a clear morning we broke camp, loaded the car, lifted Spooky in, and headed for Phoenix where we struck out north from there for the desert mountains seventy miles away wherein lay the Bard Ranch which was our destination.

YOUNG CLARA
Clockwise from left:
Clara, 27, in December
1941. Posing in doorway
in ghost town, Congress,
Arizona. Scanning the
horizon from the pink
granite rocks of Black
Mountain near Cave
Creek in 1946.

LIFE WITH BILL *Far left, top:* **Clara, Bill, Betty, and Paul at Spur Cross Ranch.** *Immediate left:* **Trying out an Indian rock used for grinding mesquite beans.** *Three photos for* Ladies' Home Journal *by Kosti Ruohomaa:* **"Crocheting," "Desert Barbershop," and "Our Cabin at Cave Creek."**

CHILDREN *Clockwise from above:* Monty's birth announcement by a Hopi artist, August 1947. With 9-month-old Sandy, July 1950. Monty, 1, in wagon with Clara in the desert—"the world's best sandbox."

Left: A "tough-looking bunch" visiting Old Mexico on "The Expedition." *Below:* Clara and the boys at South Rim of Grand Canyon near Bright Angel Lodge.

Opinion/Editorial

God go with you, storyteller ...   by Jim Willoughby

BILL PARKS *Clockwise from left:* Official Grand Canyon guide, 1946–1962. With bus tour passengers on South Rim. After removing boots, Bill examines "picture rock" on Cave Creek, winter 1942–1943. Memorial tribute from the *Courier,* June 1995.

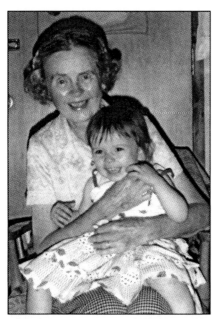

NEW GENERATION
Top: Clara at home in Stagecoach Acres with Tamara Rose Parks, her granddaughter. *Bottom:* "Ballerina" Tamara mounted on a carriage horse at Pine Lawn Ranch in Prescott, AZ.

14

At the Bard Ranch

The job at the Bard Ranch on French Creek near Castle Hot Springs had sounded extra good to us. We were to get a hundred dollars a month plus room and board, for taking care of the private estate, citrus orchard, horses, etc., of Mr. Bard, an eastern millionaire who was away most of the time. As the ranch manager, Harmonson, lived in Phoenix, we thought we would be our own bosses, for we were answerable only to him and not the range foreman who lived at the headquarters ranch called the VX. Best of all there would be no guests to cook for and cater to. Sounded ideal.

Although I was still not completely well from the bout with hepatitis, I felt able to cope with my new tasks, and I was looking forward to this new experience. After we turned off the main highway and headed toward the hills, the road became very rough and narrow, finally winding around, dipping down into washes, becoming steeper and rougher every mile until finally we began to wonder if our heavy outfit would make it.

Two miles from the ranch we crossed a boulder-strewn creek and started up another steep grade, but we knew we wouldn't make it; it was too long, too steep, but we had to try. Suddenly the motor quit, and there we were. It was late afternoon, the country was all new and strange to us, and I felt tired and very uneasy over this inauspicious beginning.

Bill set the brake and put the car in gear. Then cautioning me not to walk around outside as he had seen some bee hives close by, he set out on foot for the ranch, leaving Spooky and me alone. He was gone a long time. I waited. Nobody came by, no riders, no cars, nothing. The country seemed to be deserted. The air was hot and still.

Finally, at dusk, here came Bill in a beat-up old pickup truck that was too rickety to pull us out of trouble, so we loaded most of our stuff into the bed of the truck and drove to the ranch, Bill planning to hike back the next day for our car. On the way he told me what had happened. Upon arriving at the main house and finding no one around, he had walked a few hundred yards to a smaller house where he saw a man lying on a cot on the porch. When Bill approached, the man—who looked like some kind of cowboy—didn't get up to greet Bill and refused to help him in any way.

Finally the man, whose name was Lee, lazily suggested that Bill take the ranch pickup truck which was in the yard by the main house. End of conversation. This type of conduct was not and is not typical of the West and its people, so we couldn't understand it. But we soon discovered that many things about the place and about our job were beyond our experience and comprehension.

The large frame ranch house which was to be our new home was plain and bare, but it had a huge living room and a bright roomy kitchen, and I liked the place much better than the three smaller, more modern, plastered adobe houses above us on the hill. One of those houses, expensively decorated, with a completely modern kitchen, was the dwelling of our employer when he was at the ranch. The second, sans kitchen, was a nicely furnished guest house, and the third was for hired help, now occupied by the indolent cowhand, his wife, and three children.

We were fortunate enough to have a bathroom and running water but no water heater, refrigerator, gas, or electricity, as there was no light plant as there had been at Spur Cross. There was a big efficient wood stove, however, and for light we depended on kerosene lamps. In the living room at one end was a wonderful open fireplace which we looked forward to using on chilly winter evenings.

The place was a mess when we moved in, and when I went to fix our first meal, I was shocked. No preparation whatsoever had been made for us, the only supplies some weevily flour, rancid lard, a little sugar, some cheap white crackers, and three cans of vegetables. I had some of our own food left but not enough to last more than a day or two. Room and board? Where was the board?

We had been told that there would be a Jersey milk cow, so Bill went up the hill to ask about it, but our new neighbors were reluctant to let us have any of the milk. Finally, they gave Bill half a quart jar from the evening's milking and told him he could have evening's milk from then on, they would take morning's milk. This suited us. Later the woman whined that she never had enough cream to make butter, which we couldn't understand as the cow was a very good milker. I guess we were expected to give up our share but we couldn't have managed without it.

We tried our best to be friendly with those people, even going out of our way to do favors for them, but their hostile attitude shut us off. And they were our only neighbors within three miles.

After getting our car that first day, Bill made a trip to the commissary at the VX headquarters four miles up the creek from us, but he came back with only a handful of supplies and a dreary tale of the dirty condition of the supply room. The new flour was full of weevils, the lard rancid, the peaches canned in water, prunes as hard as rocks, the potatoes dried up or rotten, and only strong fatty bacon for meat. No fresh meat or fresh fruit, no sugar unless you forfeited ration stamps, no vegetable shortening, no eggs.

If it hadn't been for the milk cow with her rich whole milk resulting in cream, butter, buttermilk, and cottage cheese, all of which I had learned to make at Spur Cross, we would have gone down the road. We hoped that we could remedy the situation when we talked to Harmonson on his next trip from town, but all he did was make promises and usually that was the end of it. He was full of smiles and jokes, but that didn't fill my cupboards.

So I sifted the weevils out of the flour to make biscuits, and sometimes we made a whole meal of biscuits, butter, milk, and the watery canned fruit. At least it was food, and filling.

It was hot for a month after our arrival, so we put our cot out on the porch where we were protected if it rained. In spite of the heat, skimpy diet, and hard work cleaning our house and Bard's house and guest house, I began to feel well for the first time in over a year. The country around us was beautiful, we had peace and privacy for the most part, I hiked in the hills or rode horseback for the mail, and my skin assumed a healthy glow, the itching and yellow color gone, and I gained weight.

Spooky thrived on the ranch, also, for there were mice and lizards to chase, and two other cats to play with, Old Tom and little gray waif Rocky who wandered timidly down from the hills one night and joined our family after much calling and crying and a couple of fierce, brief battles with Tom to prove priority. Tom won. Both cats liked amiable little Spooky who chirped and pranced whenever he caught sight of them. He had no need to be boss.

We had to leave Chapo on pasture near Phoenix, but were permitted to have Bonnie with us, and I was also allowed to ride one of the older ranch horses, but not Bard's private mount who grew fat and lazy from lack of exercise. His name was Pancho.

As weeks went by, we began to realize that once more we had a job where, no matter how hard we worked, our efforts were not appreciated. Instead of praise, we were ordered to do more, and finally Bill was working until dark, sometimes by lantern light, putting in extensive winter lawns around the swimming pool, which was empty, and two of the houses on the hill. He cleaned weeds out of the citrus orchard, laid flagstone around the edge of the swimming pool, and repaired the road where summer rains had washed it out.

In addition, he had to take care of the horses, run the pump engine, chop wood, water the lawns, repair fences, try to fix the old pickup truck which was laid up more often than not, and drive or ride horseback to the VX for supplies. Whenever I think back, I am continually amazed at how much work Bill could do, also the different kinds that he did or was willing to try, always succeeding. He was an amazing man and a wonderful companion for me, making my life enjoyable and bearable, no matter how tough the going.

One day Bill strode into the kitchen in a fury, set a small carton of food on the table, and announced that there was no meat, not even a piece of fatty bacon.

"When I reached the commissary," he told me, "the door was wide open, and the dogs had the only piece of bacon on the ground and were wrestling with it. That was what I was offered as meat."

We looked at each other. How long could we stay at a place like this? Would we never find a job where we would be treated fairly, like human beings and equals?

Although Bill had been promised that we would get our pay check on the first of each month, Harmonson was ten days late paying us for our first month's work. This on an outfit owned by a millionaire. Bill didn't say anything, but when our second check was several days late, he took action. Bard and Harmonson were down at the barn when Bill approached them and demanded his pay. They hedged around, and Bard declared he couldn't see why Bill was in such a hurry, we were a long ways from town with no place to spend money.

When Bill insisted, Harmonson dug around in his pants pocket and finally brought out our check and gave it to Bill, whereupon Bard frowned and shook his head, remarking, "I don't understand why Arizona help is so restless and dissatisfied." From that time on we received our check on the day it was due.

I had been assured that I wouldn't have to cook for anyone but Bill. However, sometimes a roundup crew would ride through our place, and I would have to put together some kind of meal for them at a moment's notice, using up much of our rationed sugar and scant supplies of meat, coffee, and potatoes. One day Harmonson told us that a second well was going to be dug, above the first one but deeper, to provide extra water for the swimming pool, and we were to house the well-driller and feed him. I demanded more supplies, and on one or two trips to the ranch, he did bring me some extra supplies from town, and he came through with a big can of Crisco, the vegetable shortening I had been asking for.

For the first time, we received some fresh meat, a quarter of beef which we cut up and stuffed into the gas refrigerator in Bard's house on the hill, which meant that we had to run up there whenever we needed a piece to cook. The meat didn't last long, for between passing cowboys and the well-driller and his crew of two men, plus satisfying our own hunger, I used the beef rapidly, serving it morning, noon, and night to keep it from spoiling.

When Bill helped butcher a pig at the VX after the beef was used up, we received a large piece of the pork, but eating so much fat meat made us break out in a rash. We preferred the beef.

Later we were given a forequarter of beef, and those three pieces of meat, besides a couple of old roosters, were the sum total of fresh meat we received during the eight months we were there. At one of the largest cattle ranches in Arizona. We learned that the foreman at the VX butchered more often than that to feed his hands, but he couldn't be bothered to bring any meat to us even when he passed by on his way to town. He didn't seem to approve of the money spent on the luxuries represented by our portion of the ranch, and he tried to get us to quit by "rawhiding" Bill whenever he stopped by to talk to him. This was foolish, for another couple, probably not as hardworking, would have been hired to take our place.

To our pleased surprise, the well-driller turned out to be extra good company, and we enjoyed his presence very much. He was a heavy eater, loading his slices of bread with big chunks of butter and eating everything in sight, but I never begrudged him, for, in spite of his being afflicted with rheumatism, he was a hard, honest worker, driving himself unmercifully from early until late, and we respected his skill and integrity. And he understood our problems. We could discuss things with him and get a sympathetic ear, for he was having much the same kind of trouble.

A few months after we had left the ranch, Bill met him on the streets of Phoenix, and he told Bill that he had quit also, because the range foreman had been rawhiding him. Evidently the foreman didn't like the expense of providing extra water for the luxury of a swimming pool.

In the meantime, we had lost our only neighbor, the indolent cowboy. A couple of months after we arrived, Lee was asked to take his family to live in a camp back in the hills over a road only a Jeep could travel, and they had no car at all, much less a Jeep. As he had been quarreling with the foreman and both men were packing guns, this was a transparent move to get Lee off the place. Before he could be fired, he quit, refusing to be shunted back into the hills, taking his family to a dude ranch a few miles away where he had found work. We were relieved to be rid of his hostile presence and the threat of a gunfight.

The house we were living in was to be remodeled, and the carpenter and his family—which included his mother, wife, and two young children, a girl and a boy—moved into the house that Lee and family had occupied. At least I didn't have to cook for them. They had their own milk cow, a "bronc" Hereford range cow who wouldn't let a man or anyone in pants near her; the women had to milk her. One morning when I went down to the corrals wearing my jeans, this cow was loose outside the corral, and when she saw me, she started to buck and shake her sharp horns at me. I made it over the corral fence just in time.

The Jersey's milk was now all ours, but we needed it, for I had the others to feed besides ourselves, and we now had a few chickens who could use the skim milk clabber. With the cool weather, Bard visited his ranch occasionally for a few days and required fresh milk, butter, and cottage cheese.

During the remodeling, the house was in a turmoil with sometimes a whole wall gone, exposing our activities to all passersby as well as letting in flies. The carpenter was a slow worker, so we seldom had a quiet moment during the day for the next few months, and the cold winds and dust as well as flies were a constant torment. But we put up with it.

After one of the three bedrooms was finished, we were now told that a painter would be in residence to decorate the new wallboard, paint floors and my kitchen when it was redone. So I had him to feed. He was quite a character. I don't know where he came from, but he said he had some mining claims up in the hills, and he showed us some rich gold ore, which Bill told me later didn't resemble any Arizona ore but was probably from some California mine. It was a pure white quartz with gold inclusions like the ore from the "mother lode" in California, and nothing like it had been found in these particular hills. The painter thought he had us fooled, for we listened to him patiently and studied with apparent interest his ore samples and a couple of tiny vials filled with gold dust and nuggets, and he made a large, airy promise of taking us in as partners. Nothing ever came of it. If we had had a mine that rich, you wouldn't have found us slopping around with somebody else's paint cans.

After the painter received his first pay check, he bought a fancy paint horse that he couldn't get out of a walk, then went to town and got all "duded up" with a cowboy outfit and black cowboy hat complete with chinstring. I was amused at the way he tried to get me to cook fancy dishes, especially rich desserts, by bragging on the food served at the VX when he had worked up there. I cooked the way I always did, and later I learned that whenever he stopped by for a meal at headquarters, he praised my cooking to the skies in order to get the cook up there to turn out special meals for him. I had to laugh, he was so transparent.

I found the carpenter's family quite interesting as characters from the Deep South. The grandmother chewed snuff and went around bare-footed, and as she talked, she would spit into the dust at her feet, then absently work up a little ball of mud with her big toe. Even so, she seemed like a good human being, and I liked her. Her son, the carpenter, was a flabby, lazy, sheepish sort, while his wife was a giggly little thing who seemed constantly surprised that she was the mother of two fat husky youngsters, the boy about five years old and the girl, eight. The little girl was sweet and well-mannered, and she and I became friends. She didn't seem to belong to that family.

The supplies from the commissary suited these people just fine, for their regular diet consisted of fried salt pork, biscuits, and gravy.

Although the foreman and his wife drove by our place often on their way to town, they never stopped to visit or ask me if I'd like to ride in to do some shopping even though they could see that Bill had no time to take me in our old car or the broken-down pickup which had no license plates. Toward the end of November I was anxious to get my

Christmas shopping done, so one Saturday the carpenter's wife said they were going to Phoenix and would I like to go along? They had a little old sedan, and the six of us would make a tight fit, but I jumped at the chance. Bill didn't much like the idea of my going in that car over those mountain curves, but I was determined to make the trip. I didn't have much money to spend, but I wanted the fun of buying gifts for my family without having to use a catalog.

The trip in was long and uneventful, but when we reached Phoenix, I was told that the others wanted to leave soon and visit relatives in Peoria, a small outlying community. I thought of my long shopping list, but I assured them I wouldn't take long. I tore around from store to store, not having time enough to pick and choose and ended up with almost nothing from my list. I would have to resort to a catalog for my buying. I was gone only forty-five minutes, but the way they stared at me, you'd have thought I had made them wait for hours. The carpenter had been drinking and was sullen. Evidently he was anxious to get out to the relatives' house and catch up on more drinking and socializing.

We drove to Peoria where our driver, catching sight of a couple of cronies, stopped and parked the car, telling us he would be back in a few minutes. I asked if I could do some shopping while we waited, and the wife and mother looked at each other and laughed uneasily, then said they guessed it would be all right if I didn't take too long, as he would be mad if he was kept waiting. So I hurried around in the little shopping district, buying some store bread, apples, candy, and a few other things, racing back in a few minutes to where the others waited by the car.

We waited there two hours when finally at dusk the man of the family showed up, quite drunk, with a silly grin on his face. We piled into the car again, and I was hoping Bill wouldn't be too worried about our being late when I learned that we would stop next at a relatives' house outside of town. This, evidently, was the purpose of the trip to town.

We drove up to a two-room shack in a bare stretch of desert where a few straggly mesquite trees and tamarisks struggled to survive, got out of the car, and went into the house. The relatives had just finished supper, but they insisted that we eat—greasy pork ribs, doughy biscuits, gravy, and wilted lettuce drowned in vinegar and bacon drippings. There was plenty of lettuce, as several members of this family were working in the lettuce packing sheds. My companions ate heartily while I picked at the indigestible mess.

With our party, there were about twelve people present, including several small children, in that small house, but after we had finished eating we were urged to stay for the night, our hostess hospitably assuring us that we could all "double up." The carpenter's wife had had a little to drink herself by now, and suddenly she giggled and suggested that I sleep with her husband. This witticism was received with much merriment by nearly everyone present, and I politely declined the honor, stating that I just had to get home that night. I said Bill would come down the road looking for me if I didn't, and he would be very angry. I was sure he'd have better sense, but I had to think of some way to get away from there.

Finally we were able to leave, our driver quite a bit worse for wear. The little girl sat quietly next to me in the back seat, the old lady on the other side of her, the boy up front with his parents, and she watched her father and listened to his silly comments as long as she could, then piped up, "If you drink, don't drive; if you drive, don't drink." She was ignored.

On and on we went over the rough, lonely desert road, occasional jackrabbits racing across in front of us the only signs of life, the boulders and bushes and cactus ghostly shapes by the sides of the road, revealed by the unsteady glare of the headlights. The road began to curve and dip as we reached the foothills, and more than once we barely made it safely around a curve, our wheels only inches from a sheer drop-off into a wash fifteen or twenty feet below. The road was unfamiliar to me, as Bill and I had come to the ranch by the other way, but when we came to a big mudhole we had carefully skirted on our trip down, I realized that we were only about five miles from home. I breathed a deep sigh of relief and began to relax.

Suddenly our driver yelled happily, "Hold your hats, folks, here we go!" and drove straight into the middle of the mud and water, and there we were, stuck.

The womenfolk didn't say a word. They didn't dare cross this man. I didn't say anything, as it wouldn't have done any good. He got us into trouble, and now we were going to have to try to get him out. After piling out of the car on the least muddy side, we were ordered to find big, flat rocks and place them in front of the back wheels, to provide traction. My suggestion to use brush instead was ignored.

The rocks in place, the driver got into the car and started the motor. We pushed, the wheels spun—spattering us with mud—the car slipped on the wet rocks, then buried itself hub-deep. We were stuck now for sure. The "man-of-the-hour" gave a silly laugh, cursed, turned off the engine, and switched out the lights.

He and his wife decided to walk back to the cow camp we had passed three miles away to see if they could get help. They were gone less than thirty minutes. When they returned, they informed us that they couldn't find the camp, adding that some wild animals had been following them in the brush beside the road. There were mountain lions in the nearby mountains, and a truck driver had seen one sitting on the bank of a wash a couple of hundred feet from the road we were on, but I didn't think that they would harm a human.

My companions stood around uneasily and wondered what to do next. They were at a loss. Nothing like this had ever happened to them before, and we knew that no other car would be likely to come by before morning. I suggested that we build a fire, but they had no matches or paper. Digging in my purse, I produced a matchbook with three matches. Then I dumped my groceries out of the paper sack into the trunk of the car and told the others to search in the brush for kindling. They gingerly produced some greasewood twigs while I tore my hands breaking dead mesquite branches, and I soon had a good fire blazing. Suddenly everyone felt more cheerful.

So they climbed into the car to sleep, the man stretching himself comfortably on the front seat, his head in his wife's lap, while the old lady and two children got in the back.

"Crawl in," they invited me. No room for me, so I offered to keep the fire going. What else could I do? For the next two hours I wandered around in the brush searching for dry wood by the light of the campfire. It was a chilly night, so I knew that rattlers wouldn't be moving. After a while I became so tired and sleepy, I could hardly keep my eyes open, but when I sat on the ground to rest, it felt too cold and damp in spite of the fire. I opened the car door and tried to find room on the floor in front of the back seat, but there were too many feet and legs in the way. The grandmother stirred and murmured something apologetic, but that was small comfort. I was dying for sleep.

The blackness was all around us in the desert hills, dark and quiet. We were all alone in the world. No cars came by, nobody, nothing, except a couple of big range bulls, no doubt the "wild animals" which had "stalked" the man and his wife. They trudged silently by on the road, probably searching for water, perhaps this mud hole. They were out of luck. It was ours, all ours.

110

After I built up the fire, I tried sitting on the ground which was driest by one of the front tires, leaned back against the fender and dozed off. I awoke stiff and chilled through, replenished the dying fire, walked around to get my circulation moving, and stared longingly at the east as if to force the sun to rise by sheer will power. The sky remained dark, hour after hour. Clouds obscured the stars, threatening rain. I wondered what Bill was thinking. The air grew damper, chilling me through and through. To keep my spirits up and try to warm myself, I opened my precious loaf of store bread and made some toast over coals, then ate an apple with the toast.

Somewhat comforted, I settled myself on the ground for another nap, and finally after awaking and looking time after time at the blackness to the east, there seemed to be a faint glow. Morning! No, it was only the moon rising behind the clouds. I had no watch so had no idea what time it was, but after what seemed a lifetime, I looked once more, and I thought surely that is dawn coming. I stared at the western sky. Dark. I looked back toward the east. Light. Faint, but undeniably light at last. Dawn.

To celebrate the coming of "Dawn Boy," I piled the rest of the wood on the fire, dragged out some coals and made more toast which I ate with another apple.

The family in the car began to stir. It was full dawn when I opened the back car door to consult with them. The man of the family was still asleep, but the women whispered that he had sore feet and wouldn't be able to go for help. So it was up to me to do something. I stuffed an apple and a handful of my candy in my pocket and told the women that I would hike the five miles to the ranch and see if Bill could bring the pickup to pull their car out of the mud. They just shrugged and said I could if I wanted to. What a helpless lot!

I was glad to be moving, to see action after the long night. It felt good to be going along in the cool, damp desert morning, glad that the ordeal was almost over, looking back on it as an adventure of sorts, not one I wanted to repeat, however. Up and down and around I walked, crossing pretty white sandwashes, taking short cuts through the cactus and brush-covered hills, watching for mountain lions but seeing no signs of life beyond a few tiny birds just waking up and a couple of cottontails.

By the time I reached the ranch gate, a misty rain had started to fall. Bill met me in the front yard, frantic with worry and furious with the carpenter. He had to change a tire on the pickup before he could start down the road to look for me. He didn't think my adventure was at all funny. He had had visions of the lot of us piled up at the bottom of some canyon in the dark, injured and helpless, or worse. After I told him what had happened, he was more angry than ever but not at me. Before going to the rescue of the stranded party, he ate breakfast and wouldn't have gone at all if it hadn't been for the women and children.

He loaded some planks, a shovel, and chain in the bed of the pickup and went down the road. I later learned from the grandmother that Bill had driven up to the helpless car, got out of the truck, and without a single word to anyone or request for help from the carpenter, went right to work in the rain with shovel and planks, fastened the two vehicles together, pulled the sedan out, unfastened the chain, rescued the mud-covered planks, put everything back into the truck, and left them staring after him as he headed back for the ranch without having said a word. I also learned that the carpenter had helped himself to two of my apples. No one else had touched any of my food.

I was sick in bed for three days with a bad cold, and Bill and the well-driller had to do their own cooking and feed me, too, besides doing their work. That was my only trip to town for the eight months we lived in those hills. My Christmas shopping was done by mail.

That winter Bard decided to kill all the coyotes, thereby disturbing Nature's balance and letting jackrabbits take over the range. Then he planned to pull up all the giant sahuaros which he said were sapping the vitality of his land. Finally, he wanted to dehorn his cattle so that they wouldn't injure each other while fighting. At the end of our stay we saw the results of only one of these projects—cattle, dehorned during the warm spring weather, with their head wounds infected with flies, going about shaking their heads in misery, and dead cattle lying under the desert trees, finished off by the fly worms. He had disregarded the warnings of his range foreman, thereby losing far more cattle than from possible fights. It was pitiful and heartbreaking.

Bard and Harmonson had their own ideas about people. They not only didn't care to mingle socially with the help or neighbors, but tried to keep the local people from using the old road through the ranch on their way to town, in an effort (vain) to force them to go out the other way. And Bill and I were frowned at for our hospitality to prospectors or "burro men" who happened to pass our way. Prospecting, hunting, and riding through the ranch property were forbidden if you were an outsider.

Friends of management, which didn't include us, were permitted to hunt. One day when a car drove by the house with a lone man inside, we heard it stop at the reservoir a quarter of a mile away, out of sight of the house. There were some shots, then the car drove away. When Bill went to investigate, some pretty little redhead ducks were floating dead on the surface of the water, out of reach of the hunter. Tame ducks, which we had enjoyed watching whenever we rode by the dam. Special friends of ours.

We kept watch, and when the car, which had gone up to the VX, returned, Bill jumped the hunter at the gate, and the man tried to deny what he had done. When Bill accused him of lying, the man backtracked and said that he had permission to hunt, that he was Harmonson's friend. Bill expressed doubt, so the man started to get out of his car, then backed down and drove off in a cloud of dust. Later, Harmonson jumped on Bill, didn't back him up, although Bill was just following orders. Such treatment was typical of this man's lack of loyalty to his employees.

I mentioned previously in this account that we had my filly Bonnie with us, but to my dismay I found that she was becoming too strong and spirited for me. She was five years old now, and Bill had hoped to raise some beautiful colts from her some day, but she needed exercise and, as he didn't have the time to spare, it was up to me to ride her.

One afternoon when I started out on Bonnie to go for the mail at the Post Office three miles away, she spooked and balked at the reservoir, and when I turned her around, then rode her back toward the dam, she began to plunge and fight. I had on spurs but was afraid to use them for fear she might dump me into the boulders of the creek thirty feet below, which she very likely would have done. Finally, I turned her and rode her back to the house, and Bill, who was working on the lawn, took the spurs, put them on over his high-top Keds, mounted Bonnie, galloped her up the road to the reservoir, spurred her past the dam, and continued on to the Post Office for the mail.

When I told Bill I could never ride Bonnie again, he didn't try to argue with me, and we later sold her to the ranch to use as a brood mare, which meant that she would have a soft life, living on green pasture and raising colts on Bard's farm in the irrigated valley. I was sorry to let Bill down, for he loved Bonnie who was a truly beautiful chestnut sorrel, part Steeldust and part quarterhorse. But we still had Chapo who was more horse than we could afford anyway.

Along about spring we began to get restless and fed up with this job, discontented with a situation that once again drove us to the limit yet offered so little satisfaction. We had worked hard, yet received no more appreciation for our efforts than if we hadn't lifted a finger. Bard and Harmonson acted as though they were afraid a little praise might cause us to lie down on the job, and the foreman continued to "rawhide" Bill in an effort to make him do more when Bill already had more to do than one man should be expected to handle. We had been much happier working for ourselves on our mining claims at Cherry with no wage at all.

We had saved most of our money, so one day we told Bard and Harmonson that they'd better get someone else, we were through. So they fired us. Ordered us to get right off the place at once. Stunned at such treatment, for we had counted on staying a few days until they found a couple to replace us, Bill and I held a hasty conference. The Horizon Hunter needed overhauling and was in no condition to carry our load over the steep rough grades out of there, so Bill quickly found us a temporary job at a local guest ranch called Big Boulder, and the next morning we moved, Spooky with us. Bill was to assist with maintenance and chores including milking cows, while I would do maid work. In the evening Bill worked on our car.

At Big Boulder the manager was a Westerner, and he treated us as human beings, a pleasant change. I had no cooking to do, and it was a great treat eating someone else's. The help ate together, away from the guests, and we had plenty of good food to eat; although we worked hard, we felt fine.

In two weeks Big Boulder closed, and with our car fixed, we were able to head for Cave Creek where we stayed for a few days in a cabin near Black Mountain Store until we received permission to use Dan Moore's cabin again, offering to paint it in lieu of rent.

15

Life Gets Complicated

We made plans. While I did the painting, Bill would start building a cabin of our own on our own land, and later I would help him. Then we would have a refuge between jobs and a place to store a lot of the extra household and riding equipment we had accumulated including two saddles, bridles, chaps, and saddle blankets.

Happy and excited, we went to work. We had never built a house, but that didn't stop us from trying. Nor had I ever painted a house. I soon learned.

It was nearly May, and we knew we had to work fast to get our shelter built before the scorching days set in. While I wielded my paint brush, Bill hauled rocks and sand and cement to make a concrete floor inside the foundation left when a house had been moved from our land before we bought it. In the middle of this foundation was a concrete-lined cellar, six by six by six feet, and Bill had to place a wood floor with a trap door over this hole before he started on the walls. It was a problem, but he solved it nicely and planned later to paint an Indian rug design on the wood part of our floor to make it look nice and camouflage the trap door.

I finished painting the Moore cabin in two or three weeks and joined in our cabin work, feeling like an Egyptian slave as I lugged large rocks up out of the sand washes to a spot where Bill could back the car to them for hauling to our building site. These rocks were for the lower foundation, making a pretty ornamental rock and concrete wall up to windowsill height. From there on we planned to use redwood siding.

Due to the shortage of building materials, we had a never-ending struggle to find decent lumber, and much of it was poor grade, although high-priced, but we had to make it do, as time was slipping away and so was our money, We sold my saddle to pay for two-by-fours, keeping Bill's saddle as it was the most comfortable, a big old double-rigged stock saddle which fit Chapo the best. Fred's wife, at Spur Cross, had sold it to Bill against Fred's wishes. She was a really nice person and treated us well, although we didn't see her very often.

Chapo was with us, and he had a soft life, as we were usually too busy to ride except to the store or Post Office in Cave Creek. One afternoon I was riding him to the store when we started through a swarm of bees. I quickly turned Chapo and went around another way, avoiding disaster. On our return from the store with bottles of milk in the saddlebags along with two bunches of carrots for Chapo and us, we came upon a rattlesnake which didn't startle Chapo, luckily, as he couldn't hear the buzzing because of his partial deafness. When I got down to kill the snake, because it was near the schoolhouse, it disappeared before I could find a big rock or stick for a weapon.

We had several narrow escapes from rattlers that summer. I nearly walked on a small one coiled near the path from the outhouse to the Moore cabin. And Bill almost stepped on a rattler when he started out of the cabin door one night. The most startling incident was the night I threw a bucket of wash water out the door of our own cabin after we had moved in, and a rattler sang out from under the nearest mesquite tree where he had received a drenching. Bill brought a shovel and flashlight, and I insisted on finishing the snake off by myself, as I liked proving my "courage." But could you call it courage if I wasn't afraid of the snake? However, Bill said he'd hate to be a rattler with me after him.

Before our house was completed, screened, and caulked, we had to be on the lookout for other poisonous creatures. One morning a large furry tarantula perched himself cozily on a two-by-four halfway up an inside wall. Nine-inch long centipedes with hard shells and five-inch long black hairy scorpions, as well as the smaller tan deadly ones found shelter under canvas dropcloths, while Black Widow spiders made their irregular, horrifying nests in dark corners and behind lumber. We had to look twice before touching anything. After the cabin was closed up, we were able to keep the insect population under control pretty well with sprays and vigilance.

It was midsummer, the thermometer hitting 114° in the shade, and the rocks we handled were hot enough to fry us, and we still weren't through. Our tempers were frayed from overwork in the extreme heat; lack of supplies and inexperience hampered our effort, but we were determined to finish what we had started. I felt just as Bill did, and we drove ourselves unmercifully.

It was scorching August when we finally moved over to our nearly completed one-room, twelve-by-eighteen foot home, with unfurnished bathroom attached. We set our cot outdoors under a mesquite tree to get some night-time relief from the heat. We had no cooler, not even a fan, as Cave Creek had no power line yet.

There was still much to be done on our house. We had to scour Phoenix for doors and windows, hardware and nails, as usual taking whatever we could get whether it was what we wanted or not. With each thirty-mile trip our finances got dangerously low. And we still had to purchase varnish, paint, linseed oil, a ladder, and a few, simple secondhand furnishings: seven dollars for a dinette table, fifty cents each to Catherine Jones for three small chairs, six dollars for a three-burner portable kerosene cook stove, and ten dollars for a circulating wood heater.

Reluctantly we sacrificed our war bonds, the gift from my parents, and they brought not much more than the $150.00 they had cost. But we had to get our home in shape so that it could be locked up before we left. And all the time we were eating, and Chapo was eating, and the house was eating us until one dark day we realized that we were all about to go hungry.

Except for Spooky. He had a commissary well-stocked with mice, pack rats, and sometimes a young cottontail rabbit which I would skin for him. One day he appeared with a rabbit almost as big as he was, still alive and struggling. I killed it and covetously eyed the tender fresh meat as I pulled the fur off.

"Spooky," I said, "you are elected to be our breadwinner for today." I gave him the liver and heart, and he permitted me to keep and cook the remainder of his meal for ourselves, bless his loving little heart. So that night we literally ate something that "the cat dragged in." And it was delicious.

The days crept by, the heat monotonous and nerve-shattering, until I was hot and tired and sick of the whole business, and so was Bill. Life was no adventure any more. It was drudgery and prickly heat and bitterness and a quarrel over how high the kitchen sink should be, the secondhand warped five-dollar kitchen sink that we should have thrown off a cliff, said to heck with it all, and headed for the cool mountains before we endangered our wonderful loving partnership. It is sad and depressing to tell about this time in our lives, but it would be less than honest to leave it out, although I didn't include it in my *Ladies' Home Journal* article.

I couldn't take it any more. I couldn't take what was happening to us, the hard work and privation in the terrible heat, never enough to eat, just a bowl of tomato soup and bread for supper one night. Worst of all was the bitterness. Yet we couldn't leave the place until it was finished. It had trapped us. I thought, if only we had enough money, Bill could finish the house and close it up and go away for a rest and then get a job, and everything would be all right again. It might help if we had a vacation from each other.

I didn't want to borrow from my parents who would have been only too willing to help us, but I didn't want to admit defeat. So I scanned the Phoenix newspaper and found an ad for a maid job in a millionaire's home in the Biltmore Estates in Phoenix, so I replied, intending to get the best pay I could. They offered eighty dollars a month, room and board, plus a raise as soon as I deserved it, so I took the job. Bill would have respite from me; he could finish our house with the money I could send him; we would have enough to eat and no longer feel pinched and desperate.

Besides myself, there was a nursemaid for the little girl, a gardener named George, and there was supposed to be a cook, but she had quit. The house was huge, eighteen big rooms plus the small bedrooms for the help, and it was beautifully furnished, but in no way did I wish it belonged to me.

The air conditioning didn't work as wartime shortages somehow prevented its being repaired, so the house was very warm, and at night we servants were stifled in our tiny bedrooms with only the hot blast of small electric fans to move the air around. Would I never get relief from the summer heat?

I had to wear a uniform, but I chose cool white seersucker, easily laundered, no ironing needed, and the rooms where I had to work were large and airy, so I didn't suffer too much during the day. I wasn't very busy at first, for Mr. D., the head of the household, was away in the East on business, and although Mrs. D. had two house guests, they were out most of the time. As there was still no cook, they ate out a lot, except for breakfast which I offered to fix until they found a cook.

My regular duties were to serve meals, clean the living, dining, and breakfast rooms, the butler's pantry and the lanai, answer the phone and the front door. It was so much easier than the work I had been doing, and I felt almost as though I were on a kind of vacation.

The cook would keep the kitchen, hall, and servant's dining room clean, which I was doing at the moment. The nursemaid prepared the meals for the little girl and also took care of the bedrooms, baths, and laundry, although I assisted with the latter as I was fascinated with the automatic washer and large ironer, neither of which I had ever used before. On the nursemaid's day off, I took care of the little girl who was three years old, a sweet but thin and nervous child.

As for George, the gardener, his duties were clear, but his actions were doubtful. Mentally unbalanced, he told wild tales to build up his own importance, relating strange and terrible things he had done. Not realizing at first what it was all about, I took it all as a big joke, laughed, encouraged him in his delusions of grandeur, and no doubt saved my life with my friendliness.

Then one night when Mrs. D. and her friends were out, I was alone in the big quiet kitchen finishing up my chores, putting things away while the nursemaid put her charge to bed in another wing of the great house. When I was through and had turned out all the lights except for the one in the long hall leading to my bedroom, George came to the door leading into the garage and asked me if I would like to see something sharp.

Feeling uneasy but not knowing what else to do, not wishing to antagonize him, I stepped into the garage, whereupon the strange little man brought out a set of surgical instruments, shining and indeed sharp. He tenderly lifted out what he called a bone-clipper and reached for my hand, asking me to let him show how sharp it was by clipping my fingernails.

Taken aback, I withdrew slightly, my heart pounding loudly in the silent garage, the grounds beyond the drive empty and deserted, the house at my back nearly so. No other house nearby to hear me if I screamed. Realizing how helpless I was, yet knowing I must not panic, I smiled and said quietly, "No, not tonight, George. I'm too tired." Saying a friendly good night, I left before he realized what had happened.

Not wishing to frighten Mrs. D., I said nothing to her or to the nursemaid. After all, what did I have to say? Nothing had happened. I didn't want a possibly innocent man to lose his job.

One of the house guests was an Army captain who seemed out of place, as he was no particular relation to either of the women that I could tell, and the nursemaid couldn't enlighten me. But a few days after the incident in the garage, Mrs. D. came into the kitchen and told me confidentially that the soldier was there for protection while Mr. D. was away. She said that she had seen a set of surgical tools in the garage, realized that they belonged to the gardener, and had telephoned Mr. D., whereupon he had arranged for this young man to protect us. Some protection he was, away nearly every evening with the two women!

After I told her what had happened between George and me, she became very excited and asked me why I hadn't told her. I could have asked her the same thing. Evidently conscience-stricken and even more alarmed, she immediately phoned her husband and received his assurance that he would take the next plane home. As soon as he arrived, he gave George his walking papers and warned him in no uncertain terms to stay off the grounds and threatened to get the F.B.I. after him. Later George phoned me and asked for his ration book, so I had to refer his call to Mr. D. I don't know what happened, although I heard loud explosions of talk from the study.

I couldn't sleep because of the terrible heat and was desperate for rest, so one night I slipped outside, locked myself out, and stretched gratefully on the chaise longue in the backyard under the cool stars. It felt so delightful to be away from that stuffy bedroom, and I slept, not caring what might happen. And nothing happened, but my employers were quite shocked that I had exposed myself to possible danger. I didn't care. I felt that I would collapse after another hot night inside that house.

So I slept outside whenever I felt like it, locking myself out, feeling safe enough in the concealing darkness. What burglar would think to look for a defenseless woman on a chaise longue under a tree in the backyard of a millionaire's estate?

All this time Bill had been literally pounding away at our desert place, finishing the kitchen, and finally after a month he was able to close the house up. On one of his visits to town on my day off, I urged him to drive up to Indian Creek and camp in the cool pines for a week and get a good rest before taking a job. I was feeling better, but he was haggard and rundown, so finally he consented to a three-day trip, leaving Spooky with the Mitchells across the wash and putting Chapo on pasture.

When Bill returned, Mr. and Mrs. D. hired him as gardener, and he pitched in and worked hard, although he had been reluctant to take the job, working on another millionaire's lawn and garden.

As Mrs. D., hadn't been able to find a satisfactory cook, they begged me to accept the position, offering Bill and me $250.00 a month plus room and board, as a couple. As I was doing most of the cooking already, along with the maid work, I accepted, and they hired another maid to do the serving, cleaning, etc., so now I did less work for more money.

It was a wonderful kitchen to work in, all kinds of fancy equipment, a restaurant-sized gas stove complete with overhead exhaust fan and separate broiler, with plenty of supplies for fixing delicious and attractive meals, plus appreciation from Mrs. D. And an adequate wage.

After Bill and I had worked there for two weeks, Mr. D. stalked into the kitchen one morning, looked at Bill and me strangely, his eyes cold and unfriendly, and said that he had been at a party the previous evening where Fred from Spur Cross was present. He told us that our former employer had said that we were anti-social, that we didn't like the people we worked for, after which Mr. D. began to find fault with our work and fired us. So we quit.

We were annoyed by the charge that we were anti-social, but after thinking it over for a while, we decided that we were anti-social where people like Fred and Mr. D. were concerned.

Mrs. D. did pay us the wages we were still owed, and the only ones I was sorry to leave were the nursemaid and the little girl. Two years later when I met Mrs. D. on a Phoenix street, I learned that she was no longer Mrs. D. but Mrs. Somebody Else. She was charming and friendly to me and seemed much less nervous and tense than she had been. I remarked upon it, and she admitted readily that she was far happier now, that her little girl was fine and had a baby sister. We parted friends, for I held her no ill-will. She had treated me well.

Now that we had some money again, Bill and I were more relaxed, although we realized that beneath the surface lay some of the bitterness of the summer of unrelenting heat, overwork, and insufficient food. But we went ahead with plans for our desert home, having no other job in view at the moment, and decided to add a bedroom. As the bathroom wasn't furnished yet, we continued to use the outhouse which had been donated to us by a rancher friend.

Due to our reluctance to cut down the mesquite and palo verde trees on either side of the house, we decided to build the bedroom into the hill below the kitchen where its window would overlook the bedroom roof. This required a separate entrance at the back of the bedroom, which meant that when we went to bed, we would have to leave the living room, go outside and down the rock path around to the bedroom door, using a flashlight to look for rattlers. The bathroom also had a separate outside entrance which was unorthodox but okay for the desert.

One day Bill learned of a job handling horses for the winter at Brownmoor School for Girls in Phoenix. He applied and was accepted, and the wage was $250.00 a month plus room and board. He was told to show up for work in ten days' time. The year was 1945. The war had ended, but the former wrangler was still in the Army, so Bill was taking his place temporarily.

We worked hard and finished the bedroom and bought some second-hand furniture for it for forty dollars. It looked as if it had been made in a box factory, but it was serviceable. I still have the vanity which Bill had turned into a desk for me, with a well for my typewriter, and this is where I am writing this account.

New mattresses were too expensive, so we settled for a used one for five dollars. It was uneven and lumpy, but it looked clean, and we sunned and brushed it for two days. We had to pay fourteen dollars for a coil spring, second hand. Metal goods were still scarce and expensive because of the war.

Bill worked far into the night laying the cement floor in the bedroom, pouring the foundation, putting up the plank walls and roof, tacking on roofing paper, putting in four windows, and making a door, until finally he had the room finished except for the painting and varnishing inside and the fake brick siding outside. I decided to stay on and complete the work while Bill drove off in the Horizon Hunter to his new job.

I was now alone on the desert for three weeks with only Spooky for company and the Mitchells, our good neighbors across the big sand-wash, to help me with groceries and mail. And I began to make my own plans for the winter. I could have gone with Bill to the school, but I didn't see myself sitting around doing nothing. So I applied for maid work at Castle Hot Springs Hotel in the mountains where we had worked at the Bard Ranch, and not far from there. I would be separated from Bill for the winter, but I decided that it might be good for us after what we had gone through that summer, help us preserve our marriage.

The autumn days at Cave Creek were warm and peaceful, and I worked happily at the painting, and varnishing, hiring a local handy-man to finish the outside of the bedroom with the siding. My mother sent me their discarded living room draperies which she had altered to fit according to the measurements I had sent her, and I hung them in the bedroom, also using two extra pairs as makeshift coverings for "closets" in living room and bedroom. They added an attractive, rich note to our little dwelling.

I also put another coating of linseed oil to the redwood siding of our living room to keep it from drying out in the desert sun. Each night, with Spooky by my side, I would fix a simple supper, and after I had eaten and washed dishes, I would sit in the cool living room and read or write letters, Spooky purring on my lap. Beyond the windows I could sense the blackness and silence of the chilly desert night into which I must venture in order to attend to the call of Nature at our backyard "ticket office" down the hill before retiring to the cold, dark, lonely bedroom.

For these nightly excursions I would load myself with lantern, flashlight, and .22 rifle, and my back hair tingled as I left the locked living room and stepped outside, alone except for my cat, to face whatever terrors the night held for me. But all I ever saw was a coyote's gray form slinking out from beneath our garbage pail hanging in a palo verde tree nearby.

Once safely locked in my bedroom, I would check to see that a hammer was on the chest of drawers, a hunting knife under my pillow, and the loaded rifle in the corner by the bed. I braced the windows so that they couldn't be opened from the outside, fixing one so that it was open enough for Spooky to come and go. The bedroom had no screens. After examining the bed for scorpions, centipedes, and black widows, I would undress and crawl in, and with Spooky purring happily on the covers near my knees, I would lie awake, staring out into the dark through the dim rectangles of the windows and wonder which weapon I should grab first if someone stuck his head through the opening I had left.

I would drift uneasily off to sleep, waking during the night to find that Spooky had gone out or returned after one of his forays. Through the windows I would see the stars over the friendly hovering shape of Black Mountain, listen to the wonderful silence of the desert, broken only by the noise of cattle crunching their way in the granite sand as they plodded down the wash several hundred yards away, headed for water. And I would no longer feel afraid. Once more the desert was a friend. Spooky would snore gently by my side, and soon I would be asleep again.

After my three weeks alone except for occasional daytime visits from a worried Bill, I packed my bags, locked the house, left Spooky with the Mitchells who also had a cat, and got a lift to Phoenix where I sold my 12-bass accordion which Bill had bought for me secondhand, then used the eighteen dollars I received to take out sickness, accident, and hospitalization insurance with Mutual of Omaha. After which I boarded a bus which took me out to the junction at Morristown where the hotel's wranglers would pick me up.

16

We Are Apart

Castle Hot Springs Hotel, I was told, was the resort where John F. Kennedy had spent some time during the winter of 1944–1945, the year before I went there to work as a maid. The hotel was situated in beautiful, mountainous country with magnificent desert surroundings. On the ride there, however, I felt too apprehensive about my new job to appreciate fully the beauty, although the two wranglers who picked me up at Morristown were very sweet and friendly.

Once at the hotel I was given a small narrow room in the hired help's dormitory where I left my things, after which I met the housekeeper, Mrs. Jones, a plump elderly lady with a worried manner and a chronic case of indigestion. Puffing and panting as she struggled up the sandy paths, she showed me my "station" which consisted of four large bungalows and some rooms in Palm House, a total of eighteen beds to make each day with clean linen, four sitting rooms, and ten bathrooms. I was secretly appalled. Would I ever be able to get all that work done in one day when most of it had to be done in the morning?

As it was still early in the season, there were only a few guests, so I decided that I could get into the swing of things gradually before the place filled up.

Back at the linen room I was shown my basket of cleaning supplies, keys, soap miniatures, matchbooks, and toilet tissue, plus a broom, dust mop, and carpet sweeper, all of which I would be required to lug around with me as I made my rounds. The house boys would bring the linens.

By that time it was getting late and I had to get ready for supper. After I freshened up, I was shown to the mess hall by the other four maids with whom I was invited to sit. There were long tables in a large, plain room off the hotel kitchen where we were served, cafeteria style, with plain food which appeared to be well-cooked and which tasted good, especially as I hadn't had to fix it myself nor clean up afterwards. Before long, however, I understood the good-natured griping of the others, for it is hard to eat hash and stew and hot dogs and sauerkraut while right under your nose white-capped chefs are fixing mouth-watering roasts and chops and steaks for the favored ones in the guests' dining room and in the separate hall where the "white collar" workers of the hotel ate.

As a maid I was paid $65.00 per month plus room and board, although before long our base pay was raised to $75.00 a month. Uniforms were furnished, so I was able to save most of my wages plus whatever tips I might receive.

Soon after I arrived, one of the other maids quit, and I was given her station which luckily was nearest the linen room and the first to be filled with guests. I worked hard and devised an efficient system for myself to save steps and time, so was soon averaging $20.00 a week in tips which was considered very good for a maid back in those days, although waitresses made far more than that.

One day the dining room hostess asked me if I would like to become a waitress, she was short-handed and thought I would "do good" (make big tips) in the dining room, but I disliked the thought of having to juggle heavy trays, and also I preferred the comparative anonymity of the maid work in spite of the smaller tips, so I turned her down.

The guests I served usually treated me with kindness and consideration, and I enjoyed the work and saw no disgrace in doing it, although my Aunt Lydia didn't approve of my being a "domestic" as she put it. As a matter of fact, I was pleased to realize that I was making a lot more money than the top salary I had received as a secretary. And I enjoyed maid work far more, even though it is strenuous. It has a freedom and mobility to it that suited me, as I liked being active and not confined to an office desk.

Inevitably, there were a few guests who were overly demanding and arrogant, but the truly "big" people treated the help as friends. We would talk it all over in the dormitory at night, discussing one or two women guests whom the girls referred to as "hell-on-wheels" in dining room or cottage. Generous tips never compensated for poor treatment.

I had had several different roommates who came and went that fall for various reasons, but finally I had the roommate I wanted, one of the other maids, named Maude Rasmussen, an older woman who became my best friend and companion of many of my free hours. We would wander the desert and hills looking for pretty and unusual rocks, discussing the guests and the other employees and sharing our innermost thoughts. I told her about my troubles with Bill, and she urged me to return to him, although I had my doubts about that. I had become attracted to one of the wranglers who, oddly enough, resembled Bill physically, and I knew he liked me. One day he asked me if I was going to get a divorce, and I said I didn't know. And I didn't know. I was all mixed up in my mind and wasn't sure what I would do.

In the evenings after we maids "turned down" the guest beds and filled hot water bottles needed, we were free to visit the employees' canteen where a juke box played for dancing, there were books to read, a pool table, a big fireplace for friendly warmth, and a handsome cowboy to play his guitar and sing whenever he wasn't entertaining the guests. We could also buy beer, soda pop, candy, cigarettes, lotion, toothpaste, and other small necessities. Although we weren't allowed to use the swimming pool in front of the hotel, we were permitted to swim in the hot and cool pools below the hot springs, which I enjoyed as I had brought a swim suit with me.

Employees were also permitted to ride the horses if they took good care of them, in order to help the wranglers get them in shape for the guests. I had my boots and jeans with me, and soon I was enjoying the riding in the afternoon after I had my work done for the day. Then one day I was put on a big, spirited bay gelding named Rex, the wrangler over-estimating my ability, but the minute I got on that horse, I told myself, "I'd just as soon ride a mountain lion," for he moved with a prowling grace that told me of the unleashed strength and spirit hidden in that big, powerful body.

Too foolishly proud to admit my fears and doubts, I rode off at a walk, holding Rex with a short, light rein, my hand firm, but my heart pounding. We came upon some other riders performing in a field for a movie camera, and Rex immediately tried to get his head down to buck and run to join them. Quickly I turned him and headed him away and down the creek, not daring even to let him into a trot, for I felt that he would run away with me, given half a chance. Luckily the outside gate was open, so I didn't have to dismount, and presently I headed Rex up a mountain trail to work some of the excess steam out of him. To my dismay he bounded up the trail with undiminishing power as if I were no more than a flea on his back, and I knew I dared not go to the top, for the trail was very steep, and I would have to dismount and tighten the cinch for the downward journey, and I could never get back on him alone, he was so tall.

So we turned back, but when we reached the fence again, someone had closed the gate! My heart turned somersaults. What should I do? Get off and ignominiously lead my horse back to the barn? What a blow to my pride! I would be forever razzed. To my great relief, a party of riders appeared, heading down the creek toward me, and although Rex kept trying to get his head down to buck me off, I managed to hold him in check with a high, short rein until the wrangler in charge of the party rode up ahead of the others, dismounted, looked up at me with a quizzical smile and opened the gate.

I tried to smile, also, as I rode through. "He's just too much horse for me," I told the wrangler.

"You can lead him back," he grinned.

That look! Never! "No," I said, gritting my teeth. "I can make it now." Somehow I managed to hold Rex to a walk the rest of the way to the barn. When I dismounted, my legs almost collapsed like jelly, and when Rex's bridle was removed and I saw the slight curve to the bit, giving a rider very little control, I could hardly believe that I had returned in one piece. I realized later that the gentle touch of that bit was probably the very thing that kept Rex from fighting me, for, although he was spirited, he was really one of those fine big-hearted horses that will respond to kind treatment. But I never rode him again.

At Christmas and New Year's we all worked up the best spirit we could in spite of having to work as usual on those days. We employees had our own parties in our canteen, while the guests celebrated in the hotel cocktail lounge and bar. The wranglers entertained both groups, and a western orchestra played for dancing in the hotel. The canteen juke box provided our dance music. I choked down a half bottle of beer and tried to convince myself I was having a good time.

During the day I was able to maintain a cheerful and calm exterior, but in spite of the hard work, exercise, fresh air, and sunshine, I lay awake night after night thinking until the early morning hours when fatigue finally took over and I slept.

Bill and I wrote to each other infrequently and only of trivial things. I wondered, would we be able to resume our life together on the same basis we had known? Should I leave him for someone else? I couldn't decide what to do. I never wrote to my parents or brother what was going on; I just pretended everything was hunky dory. Maude was the only one I could talk to as we lay in our narrow metal beds in the dark in the little room we shared, and it was deeply comforting to have her there, even though her advice to me was always to return to Bill. I felt that perhaps time would solve my problem and why not try to enjoy life as I went along, for there was nothing to be gained by brooding.

To entertain the guests, the dude wranglers put on little rodeos each Sunday afternoon, using goats instead of calves for the roping contest. Besides the wranglers, the guests, employees, and cowboys from nearby ranches took part in the different events, and there was usually a race for us girls. Urged on by the wranglers, I entered one of the races one Sunday, an "egg on spoon" type of race, only we carried a small ball on an ash tray while riding around the arena. If the ball fell to the ground, we had to dismount, recover the ball, get back on our horse, and continue. Fastest time won. An eastern girl made a good ride, but it looked strange to see her "posting" on a western saddle. A waitress made the best ride, while I definitely lost although I made an entertaining effort, losing the ball, my hat, and my dignity, laughing wildly at my own performance, and glad I could take a joke on myself.

Dormitory life was fun, And I enjoyed being with all these different people, the maids, waitresses, laundry workers, and married couples. The single men roomed downstairs. There was very little drinking and usually not to excess. The married couple who worked in the laundry did, however, occasionally take on more liquor then they could handle, and one night the dormitory rocked with sudden upheaval when they got into a terrible fight in their room. Amid the sounds of screams and yells and curses and furniture crashing, we all stood in the long cold hall, the kitchen helpers, busboys, dishwashers, drivers, and other male employees crowding up the stairs from their rooms below, while we listened in dismay or amusement, depending on our different natures, and wondered what to do. Finally, one waitress went for the manager.

When Mr. Nord, a calm, even-tempered gentleman who was a great favorite with the help, arrived on the scene, he quietly opened the door to the scene of battle, and there on the floor sprawled the man, his eyes closed, his wife over him trying to choke him while blood streamed from her face onto her husband's still form. Mr. Nord and one of the housemen separated them, took the woman into another room where there was an empty bed, and put the drunken, unconscious man to bed in the wrecked room. They weren't fired, for they were efficient, conscientious workers, and the hotel needed them. The woman eventually returned to her man, all was forgiven, and peace returned.

Occasionally there were minor fights among the employees, disputes, arguments, as well as temporary love affairs, jealousy, hatred—all the emotions that people are susceptible to—but in front of the guests we maintained a calm exterior which revealed no hint of our private lives or activities after hours. Did they ever wonder or guess about those who served them? We knew more about them than they did about us.

We maids knew the most. We knew which people were untidy, mean, selfish, contentious with husband or wife or child, and who were messy in their personal habits regardless of their wealth and expensive trappings. We also knew which men had a roving eye, for sometimes it lit on one of us.

One elderly gentleman from the Northwest was particularly kind to me, generous with a weekly tip, and one morning when I was working alone in his bungalow, he surprised me by placing his grandfatherly arms around me, expressing a non-grandfatherly admiration. He kissed me on the forehead and said, "I could get rough with you, but I like you too much." As Maude said, "They're never too old."

I adopted a friendly, impersonal attitude as my best defense and stood quietly, not struggling, not even speaking, just smiling up at him, just waiting, until finally the old man released me. He never touched me again, and he and his lovely gray-haired wife were kind and friendly to me throughout their stay.

During the three months I worked at the hotel, I never went to town, my only outside excursion a dance at the schoolhouse three miles away, my first dance in years as Bill didn't dance nor want to. I was escorted by one of the older wranglers and had a good time, on the surface. I wanted to enjoy myself and did, up to a certain point. I was still concerned about Bill and our future together, whether there would be one.

One day he wrote to me that he wanted to see me, and we began to correspond again until finally he set a date for his visit. He arrived while we were all eating lunch. Someone had directed him to the mess hall. When I saw him come in, I stood up and approached him slowly, with all eyes on us, and a question in my eyes. When I read the answer in his face, I kissed him, after which we sat down and I introduced him to the other maids including dear little Maude who was thrilled at what was happening.

I looked closely at Bill. He was thin and looked ill. He told me he had been sick with the 'flu while living in the tent on our place at Cave Creek with no one to take care of him. After lunch was over, I had to go back to work, so we arranged to meet and walk in the hills later.

As we slowly wandered through the sunny desert that afternoon, we talked. Bill had lost his job at the girls' school as the other man who had had the place before he went into the Army, had returned and wanted his job back. So Bill had had to give it up to him, as had been promised. Soon after leaving the school, Bill had come down with the 'flu and had to live in his tent, for our cabin had been rented for two months to a Canadian couple. However, our little home would soon be vacant.

Bill looked at me. It had been lonely, living without me, he said. Would we be together to celebrate our April 12th wedding anniversary at our Cave Creek home, he asked quietly. Our fifth anniversary. My heart turned over. I suddenly realized that if I were to find happiness in the future, it must be with Bill. There was no one else for me, and I had no desire to return to my former city life, nor did I want to follow the dude ranch circuit as others at the hotel did, year after year. I wanted nothing more than to continue being Bill's partner, that the important thing was not so much to achieve the perfect marriage as never to stop trying. In the stress of our struggle with the material things, we had stopped trying. How could we, who should have known better, who had had such a promising start, let ourselves get so far off the track?

We promised each other that we would try to be cheerful, no matter what happened, that we would rest and renew our spirits when necessary, not drive ourselves to the limit of our strength and endurance. There would be no more privation, no more summers of overwork in the terrible, relentless heat of the desert.

Most important of all, we decided to have a child. Not to save our marriage, it's not fair to put such a burden on a child, but because we both loved and wanted children. A child would complete our life together and give us something to work for, give a feeling of purpose to our existence.

It was the last week in February when Bill came to see me. I decided to stay on at the hotel during March, and when our desert home was vacated and cleaned, Bill would come for me. We would spend April resting and enjoying the sunshine and spring flowers, do some light work around our place, then in May go up to the Grand Canyon where Bill had worked before the war, and he would try to get on again as bus driver-guide for Fred Harvey on the South Rim.

Now that I had something definite to work toward, I returned to my job with a light heart while Bill headed for Cave Creek. But two days after he left, I became seriously ill with a fever and a murderous headache, although my appetite remained normal. Maude put me to bed and brought my meals on a tray from the mess hall, while she and the other maids generously worked my station, dividing it up between them. Mrs. Jones, the housekeeper, was very worried about me and told me to stay in bed until I was well enough to work again.

The hotel doctor and a guest who was a physician came to my room and examined me but couldn't figure out what was wrong. They gave me a shot to stop the pain, which sent me into hysterics from the relief, and Mr. Nord arranged for a hotel limousine to take me to town to Good Samaritan Hospital. The last thing I remember as I left Castle Hot Springs Hotel was Mrs. Jones's worried face as she tried to figure where to get a replacement for me.

The hospital was crowded, but finally a bed was found for me in an eight-bed solarium ward. When I was in bed at last, I lay very still, not moving for a long time, my eyes closed, in an effort to ease my head and conquer the nausea the long rough trip to town had caused. As I lay there, I dimly sensed the comings and goings of the nurses and the movements and soft conversation of the other patients. Finally I heard one voice whisper, "She is so still."

They must think I'm dying, I thought in sudden wry amusement, so I opened my eyes and weakly asked the nurse standing by another bed if a doctor would be coming soon to see me. They needn't think I'm dying, I told myself. They can't kill me off this easily. I knew that I would get better, the way I always got over everything when my nice, cheerful, easy-going mother would always say, "Oh, you'll be all right," and I always was. She never let on if she was worried about me when I was a child and always assumed I would get well. Of course, my father made me feel very important with his worrying.

It took two doctors to figure out what was wrong with me, infectious mononucleosis, after hard lumps had appeared in my neck and groin. I was put on a soft diet and given sulfa tablets and aspirin all day and all night, day after day, until my appetite was gone. I had to drink nothing but fruit juices and water until I rebelled and begged for buttermilk to bring my appetite back, which it did, although my diet was still pretty soft and insipid.

As Cave Creek had no telephones at that time, Maude had written immediately to Bill of my plight, and he had rushed to Phoenix to see me as soon as he received her letter. He was dismayed to see me flat on my back and in pain with a headache, and for the first few days he spent every visiting hour by my side, camping on the desert just outside of town so that he would be near me.

To cheer me up, Bill spoke often of the plans we had made, and we talked of trips we had taken and others we would like to take some day. In answer to my pleas for richer food, he smuggled in small sacks of delicious candy-store candy containing chocolate, figs, dates, and other delights. It had no ill effects and helped satisfy my craving for nourishment to give me strength to fight off the illness.

Bill would also bring me bouquets of wild flowers from the desert which everyone admired and liked better than the tame displays which others received. After he returned to Cave Creek, when I was feeling better, he sent me picture postcards he had drawn of desert life, animals and birds and sketches of camps we had made, to cheer me up.

I enjoyed visiting with the other patients who were mostly old women, called "Grandma" by all the nurses and aides whether they were grandmothers or not. Most of them had broken hips or legs but were quite brave and resigned to their fate, which could be death back in those days before surgery was invented to insert pins and balls and whatever they use now for such damage, including getting people out of bed as soon as possible to keep them from getting bed sores and losing calcium from their bones.

At the beginning of my third week at the hospital, my headache was gone, so I was finally allowed "bathroom privileges" and permitted to walk the halls to get my strength back. When the nurses weren't around, I would visit the other patients in the ward, cranking beds up or down as requested, and doing errands for them, anything to help pass the time.

Finally I was given my "walking papers" and allowed to leave Good Samaritan after my insurance paid the bill, plus some extra for me for the two months the doctor said I wouldn't be able to work. Mutual of Omaha decided to settle in full, giving me a lump sum, and soon after, they cancelled my policy. They must think I'm not good for much any more, I laughed when I told. Bill. Well, I'd show 'em.

A final note about Castle Hot Springs Hotel. Years later most of the main buildings burned down and were never rebuilt, although the remaining property was used for other things.

17

Together Again

At last I had returned to our beautiful palo verde desert at Cave Creek. It was good to lie in our Mexican string hammock under the mesquite trees in our patio or wander aimlessly up and down the sand-washes, not being any more useful than one of the lizards who lay on a boulder hoping his next meal would land near him.

As Chapo was still on pasture, I couldn't ride, but I preferred walking quietly alone, letting Nature heal me and bring new strength to my weakened self.

How could I express what it was like to be with Bill again? It was as though that part of my spirit which had been missing was replaced, someone had turned a key, and my machinery was working in harmony once more. Life was bright for us both.

There was one sad note in our song of joy. Spooky had disappeared from the Mitchell's property, the fate of many a desert cat grabbed off by a coyote or a big owl. We mourned his bright presence. He had loved us, and we had had to leave him, and now he was gone. But a few years later we read an article about a rabbit-killing cat living at Payson, and the picture of him lying on a fireplace mantel looked just like Spooky! A survivor! We felt better.

By the end of April we decided that we could be on our way again. After overhauling the Horizon Hunter, we loaded it, left our cabin and furnishings in the hands of new renters—city people who wanted to try their hands at desert life—and we were out of there without a backward glance. Grand Canyon beckoned.

Arizona weather can be neither predicted nor trusted, as cold winds buffeted our tent and whirled campfire smoke in our faces in the Grand

Canyon campground. In those days people could camp for an entire summer in Grand Canyon and nothing said. Not any more!

Once again I froze as I tried to fix our simple meals over juniper and piñon coals, but the fresh pine-scented air whetted our appetites, and we thrived on the renewal of our outdoor life.

In May, 1946, Bill started work as a bus driver-guide for Fred Harvey Company, explaining the wonders of his beloved Canyon to big bus loads of tourists who stood awe struck and silent as they gazed upon the majestic and unforgettable scene before them. Finally, recovering the use of their tongues, they plied Bill with all kinds of questions, mostly about the Canyon and Arizona but also about Bill's personal life. He would answer questions about the Canyon with the knowledge that years of study and experience had given him, and parry their personal questions with reserved and good-natured replies that preserved his privacy but didn't mar their enjoyment of their trip along the Rim.

Many of Bill's former passengers will remember him as "the guide who looked like an Indian and wore a leather tie with Indian picture writings on it." Their friends who came to the Canyon asked for the driver who answered to that description. Bill had decorated a special tie with an electric pencil, using pictographs he had discovered on rocks in the hills and canyons of the Southwest. It was also decorated with many a thumb print of an admiring and interested tourist.

When the weather turned beautiful and mild, I became restless. Bill didn't want me to hike alone on Canyon trails, so to use pent-up energy, I applied for a maid job at the auto camp where the less-expensive cabins were. It was work I knew well by then, and although I had to make from twenty-five to thirty beds a day, always with clean linen, I gained weight and enjoyed being with the light-hearted high school kids and Indian girls and boys who were also employed.

Now that I was working, Bill did the grocery shopping at Babbitt's general store on his way home from work at noon or night. As we had no ice box, our perishables had to be purchased from day to day. If Bill brought meat home at noon to be used that evening, he put it in the coolest place, under the cot pad on our bed. One day he brought home a package of hamburger which he forgot about.

The weather turned hot. After three nights we began to look strangely at each other. Suddenly Bill remembered, and we almost fell out of bed laughing before he dashed out to dispose of the evidence in a distant garbage can.

Together Again

In our free time we would hike down into the Canyon part way which always gave me the feeling that it was a friendly place with its birds and little animals, lovely wildflowers and plants, not just a remote and mysterious land as viewed from the Rim.

On one of our days off we were given a free mule trip to the Colorado River, by Fred Harvey Company. It was our first time down on a mule, and my mule's name was Parrot, a big strong gentle animal, which I trusted implicitly. I was right back of the guide. Bill rode at the rear on a mule named Cricket which had been used for packing supplies and was now being trained to haul people, but Bill had no trouble with him at all. I didn't think he would. It was a wonderfully interesting trip, seeing all the formations down the Canyon walls first hand. A trip I never forgot. Some of the dude riders were saddle sore at the end, but I wasn't as I had learned how to spare myself, although I was plenty tired when we reached the Rim once more.

Some day Bill and I had hoped to hike to Clear Creek, a remote spot in the Canyon, after the summer rains were over. It would be a round trip of about 45 miles and rough, but think of all that I would see! We would have to pack our grub and blankets on our backs, but there were fish in the creek, so we counted on that for part of our food. It would be no easy jaunt, so we tried to condition ourselves by hiking part way down into the Canyon each evening after work. It was fun making plans together again, to be seeking new horizons together! To cook over a campfire, eat steaks seasoned with piñon, and talk and dream and watch the dying fire make magic pictures in the soft dark Canyon evenings. The old wonder had returned to our life and we were never so happy.

In July I went by train to Toledo to visit my parents and brother for a few weeks, after which I returned rested and refreshed to my maid work, happy to be back in the near-wilderness, living outdoors again, breathing the clean pine-scented air, being with Bill once more.

The summer rains had started, so it was quite a trick to prepare and eat meals between showers, and as the wood was wet, I had to use our campstove. But it was worth it to see and smell the freshly washed forest and sniff the tangy fragrance of wet sagebrush.

We were still planning our trip to Clear Creek when something came up that made us postpone it until spring. We were asked to take charge for six weeks of the Indian Watchtower at Desert View 25 miles east of the village, while the other couple, Bob and Ethel Fix, went on their vacation. It was too good an opportunity to pass up.

135

Before Bob and Ethel left they showed us the ropes as well as how to keep from hanging ourselves on them, and in a few days I got over my worry that I wouldn't be able to handle the cash register or do the bookkeeping properly. The work was fun, and in slack moments when visitors to the tower were few, we could go to the windows or outdoors, and there would be the magnificent colors and formations of the Painted Desert and the majestic beginnings of the Canyon.

Spread out before us was the vast mysterious land of the Navajo, a sight that expanded and brought peace to my spirit. Out there, in 1946, were 60,000 people living a simple life amid beauty and unhampered by the complexities and dangers of modern civilization. True, many were poverty-stricken, in a material sense, needing adequate food, medical care, schools, and the like, some of which they received in subsequent years. Their primary possessions were good horses, herds of sheep, simple one-room dwellings called hogans, velvet and satin clothing, silver and turquoise "hard goods" with which to adorn themselves and reveal their wealth, and a wagon or pickup truck to drive themselves to "sings" or the trading post and sometimes to the nearest town, usually Flagstaff or Gallup.

The average Navajo in his isolated desert canyons or desert seems far happier than the average city man with all of the latter's luxuries and conveniences along with the ills attendant on fast-living, overwork, and inhaling the pollutants daily in the canyons of commerce where he attempts to earn the money to pay for the possessions which are threatening to destroy him.

We had some fine young Hopi Indians working with us at the Watchtower, and what a wonderful sense of humor they had, as most Indians do, we have found. Laura, the wife of Orville Wadsworth who ran the nearby service station, cooked supper for all of us, and our meals were hilarious as we talked over the day's happenings and commented on the quirks and antics of the tourists. She was a marvelous cook, also.

Most of the visitors who came to the tower were fine people, appreciative of what we told them about the Canyon and the Painted Desert as well as the Tower, which is a replica of the ancient watchtowers built by prehistoric Indians. Then there were tourists who tried to sneak up into the tower without paying the modest fee charged. Others were tired and bored and not receptive to the beauties of Nature; they stayed only briefly, wanting to be on the move, get their trip over with, and be home again. Sad. Some people asked us personal questions: Did we actually live way out here in the middle of nowhere? To us, this wasn't "nowhere," this was The Place to be!

One woman stood and stared at Eldon Kewonyama, one of our young Hopi assistants, for a long time as he sat by a wall in the Kiva room. He kept a straight, solemn face, even when she finally handed him a dime. He thanked her politely, not wishing to hurt her feelings by refusing to take it, but later when we closed the Tower and the boys were sweeping and cleaning up, he told me about it. Then he grinned and said, "She must have thought I was poor boy." He was a school Indian as was his older brother Leroy who was a wonderful artist, painting beautiful pictures of Kachinas.

What amazes us is the lack of insight of people who speak of Indians as being "uncivilized." They are quiet people with wonderful manners, and they treat you with consideration if you treat them well.

Aunt Florence came to stay with us at the Tower for a couple of weeks, and we were all treated to an incredible meteor shower one night as we stood on the top of the Tower, the Hopis with us, along with Joe Kennedy, the District Ranger, and his wife Muriel, who were stationed at Desert View and became our friends. We were amazed at the sight of dozens of meteors every few minutes flashing brilliantly in the moonless sky, a sight none of us ever forgot.

In August our six weeks were up and it was time for us to leave our Hopi friends. We were sorry to say good-bye. They had worked well, and we had enjoyed our stay with them.

18

Pregnant, and Broke Again

As there was no house available for us in Grand Canyon village, we voted to spend the winter at Cave Creek. When we hit the road once more, our sudden freedom felt doubly delicious after our sunmer and fall of work. In spite of our deep love for the Canyon, it was a rest for us to be amid more "ordinary" scenery for a change. We were filled to the brim with grandeur, and as bread and milk taste good after a too rich diet, so the low hills and desert stretches were a welcome contrast.

We had earned our freedom, we decided, as we drove along. So why not see some new country before settling for the winter on the Cave Creek desert? Where should we go? So many places to choose from. As I hadn't seen the desert and mountains around Tucson and Oracle in the southern part of the State, we decided that after we left everything but our camping equipment at our Cave Creek home, we would take a three-day trip down into that country.

On the first night of our camping trip, we slept in a beautiful clean white sandwash in the hills near Oracle. It was so wonderful to lie there in the peace and quiet and gaze up at the brilliant stars and listen to the distant howling of the coyotes once more.

Next day we drove up to Sabino Canyon in the Santa Catalina Mountains, then back to Tucson Mountain Park where we camped for the night in a sheltered cove near the Picture Rocks which are covered with innumerable Indian pictographs which Bill wanted to copy in his notebook.

We had hoped to make a run down across the border into Old Mexico, but as the sky looked stormy, we settled for a visit to beautiful little San Xavier Mission on the desert, then drove into the picturesque Santa Rita Mountains with their rugged heights splashed with the autumn gold of aspen groves. We climbed as far as we dared in our old car up the steep road until we reached the campground near Madera Canyon where we saw several white-tailed deer whisk off into the brush. As it was too cold and stormy for camping, we turned back down the mountain, then drove straight through to Cave Creek that night, arriving exhausted but pleased with our little outing.

While we had been gone, the power line had been brought through to Cave Creek and past our property, so we decided that it would add to the value of our place if we wired our house for electricity. Filled with enthusiasm, we plunked down one hundred hard-earned dollars for a handsome little apartment-size electric range which had caught my eye in a Phoenix store, so after that it was a case of "have to" where electricity was concerned.

As metal products were still in short supply, many a trip to town was needed before we found the necessery things we needed for the wiring, and as we couldn't get an electrician to come way out there and wire the house, Bill decided to do the work himself with the help of a diagram supplied by a Phoenix electrician sympathetic to our cause.

As Bill worked, he kept declaring, "It won't work!" And just as emphatically, I would contradict him, "Of course it will work! It has to work!" When he fastened the last wire with the last piece of friction tape and turned the last screw in the last switch, then, snapped on the lights, lo and behold, it did work! I couldn't understand why Bill was so surprised, but I did understand why he felt so proud. Thomas Edison couldn't have felt any prouder.

Then our kind electrician friend gave in to our pleas and drove out from town to install my electric range in return for a ride on Chapo, the finest inducement we could have offered him. Oh, what a pleasure it was to have the electric range to cook on after the smoky smelly portable kerosene stove I had been using!

I still had no electric washing machine, but just for the two of us I didn't feel the need for one, the old-fashioned washboard and galvanized tubs were enough. It was a lot more than I had had to do with when we first started out. I sent our bed sheets to a local laundry for wet-wash; everything else I did myself by hand. As we now had power, I ironed, but only shirts, nothing else. Life was still simple, and there was no nonsense about trying to "keep up with the Joneses." Our Joneses, Catherine and Theodore of Cahava Ranch, were literally some of God's best people, living simply, wearing denim and eating beans; all you had to do to keep up with them was be honest, decent, and kind.

Now we started on the plumbing. Bill dug a deep pit below the house, lined it with concrete, and fitted it with a cover, for a septic tank. After putting up a metal water storage tank on a wooden platform and installing pipes, we had the supreme luxury of running water in the kitchen. Bill had to pump the water by hand up into the tank, no mean task, and I had to be sparing in my use of the precious liquid, but how much easier it made things not to have to carry water by the bucketful!

We bought the least expensive toilet and wash basin we could find, and soon our bathroom was a lovely, convenient reality. The tub was the least expensive item—concrete-lined, sunk into the floor and painted white. It had to be filled by hand with a hose from the wash basin, but it served the purpose besides saving money.

Instead of resting on his laurels, Bill now decided to build a small cabin among the palo verde trees a few hundred feet west of the main house. When the new place was ready for occupancy and we were broke once more, we could rent our larger cabin for the rest of the winter and live off the rent. It was still difficult to find building supplies, but gradually the little house took shape, complete with concrete floor, tiny living room, larger bedroom, and miniature kitchen, prospector-style with no plumbing or electricity. I named it the "Knot Hole," but in spite of its being so small and plain, it was really cozy, and I kind of liked it better than the larger cabin, for we had such a good time building this one.

Our construction work had required more money than we had figured on, but when Bill tried to borrow from the bank, they turned him down flat. Even though we had always paid cash for everything, we had no "credit rating." We were dumbfounded, being treated worse then the most extravagant fourflusher that walked the streets.

While painting the new cabin, I discovered that the smell of paint was becoming increasingly bothersome to me until I could hardly stand it. One day when Aunt Florence drove out for lunch with us, I fixed our favorite tomato soup and grilled cheese sandwiches, sat down with an appetite, and suddenly found I couldn't eat. What was wrong? Some strange disease? Then I found that I couldn't even look at cans of food with pictures on them without becoming nauseated. What kind of joke was Mother Nature playing on me?

Joke? Surely no joke. My mind began to work rapidly. I began to think back. My heart beat faster. I hardly dared to believe what I was beginning to believe, to hope what I was beginning to hope.

I told Bill how I felt, but we didn't dare put into words our feelings and thoughts. First I must wait a certain length of time, then see a doctor.

The day finally came when Bill could drive me carefully over the rough desert road to Phoenix where I rode up in an elevator to an office in a high building, sat impatiently in a crowded waiting room, then jumped up eagerly when it was my turn to see the doctor. He questioned me closely, examined me, then his eyes twinkled and he smiled as he gave me the verdict I was waiting and hoping for. It was true! I was going to have a baby! After all this time! It was really finally true!

When I reached the street and met Bill and told him the news, he almost keeled over, and when we went to find the car, he couldn't remember where he had parked it.

Although Bill was pretty sure he'd get his job at the Canyon again in the spring, at the present time he had no job, and we were almost broke from the high cost of eating, feeding a horse, and building a house. Yet we never doubted for a moment we could provide for this new addition to our family. We had it to do, so we would do it. This would mean changing our way of living and settling down to a more stable life, but we didn't mind. All we could think of was our happiness over our coming child.

Although I was thirty-two years old, the active outdoor life had benefited me, and I felt pretty well, even though the nausea was bad. I fought it off with snacks of crackers and apples at all hours of the day and night, and gradually it left me, until finally I began to crave different foods, mostly peanut butter, and I was pleased to be reacting to my new condition the way other pregnant women did.

As we were low on funds and our place still wasn't ready to rent, I decided to write an article and try to sell it to a magazine. I had read a story about a "perfectionist" housewife in the How America Lives section of the Ladies' Home Journal, so I said to myself, I'll let them know how an entirely different kind of housewife managed.

With little previous experience at writing, one rejection slip, and no sales to my credit, I sat down at our dining table and started. To our amazed delight, the Journal which had never purchased a manuscript by an outsider for that series, wrote that they would use mine, along with some of the pictures we had taken on our travels, for my story told of all the adventures we had had since we were married and the hardships we had undergone.

When the *Ladies' Home Journal's* check and letter of acceptance arrived, I ran leaping over small bushes to where Bill was working, and then we sat in the Horizon Hunter to get out of the wind and hugged each other as I laughed and gasped and read and re-read the wonderful message. I could hardly believe it, but I had felt sure that our unusual way of life would appeal to the Editors, and they concurred. The money was a gift from heaven. Now we could pay our bills, eat, pay for pasture for Chapo, and have enough left for doctor and hospital, diapers, bassinette and baby carriage, baby clothes and high chair and all the lovely little things that babies need to thrive and grow.

The Editors at the *Ladies' Home Journal* wrote to us that their Picture Editor, John Morris, and photographer, Kosti Ruohomaa, would travel to Arizona to take pictures of us, our home, and our horse. As these two nice young men were unable to find a place to stay in Cave Creek, we were happy to house them in our bedroom while we slept in the Knot Hole on an ancient metal bed we had purchased.

John and Kosti were with us for a week, long enough for the sun-warmed springtime desert to grip them in its spell. We drove through the friendly hills, visited neighboring ranchers and prospectors, explored deserted cabins, scrambled around in the granite boulders of Black Mountain, and showed them how we camped out. We served them a steak supper cooked over campfire coals, while an Arizona sunset obligingly painted a magical backdrop for their pictures. The ones that appeared in the August, 1947, issue were wonderful! They certainly did us justice.

Some time ago I saw the Picture Editor of the *New York Times* on the program *60 Minutes*, and his name was John Morris, so I wrote to him and asked him if he was "our" John Morris. But he never replied, so I guess he isn't, much to my disappointment.

We had been afraid that the long, rough trip back to Grand Canyon by way of the unpaved Black Canyon road would be harmful to my condition, but as we wished to avoid the heavy traffic on Yarnell Hill and the White Spar, it was the only route we could take. Aside from my feeling ill in Lonesome Valley, too tired to sleep the night we stayed in Ashfork, and worried about the Horizon Hunter's attacks of "vapor lock" on steep Ashfork Hill—renamed Nemesis Hill by us—we finally reached Grand Canyon without mishap.

As employees in the Park were no longer permitted to camp in the public campground, we rented a one-room non-modern cabin in the auto camp which had one electric light bulb hanging from the ceiling, and a tiny wood cook stove to prepare meals. Outside nearby was a water tap, while the laundry room was a block away with just set-tubs, no machines. And several hundred feet distant and across the road was the public restroom.

It was April, the nights were cold and windy with snow flurries, so it was a mild form of torture when I was forced to get up two or three times a night, put on a coat, tie a scarf over my head, take flashlight in hand, and stumble sleepily out into the deserted, wind-swept night to attend to my needs. My "pioneer spirit" began to sag a little.

When our cabin was needed for tourists pouring in to visit the Canyon, we were moved to a non-modern "prefab" which had screens and canvas flaps and three translucent windows to admit a little light. Dust blew in around the flaps and into our food and the furniture. The cabin was supplied with a small oil heater, a bed, two chairs, and a table. There was no cookstove, so I fixed our meals on a two-burner electric hot plate we had to buy. We asked again about getting a house in the residential area, but there still was nothing available, so we had to stay where we were and make the best of it, as Bill liked his guide job and found it very congenial work.

During our first month back at the Canyon, the *Ladies' Home Journal* sent psychiatrist Dr. Hohman to interview us for an article he was to write about us, to tie in with the "How America Lives" piece. When he arrived, he was astounded and continually emphasized the lack of security in our mode of living. How could we dare to bring a baby into such an insecure existence as suggested by my article? Bill and I were amused. We didn't feel in the least insecure.

Further along in the interview, he stressed that Bill, now nearly fifty years old, would be an "old old man" by the time our child entered school. Again Bill and I had to smile at each other. Being young in spirit was what counted with us, and that helped keep the body young.

When Dr. Hohman shrank back upon his first view of Grand Canyon and said that it made him "sick to look down at it," stating that he preferred the security of his own snug home in the East, we began to wonder uneasily what he would write about us. He didn't see us in a true light, nor did he appreciate the freedom and beauty of our life the way John Morris had. We feared that the doctor's article would be unfair, depicting us as irresponsible people who didn't deserve to have a baby. But we figured that John would stick up for us as he had seemed to admire our way of life during his brief stay in our desert home.

When my story "Horizon Hunters" appeared in the *Ladies' Home Journal* that August, there was no attendant article by the psychiatrist. We were given a wonderful spread, with some of the snapshots I had supplied and beautiful pictures in both color and black-and-white by Kosti. We decided the Journal editors had seen things our way, for they printed nothing to spoil the spirit of my piece, for which we were truly grateful.

Soon after the magazine appeared, we were very pleased to receive lovely letters from readers who said they had enjoyed reading about us and wanted to know more, inquiring about our child about to be born and wishing us well. Some generous people sent gifts for the baby. We were thrilled about the response, and I did my best to answer all the letters amid the excitement of preparing for the birth of my baby. I still have some of the letters which I saved.

It was a Sunday night in August. Aunt Florence had driven up from the desert and was living in a tent in the public campground in order to be on hand to give me aid and comfort. She was sitting in our cabin that evening while Bill read, and I lounged on the bed, as I hadn't felt up to our usual walk around the campground. Suddenly I began to feel strange. I said nothing until Aunt Florence had left for the night, as I saw no purpose in keeping her awake while the baby took his time appearing on the scene.

When she had gone, I told Bill that I was in labor. Not at all rattled, just his usual calm self, he helped me into the car with my suitcase and carefully drove me up the hill to the hospital. Dr. Scoles was away, but Billie, the nurse on duty, examined me, affirmed that I was in labor, and put me to bed. I didn't see much sense in Bill's sitting on the edge of a chair the rest of the night, so I told him to go home and get some sleep, which he reluctantly did. Billie gave me a capsule to put me to sleep and went to bed herself, and I was alone, she and I the only two people in the building that night, as there were no other patients.

It was very quiet, the only sound the wind outside in the pines and the occasional vibration of the windows, caused by the big machines in the Grand Canyon power house. I dozed, waking every few minutes to look at my watch in order to time my contractions which came at five-minute intervals all night long. By morning they were three minutes apart when Billie brought me a cup of coffee, and when Dr. Scoles arrived, the time had shortened to two minutes.

I didn't feel much pain as I had been relaxing with each contraction. I had read that that would help, and it did, until the second stage arrived. That was different! The doctor looped a strip of sheeting to the foot of the bed, put the ends in my hands and told me to go to work.

Aunt Florence sat and waited outdoors in the sunshine while Bill, who had spent a sleepless night, stood by my bed with anxious eyes. He tried to say something helpful, told me I could relax better with my mouth open.

I opened it enough to gasp, "Leave me alone!" He did, and he fled. I shouldn't have been so rude, I thought, but I didn't really care. I couldn't. I was too busy, a vast wave of feeling washing over me with no time for thinking or talking or being polite.

Before long, with my unceasing efforts, these new contractions piled into each other so hard and fast that the doctor and two nurses, one of them the doctor's wife, hurriedly wheeled me across the hall to the delivery room. Dr. Scoles gave me a spinal anesthetic, and, although I was fully conscious, I felt nothing while my baby was being born. I realized later that I could have finished the job with a few whiffs of ether, as I had undergone the hardest contractions with nothing but some kind of capsule. So I felt kind of cheated.

Be that as it may, my baby was there, a big handsome boy, eight pounds, twenty-one inches, Monty Edward Parks, a new Horizon Hunter, had joined his life with ours.

19

Horizon Hunter No. III

After Monty was dressed, Billie brought him in to my room and laid him on my pillow. Bill and Aunt Florence hovered over us with pride and interest.

My baby.

I caressed his rose petal cheek with one finger. "So soft," I marveled with the same lack of originality of new mothers everywhere. "The tiny hands and feet. The small nose and ears. Blond curly hair. So much of it. And a funny little 'cow lick' in the front. How he'll cuss that when he's getting ready for his first date! Doesn't he have a good nose? The doctor remarked on it first thing. Who do you think he looks like?" And on and on.

After the spinal had worn off, I wanted to get out of bed right away to keep from losing strength, so Dr. Scoles let me as he had modern ideas on that subject. I felt strong and well, not at all dizzy as I sat up and walked around. In five days they let me take Monty home to our prefab, Bill driving the Horizon Hunter more slowly and carefully than he ever had.

For a bassinet we used a baby carriage which also served as transportation for daily walks. Aunt Florence did the cooking and cleaning for me at first, but I insisted on taking complete charge of Monty. I felt equal to it, and I didn't want to miss a minute of this wonderful new experience.

As I wanted to give my baby all possible advantages, I tried hard to breast-feed him, but I couldn't seem to keep him awake and make him work at it. If he had had his way, he would have nursed in fits and starts all day and most of the night, clearly impractical. I didn't try to put him

146

on a schedule and fed him whenever he cried, but when he got me up six times in one night, Bill declared firmly, "This can't go on!"

Worn out and despairing, I sat on the edge of the bed and wept. I was a failure as a mother. When Bill gently suggested that he'd better ask the doctor for a formula, I cried even harder. "I can do it," I insisted, "I can nurse him. He needs the immunity and other advantages that my milk will give him."

I continued the battle to nurse my precious baby, hating to give in, feeding him every two hours, but when I realized with fright that he had gained only one pound over his birth weight in two months, I admitted failure and began to use a supplementary formula, continuing to nurse him, also, until he was five months old when I had to admit defeat.

From that moment Monty started to gain, and I stopped reading articles that stated that "all mothers can breast-feed their babies if they try." In three months Monty was fat and healthy, but he still cried. He cried over every little thing. He thought he had to cry to get whatever he wanted, as we could find nothing wrong with him, and even after I had attended to his needs, he cried himself to sleep. It was puzzling and nerve-wracking. I jumped when he stirred in his sleep, whenever he opened his mouth and let out the first wail, and my hands shook and I dropped things while he cried. I tried everything I could think of to help him, but when he still cried, I was frantic. The only time I felt relaxed and at ease was when I held him and fed him and he lay in my left arm and was quiet and contented.

Aunt Florence had left after helping me out for a month, for in late September the nights at the Canyon become too cold for camping out, and she had to head for the warm desert and her home in Phoenix. It had been so reassuring to have her with me, and I was frightened at having to cope with everything alone. People had commended me for my courage in camping out in the wilds. They didn't know what they were saying. Facing up to a mountain lion would be nothing compared to coping with a crying baby in the night and trying to figure out what was the matter. Now, that takes real courage.

It took me nearly a year to conquer my nervousness while bathing my baby. Monty was so strong and active, I was sure he would slip out of my arms, no matter how careful I was. He usually enjoyed his bath, but sometimes my nervousness was contagious. One warm day a locust buzzed suddenly outside the open flap of the prefab. I jumped, and Monty jerked and screamed in fright, almost pushing himself out of his little bathtub perched on our round dining table. I shook so that I could hardly finish his bath. I was a basket case for sure.

In December when Monty was nearly four months old, we decided to spend the winter at Cave Creek. As the Horizon Hunter was getting pretty old and unreliable, Bill hired Finch, one of the other drivers who was going on vacation, to take Monty and me in his car and follow Bill as he drove our '28 Chevy down the mountain grades. We went by way of the Black Canyon road again, but instead of going past Lynx Creek, we headed down into Lonesome Valley which is called Prescott Valley now. When we reached the turn-off, we saw that the dirt road to Dewey was a sea of churned mud. Nevertheless, we forged ahead, only to have both cars become mired hub-deep after a few hundred yards, with no way to turn around and go back.

Finch complained that he had a bad back, so it was up to Bill to dig both cars out time after time, mostly with his hands, while we inched our way along. Monty had been sleeping in my arms, and now he woke up and began to scream from hunger. Not knowing what to do for him, I held him close and began rocking him back and forth in my arms, as I had no way to heat his bottle, but finally I managed to take a little of the chill off by holding it against the car heater. After he gulped down a full eight ounces of formula, he went back to sleep. When we reached Dewey, he awoke and cried again, so I gave him another bottle, he drank that and went back to sleep. He was bottomless, it seemed. Luckily I had brought plenty of formula.

It was dark when we finally reached the low desert, and then Finch's car developed a flat. Our car had given no trouble at all. As Finch had no spare, Bill drove Monty and me the rest of the way to Cave Creek in our car, bought a tire, left us at the Black Mountain store and returned to Finch's car. After they changed the tire, Bill and Finch drove to the store where I was waiting, and the Franklins, who were friends of ours, gave us all some warm supper, and we went on to our house, worn out from the long trip.

We let Finch have our bedroom, while Bill set our cot up in the living room where I put Monty to bed in his baby carriage, completely draped with mosquito bar to protect him from any scorpions, black widows, and centipedes where they surely were lodging in the rafters after our long absence.

Next day after Finch left we gave the whole house a complete going-over, and from then on that was my main preoccupation, protecting

Monty from the desert's poisonous creatures. I shook out his diapers, clothing and bedding several times a day, and we bought a screened crib for him, which helped ease our minds considerably. He still cried a great deal for no apparent reason, but the baby books called it "nervous crying," from either too much attention or not enough. But which? How is a parent to know? All the reading I did about babies just served to make me more nervous and unsure of myself. Sorry, Dr. Spock.

When Monty was asleep, I would sit by his crib and gaze at him, unable to keep my eyes off his sweet little face, I was so thrilled that this was my child I had borne. When he was awake, I would cuddle him close, play with him, talk and sing silly children's songs, and even read picture books before he was ten months old, which he seemed to enjoy immensely. When his brown eyes met mine, and we smiled at each other, that was my reward for all the work and worry, and I felt that the world was mine.

I took him for buggy rides over the rolling desert roads, which he loved and gurgled with pleasure as we went along. Sometimes I would go off by myself for an hour, and Monty would stay with Bill who was adding a small porch to the Knot Hole. Monty would fall asleep contentedly in his carriage while listening to the blows of hammer and noise of sawing, music to his little ears.

Monty thrived in the desert air and sunshine, a truly healthy, handsome baby. We celebrated Monty's first Christmas at Cave Creek, decorating a four-foot-tall piñon pine with popcorn strings, colored lights, and dried yucca pods which I had gilded with gold and silver paint. He was charmed with it even though he didn't know what it was all about, of course. And he received lots of toys from relatives, friends, and proud uncle and grandparents in Toledo.

Then, two disasters. Chapo had become very crippled and almost deaf while on pasture, so we were forced to have him "put down." For a long time we could barely mention him and his sad ending, which happens to many an old horse. And we never forgot him, praising him as the best horse that had ever lived.

The other event was the demise of the Horizon Hunter. Many times in the past when it was giving trouble and we were down on the desert, we would turn to the best mechanic we had ever met. Old timers will remember Johnny Essex who had his shop in east Phoenix. But now we couldn't even get the Chevy started, not even one more "chug" out of it, and the Cave Creek mechanics couldn't figure out what was wrong,

This was financial disaster, for we couldn't afford our desert stay and the purchase of another car, even an old used one.

Reluctantly, we borrowed money from my parents to buy a second-hand 1936 Dodge sedan four-door which had pretty good rubber, appeared to be in fair condition, and cheap at the price of three hundred dollars. We thought.

When Bill drove the car home, he discovered the hitch. All the Dodge needed was a new engine. And all we needed was more money. What else could we do but borrow an additional sum from my parents who said they were only too glad to help? We were so disappointed and disgruntled with this "new" car that we could never think of it as another "Horizon Hunter." We dubbed it the "Roadrunner" and hoped for the best.

As our gloomy financial status indicated an early return to the Canyon, we were back in the prefab in March while snow was still on the ground. This made things difficult for me, as I had to leave Monty alone while I made a dash across the road to the rest rooms or fetched water from the laundry room where I also did my washing. I had outdoor clotheslines, but in wet weather I had to hang everything on ropes stretched from nails in our cabin, wet diapers slapping us in the face as we moved around.

I usually saved my clothes washing until evenings when Bill was home and could stay with Monty, as I was afraid that the cabin might burn down if I was away too long. I always managed those days to find something to be afraid of, poisonous creatures, fire, germs, accidents, a new experience for me, for I had never known such fear, not even when faced with the possibility of being broke and hungry. Fearing for one's own safety is nothing compared to the fear for the safety of someone you love. Such constant, unwarranted fear served no useful purpose, and I knew it, waged a daily fight against it, and knew I must conquer it before we could have the kind of happy home life we wanted.

When my parents arrived at the Canyon for a visit in June to see their grandson, now ten months old, I confided to my mother that "I feel so nervous I could die." I was sleeping badly and could hardly eat, so I looked thin and haggard. Rather than let me give in, my practical mother bolstered my courage with good advice, then gave me some B vitamins and iodine ration pills.

Within three weeks I was amazed at the change in myself, as they say in the ads. I felt like a different person, I was able to eat and sleep again,

I gained weight, so we all started to enjoy life. Most importantly, Monty became more relaxed as he sensed the difference in me. One night he felt so good he woke up out of a sound sleep, pulled himself up in his crib at four, rocked from side to side, and began chanting loudly, much to our astonishment and wry amusement. Luckily this did not become a habit.

After my parents left, Aunt Florence arrived for another session of camping out, which she loved and which gave her a vacation from the summer heat of the desert. As she was a real Arizona pioneer, she knew how to get the most from living outdoors. Her son James put a floor in her tent and even installed a small wood heater complete with metal chimney, and the rangers never noticed, or if they did, they didn't say anything. Try to do that these days when camping is severely limited. No way!

It was great fun for me to wheel Monty to her camp to nap in his buggy, and spend an afternoon with her in the shade of the pines and junipers that surrounded her campsite, which was a choice one. After talking or reading or just sitting in one of her chairs for a couple of hours, I would make a quick trip to my cabin and get some fixings so that Aunt Florence and I could prepare supper over her gasoline camp-stove or the campfire. I could pretend that we were camping out once more when Bill joined us and we ate our simple meal together in the glow of a Grand Canyon sunset.

After cleaning up, we would sit around the fire and talk and laugh while Monty dozed in Bill's lap, the stars far above shining softly beyond the branches of the trees. What happy evenings those were. And how hard it was to return to the clutter and confinement of our prefab. And cluttered it was! We should have had a chart to get through the tangle of table, chairs, kitchen cupboard I had been given by Ethel, our next door neighbor; double bed, oil heater, wash stand, crib, playpen, applebox bookcase, suitcases, carriage, stroller, potty chair, and clothes tree. Most of our clothes hung on nails on the wall, and some things were stored under our bed, all that would fit.

For refrigeration we had a small portable ice box given to us by my parents, which we filled with ice from the ice room at the power house and kept outside on the ground next to the shady side of our prefab. As we had no sink or drain, I had to throw dishwater out through the door onto the ground. One evening approaching visitors from Ohio almost became the target for a large pan of wash water I threw out the door.

If Ethel, my next door neighbor, turned on her electric hotplate at the same time as I did mine, power would go out until I went outside and flipped the circuit breaker, then wait until she was through with her cooking. We didn't like it but managed. What else could we do?

To look on the brighter side of the picture, our expenses were unusually low, for rent was reasonable, and electricity, fuel oil, water, furnishings, and linens were supplied without charge. So we were satisfied enough with our situation that we didn't try very hard to get a house in the residential area. We were saving money.

As we wished to avoid the financial near-catastrophe of the previous winter, Bill decided to stay on and work at the Canyon during most of the cold weather, while Aunt Florence and I took Monty to live on our place at Cave Creek, traveling in the Roadrunner, as Aunt Florence was an excellent and experienced mountain driver, even at her age of sixty-seven. She put me to shame, as I never drove after the Spur Cross fiasco.

Although I hated to leave Bill alone, I looked forward to being on the sunny desert again. A long session of being cooped up in that prefab during a dark cold winter, with not even a real window to look out of, didn't appeal to me, and plowing through snowdrifts to rest rooms, showers, and laundry wasn't my idea of fun. So Bill would have to make do, taking his clothes to be washed or dry cleaned at the laundry managed by Buford Belgard.

I couldn't have asked for a better companion than Aunt Florence. We were the best of friends, we respected each other's privacy, and she loved the desert as much as I did. And she drove the Roadrunner on our trips for groceries, ice, and mail. When Bill came for a visit, he had to take the stage from Grand Canyon to Williams, then the Greyhound Bus to Wickenburg where we picked him up and to which town we returned him when his visits were over.

At Cave Creek Monty and I slept down in the bedroom, he in his screened crib close by my bed away from walls where scorpions might be crawling, while Aunt Florence had her camp cot and other belongings in the living room. We shared the work and fun, and it was comforting to have such an understanding person with whom I could talk over my problems.

Although Monty still cried at times, I was far more at ease with him. I did worry when he walked and crawled around the cabin and into the closet where scorpions and other unwanted creatures might be lurking. One day the wind banged our outside kitchen door open, and when

Aunt Florence went to close it, she found a slender tan deadly scorpion in a tray at the sink drainboard, where it had been blown off the top of a cupboard. What if it had landed where curious little fingers might have found it? I sprayed all along the outside of the house almost daily, and I examined the inside walls and floors in every corner and looked under cupboards and furniture every morning before turning Monty loose to walk around, but I seldom found anything, and he was never stung or bitten.

Outdoors was a different matter. We had to guide his wandering, stumbling footsteps away from cactus, sharp rocks, steep trails, and possible rattlers. We never dared be far away from him as he explored the mysteries of the fascinating desert environment which looks so beautiful and even friendly, but many dangers lurk for the young and unwary. Monty's great delight, and mine, was to sit in some secluded sandwash in the warm sunshine and play with the clean pink and white granite sand. It was the world's prize sandbox.

To me, Monty was the world's prize baby. Sweet, fat, and healthy, he was growing and changing so fast, and I treasured each small change, each new word, each charming baby "trick," reporting joyfully and faithfully to Bill in my frequent letters.

Bill wasn't able to be with us at Christmas, but he arrived for a month's vacation visit the first of January when we celebrated a second Christmas with him. He was so surprised and pleased with Monty's progress during the brief time he had been separated from us, and Monty was delighted to become reacquainted with his adored "Daddenadden" as he now called Bill. For once Bill could enjoy his desert home without working himself to death, although he did apply a needed coat of linseed oil to the redwood siding of our house.

The Knot Hole had become a place to store things, as well as a home for what were called "New York tarantulas," a type of large hairless spider, as well as various other creatures including a cunning Gekko lizard who squeaked in panic when we tried to catch him. We left him there to work on the insect population.

Our plans for our Cave Creek home hadn't worked out the way we had hoped, for it was difficult to find renters, but at least the property meant a source of possible financial gain if we should decide to sell it. In the meantime we enjoyed our stay, little realizing that it was the last time we would live there.

20

Horizon Hunter IV

Something happened that winter that eventually led to our putting our Cave Creek home up for sale. After Bill returned to the Canyon the first of February, I discovered that I was pregnant again. I was thrilled, but I couldn't help wondering how Bill would take the news, for we hadn't talked much about the possibility of our having another child. I underestimated him. He was just as happy as I was. Now we wouldn't have to raise Monty as an only child. He would have a companion, a brother or sister, to learn to live, play, and get along with. I almost said "fight with," but we decided right from the start that we wouldn't permit the all too usual teasing and fighting. I hadn't enjoyed it when I was little, and neither had Bill when his older brothers came down hard on him.

The same old morning sickness gripped me twenty-four hours a day until I could hardly think of anything else. It was worse this time, and nothing seemed to give me relief. One night at the end of my second month when Bill was with us at Cave Creek for a short visit, I had a sharp pain and began to hemorrhage. I was losing my baby!

Next day after a frantic Bill had the Cave Creek nurse visit me, he piled the back seat of the Roadrunner with quilts, pillows, and blankets, gently lifted me in, then drove me to Phoenix to a doctor who had me admitted to a hospital. Once again I was in a ward with several women who helped take my mind off of myself. I listened to their troubles and problems, and they listened to mine. I read everything I could get my hands on when I wasn't swallowing medicine, taking shots, or getting bed baths or back rubs, eating light meals, and following all the rest of the usual hospital routine.

On my second afternoon, an old woman who was terribly ill was put into the bed next to mine. When she was alone, she continually asked for her husband and daughter and moaned from pain which was unrelieved by shots or other drugs. Several times in her delirium she tried to get out of bed, almost falling, once knocking a screen over onto my bed, and I was frantic with worry that I couldn't help her, as I wasn't allowed to be on my feet.

When I called for the nurses, they were slow in coming as they were shorthanded and the hospital was over-crowded. That evening a nurse's aide whispered to me that the poor old woman was going to die. I was too wrought-up to sleep until I was given a pill, after which I dozed for maybe a couple of hours, then awoke to see a low stretcher being wheeled away in the dim light of the big room, and the rumpled bed next to mine was empty. The poor old women had died, all alone, while I was asleep. I learned that she had had an intestinal obstruction, and the odor in that room was almost more than I could stand. If I had been going to lose my baby, it would have been right then. And for months afterwards my back itched constantly, my back that had been turned toward that poor woman. When a doctor said it was from nerves, I knew what had caused it. Eventually it disappeared.

On my third day in the hospital, the doctor said that I might have to spend the next seven months in bed. I wept. We couldn't afford it. Monty and Bill needed me. I would lose all my strength. I couldn't bear the thought of constant confinement. When I told Bill what the doctor had said, he asked me how I felt. As I said that I had had no further trouble, he demanded that the doctor release me. On the fifth day I was permitted to leave, and we found a different doctor, in Sunnyslope, a very capable, kindly young man who made a thorough examination, took all kinds of tests, then declared that I was not only strong enough to be up and around, but that I should be able to make the trip to Grand Canyon inside of a month without any trouble.

And he proved to be right. Gradually the nausea went away, and I became strong and more active. So the end of March found Bill, Monty, and me on our way north, while Aunt Florence returned to her family, which had moved to California.

Back at the Canyon, I was appalled at the thought of taking care of two small children in the over-crowded prefab, so Bill applied again for a house, and finally in June there was one vacant, three rooms in a duplex, plus a glassed-in porch and a bathroom! A kitchen, a separate kitchen! A separate bedroom, a living room, and a bathroom with a bath tub! Such luxury! When we first moved in, I wandered around the rooms glorying in all the space, the wonderful spaciousness of it all. And the windows with real glass in them that I could see through! The big backyard! A separate pantry by the kitchen! A sink and running water, hot and cold!

What happened to my old pioneer spirit? I wondered. Has it really left me? But a woman needs a house when she has babies, I told myself. When our children are older and there are no more diapers and bottles, play pens and cribs, I'll be back to my old self.

To furnish our new dwelling, Bill made a trip to Cave Creek for a few things, but outside of the stove and crib, our furniture wouldn't have brought forty dollars at auction. We used the ancient kitchen cupboard that Ethel, my former neighbor, had given to me, and I painted it white, using it for baby clothes and toys. We made our living room settee from an old car seat, some oiled boards, padding, and a cotton "Indian blanket" carefully tacked in place. We left the scarred floors bare until we received a gift of linoleum from my parents. The living room draperies were from our closets at Cave Creek. Kitchen curtains and draperies for our bedroom were made by my mother who also gave us a plastic curtain for our bathroom.

We had a secondhand ice box on our back porch, and we dined at an oilcloth-covered card table. The one living room chair was a rusty metal one previous tenants had discarded and which I painted and covered with our Navajo saddle blanket which Phyllis, one of my helpers at Spur Cross, had given us for Christmas our second year there.

I was satisfied. The fewer things we had, the easier my housekeeping. No knick-knacks to dust. No rugs to beat or vacuum. No vacuum cleaner. Ironing was at a minimum, shirts and jeans and Bill's guide clothing. No doilies or table linens to wash and iron. Life was simple and uncluttered. After all, no house is bare which has children and love and happiness within.

As Dr. Shnur, the new Canyon doctor, wouldn't promise to give me a spinal when my second baby was to be born, I decided not to have any anesthetic at all. I had read the *Reader's Digest* condensation of "Childbirth Without Fear" by Dr. Read before Monty was born, and it had been very helpful. So I secured the book itself and now read it thoroughly, so I was sure I knew what to do when the second stage of labor began and that I could go ahead as advised in the book. If I couldn't, there was always ether.

On the afternoon of the thirtieth of September, 1949, while Bill was driving his bus to Hermit's Rest, I began to feel my first contractions. I didn't call them pains, for to me they weren't pains, they heralded the coming of a child, to me a joyous and not a painful thing. While Monty napped on our bed, I lay beside him and timed the contractions. Although they were five minutes apart, when I arose to do some necessary work, they almost disappeared. Not wanting to go to the hospital until Bill could be home with Monty, I stayed on my feet the rest of the afternoon, doing my work, taking care of Monty, and fixing supper for him and Bill.

When I was sure that Bill was back at the bus garage from his run, I called and told him I was in labor. Then I phoned the hospital, and after he got home Bill drove me there with Monty along. When Dr. Shnur examined me around 6:30 that evening, he told me that I was indeed in labor, so the nurse put me to bed, brought me a light supper she had prepared, then prepped me while Monty and Bill went home to eat their supper.

Alone in my hospital room, I lay quietly, relaxing with each contraction the way I had planned, happy over the thought that my baby would soon be born. When the contractions became more severe and different, I began to bear down and work with them, almost falling asleep in between times. I could feel my baby moving down in the birth canal, and I knew it wouldn't be much longer, when suddenly Dr. Shnur came into the room. He asked me how far apart the pains were, and I told him I thought about two minutes, but I was too sleepy to keep exact track of them. It was working out just as Dr. Read said it would.

"Imagine being sleepy when you're in labor!" Dr. Shnur remarked, then examined me. I was ready for delivery. Once in the delivery room, the doctor told me to breathe deeply while he washed his hands and got me ready. I lay there on the table quite peacefully, although my legs trembled a little from tension over which I had no control, and when the doctor and nurse were ready, the contractions obediently began again, hard ones this time, and I really got to work.

As I gasped and grunted with effort, the nurse tried to fit an ether cone over my face, but when I shoved it aside, Dr. Shnur told her quietly, "She doesn't want ether." As my efforts became more fierce and I almost strangled with the intensity, the nurse who was young and seemed quite nervous, asked the doctor if he needed forceps.

"No!" I gasped in sudden fury. What business did she have asking him that? I was doing the job myself!

"No," said Dr. Shnur, "I won't need them." Good man!

The nurse insisted on placing the ether before my face again. Weakening, wanting a moment's respite, I took a deep breath, but the ether did nothing to dull my senses, and it didn't matter, for at that moment I could feel my baby slide easily out, and it was all over. I had felt my baby being born! Exultation and pride swept over me, and a glorious feeling of accomplishment as I heard my baby's first cry.

"It's all over," said Dr. Shnur unnecessarily. "It's all over."

"I know!" I gasped, as I lay panting. "Is it a boy or girl?"

"A boy, a fine baby boy," he pronounced emotionally, covering me up to my chin with the sheet. "You worked like a Trojan," he added, patting me on the shoulder.

Another boy. A companion for Monty. "Please call Bill," I asked the nurse. A wave of delight swept over me, thinking about Bill's sure reaction.

After Bill and Monty came, Monty stared coldly down at the sleeping child, not knowing what to make of things. After all, he was only a bit over two years older than our new arrival. Bill, of course, was thrilled and happy that it was all over. Our new baby boy, so dear and sweet and pretty. Seven pounds, twelve ounces. Fine, blond curly hair. Double "cow lick" in the back. Cleft chin, taking after his daddy's side of the family. Pink and white skin. Perfect little head. Flat, tiny ears and sweet, full curving lips. William Sandelin Parks, to be called Sandy by family and relatives, Bill or Billy by friends and outsiders later on. Our fourth "horizon hunter" had arrived!

I lay awake all that night, tense with happiness, my mind going over and over the details of the birth. I was so proud of myself, so completely happy. Nothing else could compare to that time in my life.

Next morning I felt wonderful and was allowed to be up and around as before, and as Sandy's bassinet was placed in my room, I was permitted to help take care of him, much to my delight. He was such a good baby, so strong and healthy and hungry and happy. I held him close in my arms, cuddled him, and talked to him softly while I nursed him and all the time he was awake and much of the time when he slept, enjoying our closeness those five days when we lived for each other alone.

Bill took several days off so that he could take care of Monty and do the housework, such as it was, and they visited Sandy and me as often as possible, although Monty still didn't show much interest in his new brother who seemed to do nothing but sleep.

As I continued to feel strong and well, I was allowed to take Sandy home in five days, and for the first five days at home, a neighbor, Mrs. Capell from across the street, came in for one or two hours in the morning to wash dishes, mop the floor, and wash the baby clothes. As Monty wasn't potty-trained yet, I had two in diapers; no disposables back then to make things easier, although I doubt if I would have used them or been able to afford them.

As before, I took complete charge of my new baby, took care of Monty's needs, and did my evening chores with Bill's help when he wasn't working. Some evenings he was on duty, driving guests from El Tovar Hotel and Bright Angel Lodge to the train station.

Now, I told myself, with Sandy I am going to do things differently. I fed him whenever he opened his mouth, even if he had eaten only ten minutes earlier. I didn't let him cry his heart out. As I couldn't nurse him enough to satisfy his needs, I put him on supplementary formula right away, and after two months he was strictly on the bottle. I adjusted the formula until it satisfied him. I wasn't afraid to follow whatever course my common sense dictated. And he thrived. By six weeks of age, he was sleeping through the night. He put himself on a three-hour schedule at two months, and he seldom cried, even when he was hungry. He was never upset, even after I started him on solid foods at three months. Fat and strong, he was the happiest baby I ever saw.

I thought to myself, if only I had had the sense or knowledge to take care of Monty this way when he was tiny. Letting him "cry it out," as I had been advised, was a big mistake.

Sandy was a thumb-sucker, but far from deploring the habit, I thought it looked cute, was glad that he had the comfort, and never tried to deprive him. He gave up the habit before he was three years old, of his own accord. He was standing in his crib after a nap one afternoon, took his thumb out of his mouth, looked at it with distaste, said "Wet sum," wiped it off on his pants, and that was that.

I was just as easy-going with Sandy's cup-training and later his toileting, waiting until he was ready to learn. As a result he never became belligerent or formed any strong dislikes or inhibitions concerning new habits I wanted to help him learn.

Monty soon became interested in his new brother after I brought him home from the hospital, not showing jealousy or fear of being displaced, as I was careful to give Monty more than his share of attention, reading stories or singing to him while I fed Sandy. And I began to enjoy Monty much more than I had before, no longer nervous or frightened when I had to make decisions about solving the problems all mothers have to face. I felt like a real mother at last. I loved my children deeply and enjoyed them. I had been trying too hard, and my previous inability to relax and take it easy had almost wrecked me. I was a different person, and Monty could sense it. We had become a happy family, one that Bill was enjoying, also.

21

Settled Down, Sort Of

When Sandy was nine months old, my parents and my brother Alfred drove from Toledo to Arizona to pay us another visit to get acquainted with our new baby, their second grandchild and nephew, respectively. Charmed with both boys, my parents were also delighted to see us finally living in a more or less civilized manner, in spite of our plain and scanty furnishings. We were apparently settled now, and that pleased them. They knew that it was the children who had brought about this transformation, and they were glad that we were facing up to our responsibilities.

No other course had entered our minds, as we had no intention of letting our finances reach their former precarious state so long as we had our little ones depending upon us. That did not mean that we had given up on the idea of outdoor living, for we could look forward to all kinds of short outings as well as extended camping trips in our beloved desert and mountains as soon as baby Sandy was out of the bottle and diaper stage. Such trips would come during Bill's vacations with pay, but to know that we had them to look forward to kept us from feeling too tied down.

My mother was pleased to see that I was wearing dresses again after all those years of jeans, even if they were only simple cotton house dresses, usually the kind that didn't need ironing, as I had discovered that dresses were much cooler than jeans or even shorts for hot weather. I still preferred jeans for winter and for trips.

Now that we had a good house to live in at the Canyon, we decided to stay there year 'round except for vacations, and as it would be foolish to leave our Cave Creek place vacant and subject to deterioration or vandalism we put it up for sale. In the autumn of 1950 we found a buyer, a wealthy Chicago couple named Alberts who wished to have a desert home to use for winter vacations. We realized only $3,500.00 on the sale, small return for all the work we had put into the place, but we felt rewarded when we used a good part of the money, $2,200.00, for the purchase of the car of our dreams, a gleaming new Plymouth Suburban in a desert tan color, which would be the perfect car for our family-type traveling and camping, our first and only new car. If we had kept our Cave Creek property with its four-and-a-half acres and good well, today it would be worth tens of thousands of dollars, but we needed that car, so it's no use having regrets this late date.

To give the station wagon and our children an easy trial run, we decided on a trip down into the desert to Yuma and Ajo that same fall. As I had a feeling it was going to be rugged with a couple of small boys who could easily get cranky and tired at being confined, I was pleased when Aunt Florence accepted our invitation to accompany us.

Although we stayed in auto courts and did our own cooking and laundry, the trip was rugged. Sandy was teething and became upset, running a fever the first two days. I was in the back seat with the boys, and when they became tired, they took it out on each other and me, while I tried to get them settled for naps. By nightfall I was worn out, yet I had to prepare bottles, boil diapers, and help with supper, as well as feed Sandy and put him to bed in his folding crib.

Things eased off as we became accustomed to traveling again, and I was glad we made the trip, for we saw some new country, the sand dunes near Yuma, the huge open-pit copper operation at Ajo, the organ pipe cactus in the National Monument south of Ajo, and an interesting bit of Old Mexico when we crossed the line into Sonoyta, a tiny unspoiled village on the road to Puerto Peñasco.

Oh, that car! The luxury! The beauty! The efficiency! The power! The sheer joy of owning a good car at last! It climbed in high gear hills that the poor old Horizon Hunter could make only in low. No one appreciates the miracle of a good car the way we did on that trip. Only people who have done without can truly enjoy what a good new car means. We now had Horizon Hunter II which was our friend as well as our key to new adventures, new horizons.

In the months following, we took several one-day picnic trips, and a year after our initial trip to the desert with our boys, we decided on another journey, this time to the State Fair at Phoenix, following which we drove to California, staying at auto courts in Blyth and Needles, then going north through the Mojave Desert, on past Davis Dam, and over to Kingman where we stayed for two nights. Now that Monty and Sandy were ages four and two respectively, they were enjoying the trip and so were we.

From Kingman we took a side trip to lovely Mojave Lake, created by Davis Dam, and hiked and prospected in the Kingman country, which proved to be the best part of our trip. At four, Monty could almost out-hike Bill, going through the rocks like a chipmunk. While he and Bill searched for worthwhile prospects, Sandy and I played near the car, looking for pretty stones and digging in the clean sand, fun for us both. He was such a charmer! Big brown eyes!

If Bill and Monty didn't return from their hikes within a reasonable time, I would worry a little, although I knew that Bill was an expert hiker, never got lost, and would be extra careful with Monty along. They always returned safe and sound.

During the previous year I decided to resume my writing career if possible, and although the *Ladies' Home Journal* rejected a short story I sent them, they gave me enough praise and encouragement to make me want to try again, and they accepted the next short story I sent them called "Tiger in the Closet," which they published in their November, 1951, issue. The story was about a little family in which there were two small boys like Monty and Sandy and their problems, and readers wrote some very complimentary letters, although one or two unbelieving souls stated that I couldn't possibly have ever been a mother! The story was based on Monty's fear of a tiger in our own closet and our efforts to banish the beast. We weren't allowed to have a kitten as the parents in the story did to solve their problem, but our tiger finally did get tired and went away of his own volition.

Through the sale of the British serial rights to my "Tiger" story, it was published by *Woman's Journal* in England, and I acquired an agent, Anne Curtis-Brown. She gave my career a boost with her help and encouragement and the very welcome sale of two short stories to *Collier's*, "A Gift for Teresa" which appeared September 13, 1952, and "Dark Hour" published in the January 10, 1953, issue. Both stories had authentic desert backgrounds and were well-liked by my Arizona friends especially. The British and Swedish rights to the "Teresa" story were sold as well as the Danish rights to "Tiger" and the Swedish and Danish serial rights to "Dark Hour." The "Teresa" story was published by *Woman's Journal* in

England as "Storm Harvest," and the "Tiger" story as "Tiger in the Cupboard," of course!

I sometimes found it hard to believe the success I had achieved, but
life went on as before, and in spite of continuing to write, I made no
more sales. But I had earned more than four thousand dollars with my
writing, a welcome boost to our financial status, enough of a "cushion"
to see us through future emergencies.

22

The Expedition

In the spring of 1952 we piled into Horizon Hunter II, still our dream car, and made a joyful trip through the Painted Desert, fascinating to our boys, then on up over the Kaibab Plateau until we reached Kanab, Utah, where we stayed in an auto court cabin for two nights so that we could make a one-day trip to incredibly beautiful Zion Canyon which our sons and I hadn't seen yet. Wild flowers were blooming, the weather was warm and perfect, as we walked along the trail by the Virgin River and looked up at the tremendous cream-colored cliffs that towered high above our heads, and exclaimed over the beauty that is Zion.

As we had had such a wonderful time on our previous trips, we decided that fall when Monty was five and Sandy three, we would go on The Expedition, our first camping trip, the real thing this time. We chose October, as the nights would still be mild enough to sleep out. The boys fell in with our plans with great enthusiasm. They had either inherited or been completely caught up in the contagion of our love for the outdoors. They cared little for the city. Its pleasures meant nothing to them. Their idea of a good time, as with Bill and me, was exploring in the desert and mountains and learning about the wonders of Nature.

For this trip we decided it might be a good idea to invest in a small camping trailer, so we did, but while dragging it the sixty miles from Williams where we had bought it, to Grand Canyon, we were dismayed, The Thing acted as if it were alive, seeming to creep up behind us and tug at the car like an angry fish. How could we travel over mountain roads with a thing like that on our tail? We abandoned the idea and parked the trailer in our backyard to be used as a playhouse. It was a homemade object that had cost us only ninety dollars, so we weren't heartbroken over the loss.

This trip was to take fourteen days, starting on October fourth, and planning our load through previous experience, we included: a new gasoline campstove, coffee pot, double boiler, dish pan, plates, bowls and cups, and "silverware"; paper goods of all kinds, coffee, sugar, cereals, crackers, and other staples in plastic containers; soap and detergent powder; pillows and bedding and air mattresses; camp folding table, camp chairs, and the boys' small folding table and chairs; shovel, axe, and tire chains; steel cot; three changes of clothing; towels and wash cloths; plastic bags for leftover foods, soiled clothes, etc.; small portable ice box for milk, butter, cheese, and meat which we would buy as we went along, including ice; bucket, two large canteens of water, and a two-gallon jug of boiled water for Monty and Sandy; potty chair; first aid and snakebite kits (never used); battery lantern, flashlights, and canvas tarps, no tent as we preferred to sleep out in the open; tools, mosquito candles in glass bowls, and other miscellaneous items. The candles turned out to be a nice little camping accessory, they made good night lights, and their cheerful gleam kept animals from prowling around the food supplies. Each candle was good for fifty hours.

We loaded our heaviest stuff onto a metal cartop carrier we had acquired, piled bedding and pillows inside plastic covers into the back seat and floor to make a nest for the boys, and everything else in boxes and a couple of suitcases which fit neatly in the rear area of the Suburban. It would take some doing to get used to where everything was as we went along, an old story, but we always managed.

The four Horizon Hunters were on their way at last! As we made a rather late start, our first night's camp was no farther than the junipers near Canyon Diablo east of Flagstaff. The weather was perfect, and it was a delightful camp. Volcanic ash, with no cactus nearby, gave Monty and Sandy a soft, safe, and pleasant playground while Bill and I set up camp, and I prepared supper.

Right from the start the boys took to camping like old-timers. They did have trouble getting to sleep that night, their giggles and upheavals continuing long after their usual bedtime, but we didn't get tough about it. We had to smile as we lay in our bed by a big old juniper tree and listened to them. The air was cool with very little wind, and a full moon cast its radiance over the friendly juniper forest.

In the middle of the night pitiful wails issued forth through the open back window of the car. It was Sandy. When I put on my shoes and jacket and hurried to the car, opened the door and asked him what was wrong, he sat up, crying his heart out. I edged myself into the dimness of the car, squeezed myself a place to sit, then held Sandy close, snuggled in a blanket, and tried to comfort him. Was he sick? Was he frightened? What was it? All I could make out from his muffled words was that he had had a bad dream and his feet hurt.

I rubbed his feet and managed to quiet him finally, then tucked him back into bed beside Monty who had slept peacefully throughout the disturbance. Then I returned to bed. The same thing happened a few other nights during the trip, but as it also occurred at home sometimes I didn't blame camping out and decided it was just "night terrors" which he would get over some day, and he did.

After we were on our way again the next morning, we turned off on the Meteor Crater road east of Canyon Diablo and paid a visit to the Museum where we were entranced by Dr. Nininger's wonderful collection of both metal and rocky meteorites and listened to the interesting things he told about his trips in search of new specimens.

While there I bought a small meteorite and admired a beautiful Navajo-made silver bracelet set with a polished metal meteorite, the most interesting piece of jewelry I had ever seen. Although I had no hope of possessing it, to my surprised delight it turned up the following month at Grand Canyon on my birthday, a gift from the heavens and from dear Bill. I still have it, and it is more precious to me than any earthly gem.

Our second night's camp, near Showlow, was also in a juniper forest, again a pleasant place, but no volcanic ash this time, just small lava rocks and dried grass plus a few small cacti which had to be removed before we could let the boys play. As we were on an old road quite a distance from the main highway, there were no traffic noises, and it was a peaceful, quiet, and lovely spot. We felt very far away from everything.

As it was dusk when we made camp, our cooking, eating, and dishwashing were done by lantern light, and later we went to bed by the light of the moon which was still nearly full. The boys were soon asleep after their long, busy day, and we had a marvelous night's rest in the sweet fresh air.

Next day we drove through the steep, colorful Salt River Canyon until we finally reached low desert country. Then on and on we traveled, past Coolidge Dam, making camp our third night in the pretty greasewood desert near the Gila River bottoms. The air was warm, almost hot, and we had to caution Monty and Sandy to stay seated at their little table to play, for rattlers would be moving on such a mild night.

We made a campfire from sticks gathered by flashlight, rolling the wood over with one foot and examining it for poisonous creatures before picking it up with gloved hands.

After supper Monty and Sandy were permitted to toss twigs and bits of paper into the fire and poke it with long sticks under Bill's watchful eye, while I cleared away the leftovers and packed everything back into the car. That night I used paper dishes as we had made camp so late, and that became my custom from then on whenever we were late making camp.

Then the four of us lay on the cot which was set near a fragrant greasewood bush, and we talked and giggled and looked up at the sky to watch for meteors. When the air turned cool, we put Monty and Sandy to bed in their nest in the car. They were taking to the camping life as though they had been born to it.

In the morning two little blond heads would poke up into sight, and we would hear giggles and cries of "It's morning, guys! It's morning!" and the car would tremble and rock with the romping and wrestling that followed as we waited for the sun to warm our camp before we started our day.

Instead of undressing the boys and exposing their sleep-warm bodies to chilly morning air, I scheduled their baths and clothing changes in the heat of the day, although they were just as pleased if baths weren't too frequent. They were having too much fun to be bothered. And I decided to relax and take things easy myself, enjoy the trip, and do a minimum of work. So long as faces, hands, and feet were washed daily and clean clothes supplied when needed, that was enough. We were camping out!

That day we drove to Safford for supplies and news of the last game of the World Series as Bill loved baseball, after which we headed for Graham Mountain looming out of the hot desert south of town.

Each day we decided to start looking for a camp site early so that I could do my cooking and other camp chores in daylight, but that was easier said than done. So often a suitable place wasn't available, but that afternoon as we drove up and up over the rough narrow dirt road, it was still early, so we felt pretty sure of finding the kind of spot we wanted. As the mountain was steep and the canyons narrow, and figuring that the situation would be worse farther up, we stopped in daylight at the picnic ground in Wet Canyon through which a pretty little mountain stream rushed and sang.

It was hot out in the sunlight, but as Wet Canyon was narrow and east-facing with numerous tall trees crowding the steep slopes, no sunlight penetrated at that hour, and the creek and a strong down-draft added to the chill and dampness, so we dubbed this the Camp of the Icy Breath.

In spite of the cold and wind which made us hurry for sweaters, jackets, and caps, we found it an exciting place with the dark mysterious rock-strewn cliffs hinting of bears, mountain lions, lynx, and other wildlife which inhabited this region.

Outdoor-wise Bill quickly set up a large canvas windbreak between two trees, then clambered over the slopes to find firewood, after which he built a roaring fire against the rocks to keep us warm while we ate a hearty supper. After I washed the dishes, we raked out some of the campfire coals and toasted marshmallows and popped corn with our old-fashioned wire basket popper, while all around and above us the wind roared and tossed the trees.

After the boys were bundled warmly into sweaters and tucked into their bed in the car, we dressed ourselves in everything but the bark off the trees, placed our cot between the car and the fire, with the windbreak at our heads, and crawled between the piles of covers. With the red eyes of the dying campfire and one of the friendly little mosquito candles glowing in the dark by the cliff to keep animals away, I felt perfectly safe as I dozed off under the wildly tossing trees. A mountain lion or bear would have had a tough time getting at us in that jumble of clothes and blankets. He'd have given up in disgust at the first mouthful of quilt, blanket, and canvas tarp.

My worst fears on that trip weren't the wild animals. I was far more afraid of reckless or drunken drivers while we were on the road. And while camped, our greatest danger was from the occasional outlaw or fugitive that might escape from the prison at Florence and roam the southeastern part of the state. As a precaution Bill kept our loaded .22 rifle under our pillows at night, unloading it each morning for safety, and later I bought a large knife which was so sharp that Bill was certain I would cut off my own hand with it. Although I never had to use it for protection, I nearly sliced off the end of my thumb while dealing with a cold watermelon that defied me later on our trip.

When the early sun had warmed our Camp of the Icy Breath a bit, we arose and enjoyed a campfire breakfast with appetites whetted by our night in the cold fresh air. By now Monty and Sandy accepted everything in their stride, and they were as much at home eating their cereal and drinking their milk in that wild canyon as they would have been in the coziest little breakfast nook. They loved the freedom of camp life, and their store toys were ignored in their enjoyment of all the interesting things about them.

The stream was of special fascination at our present camp, and they would have been willing to live there from that time on, but after a session of throwing bark "boats" into the water and watching them tumble down the little rapids and whirl slowly in the small pools, we managed to tear them loose for a drive up the mountain and on to Heliograph Tower, about 10,000 feet elevation. From there the desert looked vast and hazy and mysterious. It was worth the hair-raising drive. Some of the mountains we saw from there were in Old Mexico, a magnificent sight.

I hadn't really wanted to make the drive over the narrow road which, in places, overlooked thick forest hundreds of feet below. I was sure we would meet a car or truck which would shove us over a cliff, but I managed to relax, and the view was reward enough for the seemingly perilous journey. Bill was an extremely careful driver, experienced over many years on all kinds of mountain roads, and we were safer on that trip than we were in the crowded streets of some of the towns we passed through. We were glad that we weren't dragging that little camp trailer we had bought, as it would have limited our side trips and explorations considerably.

On top of Graham Mountain we saw thousands of ladybugs for which this area is famous. They made an amazing and colorful decoration for the silvery weathered wood of the little barn and corral standing near the lookout's cabin at the Tower. We understood that the insects migrate to the mountain and found that it was really true.

That night we camped on the desert near Dos Cabezas southeast of Willcox, under a cutbank where the highway department had removed material for road-building. Protected by the wind, with no brush around to conceal rattlers, we thought it an ideal spot. So that night it was the Camp of the Cut-Bank. The next morning the name changed.

While I was washing dishes at our card table, yellow jackets began to appear, first one, which I swatted as it lit on the dishpan, then another flitted around and decided to stay. Then another and another. Bill was relaxing on the cot and reading the paper. He would break camp as soon as I finished the dishes and packed things away. There was no hurry. We had plenty of time, no set schedule. The hornets had other plans. When six of them ganged up on me, I yelled for help.

"Bees, Daddy," said Sandy in alarm, "bees!"

Bill glanced up absently. He was used to our "much ado's about nothing." Realizing suddenly that this was serious, he went into action. I wish that I had a movie of him going after those insects like a badminton player, only his bat was a pink plastic flyswatter. We made the boys sit quietly at their little table on the other side of the car while I finished the dishes and put everything away and Bill fought off the hornet brigade which had been attracted by the smell of the dishwater and wash water we had thrown on the ground nearby.

After we finally were able to break camp and find refuge inside the car, we were only too glad to depart from the Camp of the Yellow Jackets. Luckily none of us had been stung, for the postmistress at Dos Cabezas, when we stopped briefly at the Post Office, told me that one had stung her and made her sick for a week! When we saw the tumbledown adobe buildings there, we realized where the hornets made their homes, and the air in that little settlement was alive with the creatures. On one wall of an empty old house were the words, "Barefoot Charlie lived here." Had the hornets chased him out, also?

From Dos Cabezas we traveled steadily southeast to the weirdly magnificent spectacle that is the Chiricahua Wonderland of Rocks where gigantic boulders piled one atop the other form strange, realistic, and often surrealistic statues of men, animals, birds, and other objects.

After a picnic lunch at Massai Point overlooking the heart of this scenic country, we decided to spend that night at Cochise Stronghold in the rugged Dragoon Mountains where the great Apache chief Cochise had successfully withstood the efforts of the white soldiers to conquer him.

As you approach from the floor of the valley, the Stronghold looks something less then imposing, but when you drive nearer and head up the canyon, you begin to realize the possibilities of this place as a hideout for fleeing Apaches. Yet, there is more to it than that. It is serenely majestic and beautiful with the towering boulder-strewn cliffs hovering protectingly over the floor of the canyon where oaks, yuccas, squaw grass, and brush grow in abundance. Here you can picture what must have once been a common sight, the sprawling nighttime camp of the Apaches with the strong copper-skinned bodies gathered around council fires, dark eyes determined and menacing under tangled fringes of coarse black hair, as the warriors debated how to take revenge on the white man who had stolen their hunting lands, broken sacred promises, and killed and captured others of the tribe, some of them helpless women and children.

Much has been said and written about the ferocity and cruelty of the Apache, but he was fighting for his rights in the only way he knew, a way dictated by the rugged land in which he lived. And when he was betrayed by the white men who had pretended to be his friends, his hatred and desire for retribution knew no bounds. Anyone who wishes to know more about this shameful chapter in our country's history can read of John P. Clum's experience in the book Apache Agent by Woodworth Clum. As an Indian agent on the Apache reservation, John Clum was the Apaches' friend, and they loved and respected him for his kindness and integrity and the just manner in which he treated them, but one man did not have the power to undo the harm caused by many.

It was nearly sundown when we reached the picnic grounds in Cochise Stronghold, and Bill and Monty went off on foot to explore for the best campsite while Sandy and I stayed at a table near the parked car. All around were picnic tables and fireplaces to accommodate visitors, but the place we settled on was on the far edge of the campground and hidden behind the trees and bushes. There was a nice big table under an oak tree, and near it a handy fireplace made of the native granite rocks. A clean new outhouse stood not too far away for our convenience. Bill and Monty had chosen well.

There were no other campers, and the place was very quiet and peaceful as we unloaded the car and set up camp. While I prepared supper, Bill gathered dead wood for a campfire, and Monty and Sandy played happily at their little table. We didn't want them wandering around by themselves, for we weren't sure yet about the rattler situation, but the boys were always good about staying put when they understood the necessity for it.

It was very still, no wind stirring the trees, and as it grew dark, I glanced uneasily up at the boulder-made caves which, I thought, could very well harbor mountain lions or lynx. Bill cautioned me in a whisper not to leave the rear of the station wagon open, as he had heard of lynx coming boldly into camp and swiping unprotected food right from under the noses of campers. This did nothing for my peace of mind, and I stole glances over my shoulder occasionally as I went about my chores. Until we had children, I had never been uneasy about camping out in the wildest country. My uneasiness was for their safety.

A cheerful campfire near which two healthy, happy little boys sat on a log and giggled and chattered did much to dispel my fears. Bill and I smiled at each other as we sat on our camp chairs and listened to them as they talked their own special brand of little boy nonsense. That was the sweetest sight in the world to us, and how happy we were that we had two little guys to keep each other, and us, company.

I marveled at how oblivious the children were of the brooding cliffs all about us, but it was to be expected, for the mountains and desert and forests were almost all they had known from the time they were born, so they felt most at home in them.

When Monty and Sandy were asleep in the car, and Bill and I were bedded down in our cot with a canvas stretched back of our heads in case the wind should come up, everything changed. The dying fire snapped and crackled, there were constant rustlings in the dead oak leaves that covered the ground, coyotes howled far off in the desert, and a lone owl hooted in the canyon below our camp. Again and again I would rise up on one elbow to peer off into the brush with my flashlight. I tried to reassure myself. Surely no lynx or mountain lion would venture into camp so long as the campfire coals still glowed and the friendly little mosquito candles burned. I had both of the candles lit this night, one at each end of the camp, for a few tiny mosquitoes had pounced on us while we were getting ready for bed.

Finally, in spite of the night noises, fatigue and fresh air got the best of me. When I awoke three hours later, a waning moon cast a radiance on the hills around us, and the sight was no longer gloomy or forbidding. After I checked to see that the boys were covered, I went back to bed for a welcome and refreshing sleep.

The spirits of the dead Apaches must have approved of our presence, for the following morning was beautiful and friendly. Sunrise touched the huge boulders with a pink glow, and I felt that this was the most wonderful and exciting camp Bill and I had ever made. Suddenly it seemed like a home, as our favorite camps already did. Although we were out of milk except for canned and dried kinds, we voted to stay another night, giving us a whole lovely day to hike and rest and wash clothes and take baths with the rather rusty water supplied by the nearby covered well.

The day was warm and quiet, and at noon I had the boys stripped and began to bathe them in the sunshine of our secluded little retreat. As usual, they were delighted with the novelty, taking to primitive methods like happy little savages.

Later, as they explored our surroundings Sandy named our camp. His name for the large soapweed yucca thereabouts was "fondry," so this became the Camp of the Fondries. There was one big mother "fondry" with a baby by her side, toward whom we felt quite friendly, although carefully avoiding their long sharp "arms."

In the forenoon while Bill and Monty went for a hike up the steep canyon, I bathed behind the bushes while Sandy sat on the ground under a small oak tree and played contentedly in the sand with stones, twigs, oak leaves, and acorns, ignoring his store toys in favor of the toys of the Apache children who had lived and played there long before his time. That's usually the way with children, at least with our two. They preferred objects they could manipulate with their imaginations, and when at home, they liked best their blocks, tinkertoys, erector sets, paper, clay, paints, pencils, blunt scissors, and cardboard cartons, along with books that I could read to them and did, every afternoon and evening before bed.

As Sandy played and I bathed, he discovered what had been causing the rustlings in the leaves, a friendly gray lizard who suddenly appeared at our fireplace and made himself at home on the warm rocks. As he was absolutely fearless, we named him "Cochise's Spirit" and tossed crumbs to him, which he proudly ignored.

Although we kept close watch, neither Bill nor I saw any rattlers or snake tracks, nor the tracks of any large animals. The only creatures we saw evidence of were skunks, porcupines, a few birds, and the lizards. There were no hornets to contend with; only butterflies, a few mosquitoes and flies, and ants comprised the insect population of this strange, lovely country. The lack of running water accounted for the scarcity of wild life.

That afternoon when Bill went on a long hike alone, he realized that we weren't in the Stronghold proper but only in the outer edges, for when he reached the top of the canyon, he saw far below him the tops of the trees of the inner Stronghold. We planned that when the boys were older, that was a sight we must all see some day, because the place captured our imaginations and we must journey to the innermost recesses of Cochise's hideaway to explore its wonders and experience its strange beauty. Sadly, we never returned.

We had another delightful evening around the fire, happy after our day of rest and exploration. On a line strung between some nearby oaks hung our drying laundry, and I felt as though I had accomplished a great deal that day, as Apache women might have felt in the distant past.

In the night I awoke and heard some louder rustlings and snapping of twigs, and when I investigated with my flashlight, I spied friend skunk nibbling at the grass and weeds a few feet from our car. He ignored me, and after I had discreetly admired his black and white tail from a safe distance, I left him to his supper, peeked at the boys to see that they were covered, and went back to bed. All was well at the Camp of the Fondries.

Next morning after I was through with my chores and while Bill was breaking camp, I went on a short hike of my own. After I had climbed up one of the ancient Indian trails a way, I sat down to rest on a huge granite boulder where I had a view of the canyon below and the dim, hazy, pastel-colored desert beyond. I thought of the young Apache boys who had played and climbed in those very same rocks which surrounded me and how they must have sat and gazed at their beautiful country, their hearts filled with emotion at what was happening to their people. And tears came to my eyes, and I was sorry and ashamed and wished that I could tell Cochise, Eskiminzin, and the other Apache chiefs who had tried to be friends with the white man, that I was sorry for the wrong that had been done to their people.

Now this wonderful land of theirs which had resounded to their songs and laughter was silent, empty and deserted except for occasional visits of a few apparently unappreciative city people whose only evidence of their brief stay was in the form of scattered tissues, paper plates, bottles, and tin cans, that dreary scourge of so many of the West's otherwise beautiful desert and mountain parks.

As Bill wished to do some prospecting in the Swisshelm Mountains, we drove that day to the towns of Bisbee and Douglas down near the border in a fruitless search for detailed maps of the area. In spite of not having the necessary information, we decided to try our luck without it, so after purchasing food at Douglas, we headed north and made our "Camp of the Old Corral" not far from a running stream in the Swisshelm Mountains.

There were few trees and no dead wood to be found, but as the ground was covered with dried cheat grass, we couldn't make a campfire anyway, so all of my cooking had to be done with the camp-stove. Although we were near water, there were no mosquitoes, and we congratulated ourselves on our interesting and pleasant campsite. It was quite different from our previous camps, as there was nothing to shut off our view of the mountains. Not far off was an old splintery loading corral which gave our camp its name, and farther down the creek the lights of a ranch house gleamed in the darkness. We were closer to the dirt road than we really cared to be, but there were few cars passing to raise a dust in our direction.

We didn't bother to load the rifle, for when we are so far from the main highways, we have little fear of undesirable characters bothering us. However, two weeks after we reached home, we read in the newspaper that several fugitives were on the loose in southeastern Arizona, including a couple of dangerous killers, so we felt doubly justified in having taken the rifle with us.

The night was cool and quiet, and the velvety sky was studded with stars, the most brilliant display we had yet seen, for the moon rose late and the mountains were far enough away that they didn't cut off much of our view. Rather, their dim black silhouettes enhanced it. And when coyotes sang for their supper, we thrilled once again over the renewal of the life of freedom we had known.

The morning was fresh and beautiful, and we were tempted to linger, but the presence of that stream of water warned us that we might expect an invasion of hornets, so we hurried through our chores, but, sure enough, before we could break camp, the devilish little creatures began to haunt us with their legs dangling as they hovered overhead looking for a landing field. This time Bill made the boys and me go out and walk briskly up and down the road while he fought off the attack and attempted to load the car at the same time.

After he cleared the car of the insects and shut the windows tight, he drove out and picked us up, and we tried to find the place where he had hoped to do his prospecting. But wherever we went, the hornets were sure to go, so we surrendered and decided to drive back to Douglas and from there cross the border to Agua Prieta in Old Mexico.

Not wanting to unload our car for examination upon returning to this country, we parked at customs on our side and walked across the line. As we wandered down the hot, dusty main street, I glanced at Monty as he walked ahead with Bill, and I saw then that the granite boulders at Cochise Stronghold had inflicted considerable damage to the seat of his jeans. When I mentioned it to him, he grinned and seemed proud of the distinction of going into Mexico with a hole in his pants, and Bill and I had to laugh. For some reason, both boys liked to wear patches in their knees and brag about them to each other, which showed that they were learning the true values in life. Fun in patched denim was better than boredom in broadcloth and serge.

We all looked rather shabby and wrinkled in our camping clothes, but that gave us a certain protection from being importuned by curio salesmen, and we could enjoy our wanderings in the freedom of obscurity.

However, the October day was too hot, and after a brief visit to the church and a few minor purchases, we decided to leave. It was too far for the boys to walk around the more interesting outlying section of the town where we could have seen the people going about the daily business of their lives amid their little adobe dwellings and their gardens and chickens, cats, and dogs. We had hoped to make a real camping trip some day into Mexico and become better acquainted with our neighbors to the south, but we never got around to it. There were too many other places that had priority.

As always, we had the fun of making up our itinerary as we went along, so we now decided to camp that night in the Huachuca Mountains to the west. That afternoon we crossed the San Pedro River in the beautiful valley in which Coronado had made his entrance hundreds of years before. What a tempting sight this lush country must have presented, inevitably leading him on to further eager explorations. It was then that I sighed and turned to Bill and said, "Home will seem small and stuffy after all this," to which he wistfully agreed.

When we reached the Huachucas, we chose Miller Canyon for our night's camp, but the road proved too rough and steep, and we were forced to turn back. Ramsay Canyon was beautiful, but it was taken over by rich dudes, and their fences told us we weren't welcome, so we drove on to Carr Canyon where in spite of evidence that city people were taking over here also, we found a beautiful campsite under some huge oak trees.

There was plenty of dead wood, and after a cheerful campfire supper, we fell sleepily into bed, ready for a good night's rest. But an hour later we were awakened by the anguished bellowing of a range cow who had lost her calf, and when the calf joined in with a series of desperate replies, we resigned ourselves to a wakeful night at our "Camp of the Diesel Cow." They finally wandered off and eventually subsided, so we were able to sleep once more.

No hornets marred our enjoyment of the following morning, and we lingered happily over our chores, although Bill muttered that he seemed to spend most of his time making and breaking camp. This was true, but we couldn't help it if we were to cover ground the way we had planned. On our next trip we would choose one particular place to camp and stay there for a week or two if conditions were favorable. Now there were certain things we wanted to see and explore, so we had to keep going and make all these different camps even if it did mean a lot of extra work. But we felt it was worth it and didn't really begrudge the continual upheaval.

The boys took to the life like born hoboes, for they acted as though each new camp were a home, just as we did. How glad we were to learn that they were so adaptable and interested in the same kind of recreation that we were. Later that morning when we crossed the San Pedro again, this time en route to Tombstone, we saw a man washing a small black sedan, inside and out, in the river crossing. Immediately suspicious, we wondered just what he was washing from the upholstery. Blood? Aha! Was this one of our outlaws? More likely he had run over a skunk.

When we reached the historic mining town of Tombstone, to our mild disappointment we discovered that although the town was still pretty interesting, it was quite commercialized, even unto the tidying up of Boothill Cemetery where the early day outlaws are buried. So we lingered only to buy food and papers and see the fascinating mementos of an earlier day in the Schiefflin Museum and the Bird Cage Theatre.

As we sat in our car and lunched on hamburgers and soft drinks, we watched with dismay a gang of small white and Mexican boys heedlessly roping each other as they tore madly around on the nearby sidewalk. Finally Bill could stand it no longer. He got out of the car and went over to warn then of the dangers of their game. All he got for his trouble were blank or hostile stares, and when he returned to the car, the game continued as before. We hurried with our meal and were glad to leave, not wishing to view a tragedy which we were powerless to prevent.

With a couple of cartons of ice cream, we left Tombstone in the early afternoon and drove out into the desert to enjoy our dessert, before going on through the beautiful rich cattle country that leads to Patagonia.

At Patagonia we made careful inquiries about hornet-free campsites and were told of some that would be perfect for our needs. Following directions, we turned at a dirt road and drove slowly along, exclaiming with pleasure over the various possibilities, the huge trees, and the large quantities of dead wood.

After making our choice, we parked the car under a large willow tree by a steep cliff and piled out to look around. To our dismay, a few hornets appeared and hovered around us.

"There must be something about us that attracts them," Bill declared, trying to joke about it. "Perhaps the color of our car."

"Maybe we're too near this cliff," I offered uneasily, "just like at the cutbank at Dos Cabezas. I don't like this place. There are spiders and ants all through the grass, also. Maybe scorpions and centipedes this near the border. Let's camp over there in that clear spot by the dead trees."

The hornets followed us. They liked our looks. After Bill dug up some small cactus that menaced the boys, he made a fire. "The smoke will drive the hornets away," he stated, "and in the morning we can get up early and get breakfast out of the way before the sun rises, and make an early start before the hornets come around."

Frantically I gathered leaves and grass to make a smudge on Bill's fire, but to my horror the hornets seemed to thrive on the smoke. Evidently a tough breed, they loved it and came in ever-increasing numbers from one of the nearby dead trees which we now discovered was their cozy little home.

"We can't stay here!" I declared desperately. "I won't! I'll sleep sitting up in the car. I'll do anything, but I won't stay here."

Without another word, Bill began to put things back into the car and tied the cot frame on the bumper, then we hastily shoveled a lot of dirt on the fire, jumped into the car, closed it up tight, and took out of there.

"We made an early start, didn't we, Daddy?" Sandy piped up from the back seat.

So that was the "Camp of the Early Start."

Our second choice was by lovely little Sonoita Creek, farther down the main highway, where some magnificent willow trees made us a charming roof. The wind was blowing, but with our large canvas windbreak we were protected and comfortable, and there were no yellow jackets, not one. As we sat by our crackling fire and devoured our fish and potato soup, we gazed about us in pleasure.

That night as we lay on our cot and listened to the music of the creek, a fox barked on the hillside and a car full of singing Mexicans drove past on their way up the canyon, giving our camp a delightful atmosphere of the southwestern out-of-doors. It was almost like being in a foreign country.

This was the second most beautiful camp we made, and we had the hornets to thank for chasing us there, so an ill wind did blow some good that time. But next morning we had some uneasy moments when three drunk young Mexican boys stalled their coupe in the creek at the crossing, and they talked and laughed and swore as they tried ineffectually to push the car out of the water. We lingered over our chores, for we knew we wouldn't be able to cross until they were out of the way, and we had no intention of punishing our heavily loaded station wagon by pushing or pulling them. Finally a ranch pickup came down from the hills, and, to our relief, the driver pushed the disabled car out of trouble and out of our way.

Before we left the "Camp of the Willows," I wandered alone up the creek under the giant trees, and as I gazed up and up the huge trunks and feasted my eyes on the soul-stirring scene about me, I hoped that I could return here once again before I died. It was places like this that made me feel the presence of God more than any man-made place of worship, and I could thank Him at those moments for the fact that I was alive and able to experience such beauty and such joy. But I returned there only in memory.

As we were so near the border, we decided not to pass up the chance to see Mexico again, so we drove to Nogales, parked the car, and walked across the line to Nogales, Mexico, where we wandered in the little town park and watched the happy crowds walking under the trees or sitting on the many benches, and we also sat on a bench for a while and looked at some caged parrots.

When we strolled along the streets past the shops, we soon discovered that our old clothes were no longer a protection from curio sales people. Finally we succumbed to the tune of a small wool blanket and some funny straw hats for Monty and Sandy. Then we had our picture taken by a street photographer, which revealed to us how hot and shabby we really looked.

We were soon surfeited with the over-crowded shelves in the shops, deciding that this kind of thing was not for us. And as the boys quickly weary of city streets, we returned to the United States and headed our car north.

After a brief stop at the Tumacacori Mission where we enjoyed the museum and the garden with its fish pond, we drove on through the hot desert to Tucson. Here we rented a cabin in an auto court, for the first time on this trip, as we wanted to see a movie at a drive-in theatre that night. It wasn't worth it.

Our room felt so stuffy after our outdoor living that we regretted our decision and were only too glad to leave next morning. We did a little shopping in Tucson, but the crowded city traffic bothered me, and I recalled in grateful retrospect the peace and safety of our drive up the steep, narrow grades of Graham Mountain!

Continuing north, we bought a late watermelon and stopped in the hills near Oracle for some refreshment. From there we drove on to Winkelman, but finding no suitable place to camp in the desert, and as the day was getting too windy, we resigned ourselves to finding another cabin in an auto court. However, when we started up the steep narrow road from Winkelman to Globe where we hoped to spend the night, I looked in dismay at the winding curves ahead and the rock-strewn pitch-off below. It was nearly dusk, the worst time for mountain driving, and I was just too tired to face it.

"Goodbye, cruel world," I sighed cravenly, as we rounded the fifth curve. I had an ominous feeling about this journey. We won't make it, I thought. We're playing with Fate once too often.

Bill took one glance at my strained expression, stopped the car at the first turn-out, backed and turned and headed back down the mountain.

"What's the matter?" I asked him in surprise.

"You don't want to go this way," he said understandingly.

"No, I don't," I admitted gratefully, but feeling a bit guilty.

So we made a fresh start by way of the rough, dusty road that led past Hayden and on up to Ray and thence to Superior, seeing few other cars and only an occasional, seemingly deserted habitation until we finally reached Ray where we had a light supper which we were almost too tired to eat. From there the road became wider, and after what seemed an age we were at the little mining town of Superior where we rented a cabin, lifted our tired, sleepy, dear little boys out of the car, moved in, and went to bed. And it was lucky that we were under shelter, for in the night a fierce, strong wind known as a "Santa Ana" blew up, and a desert camp would have been a shambles, not to mention the dust and sand that would have poured into all our food and equipment.

From Superior we drove on through the hot, bright desert to Phoenix and then to Wickenburg where we made camp in the ocotillo desert east of town. We immediately chose this spot as the place we'd like for a winter home some day. The ground was carpeted with clean granite sand, while ocotillos, greasewood, and palo verdes enhanced the charm of our site with their own special beauty, and the stars overhead were never so bright. And it was so good to sleep out again after the impersonal, dusty stuffiness of an auto court cabin.

However, as Horizon Hunter II needed working on after our long, arduous trip and the weather had turned quite cool, we were forced to stay in another cabin when we reached Prescott on the last lap of our journey. But the cool mountains were a reward in themselves after the late heat of the desert, and we inhaled gratefully the good pine- and juniper-scented air.

The "cloud buzzards" were flying the next afternoon when we left

Prescott and headed for Grand Canyon and home, congratulating ourselves not only on our happy, safe, and successful trip but on the time we had chosen for it. We couldn't have picked a better time, we gloated, as we eyed the angry red of the sunset clouds.

And now we knew that our boys were not only born Westerners but born "outdoorsmen," and we could look forward to many more wonderful trips with them. The company of the four "Horizon Hunters" was now a fact and not just a dream. The best was yet to come, but tragedy, also. And Monty and Sandy (young Bill) were to seek and find new horizons thousands of miles from home some day. More about that later.

23

More Horizon-Hunting

During the last few miles of our journey home from our long camping trip, I went over in my mind the interior appearance of our house at Grand Canyon, reflecting on the tasks I was about to resume, trying to prepare myself so that a return to confining routine would not be too much of a blow after so much freedom. To my pleased surprise, I was able to take over my household duties, also my writing, with renewed zest after the two weeks of rest and relaxation, so to speak, just the way the boys happily resumed playing with their toys.

With regard to my writing, some of my friends wondered how I could find time for it with a house to take care of and two small, noisy, active, inquisitive boys to raise. It wasn't easy. Often when inspiration struck, my hands were in dishwater, the house looked as though a cyclone had followed a herd of elephants through, dust mice were playing tag under the beds, cobweb spiders were hanging curtains, large holes appeared in small jeans, the laundry hamper bulged, and two little blond heads resembled Robinson Crusoe. But somehow I would find time to get some words on paper, returning to my typewriter and revising after thinking things over while doing my chores.

I don't believe a mother should devote all her time and energies to her children, but I refused to put mine in second place to my writing. How could I sit down at my typewriter when outside the sun was shining, the snow was just right for sledding or skiing, and two rosy-cheeked, snowsuit-clad bundles begged me to join their fun? And who could concentrate when the spring air was warm and fragrant with pine, the vireos were whistling, and a friendly forest was beckoning eager explorers?

But I wasn't perfect. Sometimes I would become frustrated and irritable at the noise and interruptions, and I would yell. Later I would apologize which wouldn't excuse me, but Monty and Sandy were satisfied, and intrigued, with the sight of a grown-up apologizing. I would offer to give up my writing, and they would yell, "But we want a ranch!"

My writing was supposed to be so successful that it would bring us a ranch. They didn't want to be rich, just have a small spread where we could work hard, be together, have animals to care for—horses, a milk cow, chickens, cats, and dogs—and a garden to tend. It didn't happen. Some day we would have an acre, a horse, and some cats, strays that we took in. Also a small garden. More about that later. We continued to have our camping trips.

With my writing earnings we did purchase a few things for our home, a dinette set to take the place of the rickety card table, a comfortable bed without lumps, a sofa-sleeper for guests, a radio-phonograph and records, a vacuum cleaner, an apartment size gas range and water heater so that we could get rid of the fuel oil outfit; and my generous family gave us a new electric wringer-type washer with drain pump, a toaster, and an automatic iron. Such riches! Compared to what Bill and I had started out with, these things represented the ultimate in luxury. There was nothing else I wanted; even when television came to Grand Canyon, we weren't interested. In fact, we never did get a television set until 1968 after both boys were out of high school.

We were happy with what we had and the way we lived. Bill had a job he enjoyed and was good at, and his work was appreciated by his employers and the visitors he drove on the South Rim and out to the Indian reservations. And it provided us with a good living, also giving Bill time to enjoy his family and take us on outings. Even though he was nearly fifty years old before he had his first child, he was gentle, calm, patient, and understanding with his boys, and they couldn't have asked for a better father.

Grand Canyon village was a good place to raise a family. In spite of being sixty miles from the nearest town, Williams, we never felt isolated from the world, for the world was continually pouring through there in the form of millions of visitors per year, not only from this country but from all over the world. And it was a wonderful playground for children with the beautiful outdoors and plenty of congenial playmates.

There was a fine grade school to which an annex was added later, also junior high, and later a high school, and the school staff was well-trained with pleasant teachers who managed to make learning enjoyable for our children, also becoming their friends. For recreation the school had an indoor playroom, and outdoors there was a large playground with swings and other equipment, a basketball court, and a baseball field.

Although we weren't allowed to have pets in a National Park, the children saw plenty of animals every day, deer, squirrels, and chipmunks running through our yard, as well as numerous birds. The deer could be pests, especially the bucks, as Canyon visitors insisted on feeding them in spite of signs forbidding it. One "tame" buck became so dangerous that he attacked an elderly woman and put her into the hospital, so the Rangers had to shoot him. You never saw the regular residents feeding or trying to pet the deer. We all knew better, and the children were all forewarned.

Grand Canyon village was a very safe place to live because of the many Park Rangers, the Santa Fe special police, a Deputy Sheriff, and a constable, a better and larger police force than any town several times its size. Crime was almost non-existent, but if something did happen, a criminal had only two roads out of there, so that simple roadblocks could trap him before he could make a successful getaway. As for fire fighting, this police force plus Fred Harvey, National Park, and Santa Fe employees served as volunteer firemen, so any blaze was doomed in a matter of minutes.

We were happy living at Grand Canyon, but we continued to leave there every once in a while for our camping trips to refresh us and keep us from feeling too isolated. One year on Bill's vacation we went out to the Navajo reservation to camp and took along the baby clothes and other things that the boys had outgrown. One was a small pink woven baby blanket which my Aunt Lydia had sent to me among other gifts. The next year when Bill took a carload of visitors out to the Painted Desert and other sights, he made a stop at Gray Mountain Trading Post (which burned down later), and saw four beautiful Navajo-made hangings in three dimensions, one of which he purchased. It shows a Navajo woman sitting at a loom on which her partly made blanket is displayed. Beside her is a basket with yarn balls. She is dressed in satin and velvet, and her black hair is tied back with string. On her sash are four silver conchos. She is sitting on a white "sheepskin." It is a very colorful and well-depicted scene, very realistic.

When Bill gave it to me and I examined it carefully, admiring the workmanship, I exclaimed, "Why, that's the boys' baby blanket that Aunt Lydia sent!" A Navajo woman had cut the blanket into four pieces for her marvelous, imaginative craft work. It is now over forty years old and on my living room wall for everyone to admire.

During the fall of 1952 we drove to Escondido, California, to visit Aunt Florence and her family, camping in the desert all the way over and back except when Monty became heat sick and we had to stay one night in an air-conditioned motel in Indio. While at Escondido we took the boys to the San Diego Zoo and also up to Julian in the mountains to the Apple Festival. They were learning about new horizons at an early age.

We were still carting along the boys' potty chair for convenience, but on the way home from this trip, we burned the potty chair one morning at a desert camp among mesquite trees, which delighted the boys and pleased Bill who was tired of packing and unpacking it, trying to fit it into the car at the last moment before departure. I tried to compose a little verse about the event, starting, "On one peaceful desert morning, we burned the pot chair without warning." I can't remember the rest, but it elicited joy from all concerned.

In spite of being tied down for the first time in his adult life—since leaving the Army after spending a year and a half in France during World War I—Bill never complained during his sixteen years while guiding around two hundred thousand Canyon visitors by bus on the South Rim and on "specials" by limousine to the Indian country.

Some notables whom he took care of were Mayor Daley of Chicago (friendly), the Shah of Iran (aloof), Batista of Cuba (friendly), Queen Frederika of Greece (very nice, but worried about her hairdo in the sandstorms of the Indian country), Frank Lloyd Wright (angry over charges he had to pay for transportation, which he thought he should get for nothing), and Prince Faisal of Saudi Arabia before he became King (very polite and nice).

In the summer of 1953 Bill was left at the Canyon to work and fend for himself while I took Monty and Sandy to Toledo by steam train to visit my family, stopping first at Chicago where my brother, Alfred, met us to help us change trains and where we stayed overnight at a hotel before going on. The boys, of course, were more than delighted with the train ride, as I had been when I was little, and my parents were happy to see us. They had driven to the Canyon twice to see the boys when they were babies, but this was a new experience for all of us, especially when my father drove us to Cleveland to visit the Edgertons, Aunt Lydia, Uncle Arthur, and Boydie, who took us out to the Cleveland Yacht Club for dinner.

During this stay we also took the boys to the Toledo Zoo where a small elephant got loose and gave us a scare. And there was a fishing excursion to Toledo's Walden Pond with neighbor Mr. Schwalbe and Alfred, when Sandy caught a small fish which my mother fried for his supper. We have a picture to "prove it." The boys talked about their Toledo trip ever after.

In October of that same year when Monty was six years old and Sandy four, we took them on a camping trip to Death Valley by way of Death Valley Junction, enjoying all the special points of fascination, including the Devil's Golf Course, Bad Water, the Panamint Mountains and the Funeral Range, Furnace Creek Ranch with its date orchard, and the huge engine which failed years ago to haul loads of borax when substituted for the twenty-mule teams. We slept on the sand at Stovepipe Wells, the boys in the station wagon as usual, our bed next to a bush where pack rats had built their nest. Rattlers could have been living in the nest, also, but as the nights were too cold for snakes to be out and around, we refused to worry about it. Next morning we all played in the beautiful sand dunes.

And we took the boys to Death Valley Scotty's Castle, which was closed at the time, but Scotty was sitting out in front and let me take our boys' picture sitting by him, a very special shot with Scotty and his two dogs, a framed enlargement of which hangs on my living room wall today. A few years ago a columnist wrote of Scotty as a "spare little man," but actually he was robust as he had been most of his life. But a couple of months after our visit Scotty died from a gastric hemorrhage on January 4, 1954, and was buried, as he had requested, on a barren hill called Windy Point, directly overlooking the Castle. He said he didn't want "no fancy marker, just put up a sign saying, 'HERE HE IS.'" I don't imagine his request was honored.

While talking to Scotty that day, we soon realized that he didn't want to talk about himself, he wanted to hear the news about the polygamists at Short Creek and what was happening to them, but we had little to offer on that score. When he talked to visitors, he never asked them where they were from but where they were going. If they were riding in big, fancy cars, he said "They're driving in their bare feet," meaning the cars weren't paid for, they were in debt for them. Scotty's motto, he told us, was "Never complain, never explain," a saying which other people have adopted as their own.

I have a fine book about Scotty called *Death Valley Scotty, The Man and the Myth* by Hank Johnston, published by Flying Spur Press of Yosemite,

California, in 1972, with interesting text and many wonderful pictures of Scotty from the time he was a handsome young man acting in Buffalo Bill's Wild West Show in 1893, until shortly before his death in 1954. The book gives the story of his mine and riches (non-existent) and his wealthy sponsor, Albert Johnson; Scotty's marriage and pictures of his wife, Jack; his only son, Walter Perry Scott, a fine looking boy aged fourteen; and several of the Castle and its interior.

Bill visited the Castle years before I met him and was amazed at its beauty, inside and out. Even though it has always been referred to as "Scotty's Castle," it was built by Albert Johnson who permitted the myth to exist. It was fun for us to meet Scotty, but we didn't impose on him or question him, as we knew it would annoy him and put us in the same class with the "annoyers," people who can't resist asking personal questions as they did with Bill when he was a guide at the South Rim.

After Bill had his novel of Old Arizona *The Mestizo* published, he continued with his writing in spite of many interruptions, turning out several interesting short stories based on knowledge and experience, and eventually working on a 100,000-word novel about the Navajo people titled "The Seventh Horizon" which he sent to McDonald & Co., Ltd. in England, who kept it for a very long time, finally returning it with regret, praising it for its lovely "delicately told love story" and "the beautifully recorded background of the countryside in which the tale is set." But they turned it down as Bill's name was not widely known in England, offering to publish it if it was published first in this country. After Bill died at age ninety-seven in 1995, I spent that summer retyping it with the changes and corrections wanted and have been trying to find a publisher for it ever since.

"The Seventh Horizon" is a "people story," one which the Navajos would enjoy themselves. It was set in the 1950s with the main character an ex-Marine who had fought in Korea and was returning to his reservation to live and to help his people with their transition to more modern ways.

We continued to have dreams that Bill's novel The Mestizo would be made into a movie stressing characterization and background and a plot that didn't rely on outrageous "shoot 'em-ups" for action, but in spite of all our efforts, and the encouragement received from excellent reviews of the book, this did not happen.

Another camping trip we took back in the 1950s was to New Mexico and Texas, first to visit amazing Carlsbad Caverns and then to El Paso to see a softball game played by Eddie Feigner, the King and His Court, with only a catcher and three or four fielders, he was such an astonishingly good pitcher, the best we ever saw in all the softball games we ever witnessed, mostly at Williams and Prescott, Arizona.

On the way we stopped for a picnic in a small town in New Mexico where no one was in sight; it was siesta time. Suddenly the boys saw some beautiful and unusual butterflies, and being avid collectors at the time, they jumped out of the car with their nets and started running around, yelling, "I dibs it! I dibs it!" their battle cry for claiming each butterfly they were after. For years afterward we wondered what those people trying to rest in those little houses thought of what was going on.

Another trip we took while living at Grand Canyon was suggested by Bill. The boys and I had never seen Monument Valley even though he had been there many times with tourists, and he decided it was important for us to enjoy that truly spectacular area of the Navajo country. It would be a three-day camping trip, over and back.

It was a fairly nice day but rather windy when we started out that spring morning, and when we reached the reservation by early afternoon, the wind had picked up considerably, sand drifting in ghostly waves across the road. Bill predicted that when we reached Marsh Pass there would probably be some protection from the sandstorm and we might be able to go on, but by late afternoon we realized it was a lost cause. It was too late by then to go back, so we drove off the road a short way into what we thought would be a cove of protecting rocks and closed the car up as tightly as we could. However, the fine sand seeped insidiously through tiny, invisible cracks, while we ate our cold supper and then settled down to an all-too-familiar night of sleeping sitting up, the boys having the best of it in the rear of the station wagon with their pillows and blankets.

Our hope that the wind would abate by morning, so that we could continue with our journey, proved false. It was blowing even harder, and we knew that we would have to return home without so much as a glimpse of the wonders of Monument Valley, to be postponed for another time. After a cold breakfast, Bill maneuvered the car back into the dirt road when we soon discovered that here, also, sand was drifting across the way. But we were able to make it as far as Tonalea where the road had become completely impassable with deep drifts and couldn't be traveled until cleared.

We were permitted to stay in a cabin there for a small charge while the road was being cleared for us and other travelers who were waiting, and finally we reached home late that evening, our windshield badly pitted, also the chrome. The windshield would be replaced, the chrome not, a souvenir ever after of our abortive attempt to seek a new horizon.

In 1957 while my brother, Alfred, was visiting us that fall, my mother phoned and told us that our father was dying, so Bill drove us all to Flagstaff where Alfred and I took a plane to Tucson where we caught another plane to Chicago and a third one to Toledo, a long roundabout trip which caused us to arrive too late to say goodbye. Our Dad had died all alone in his hospital room while my mother was downstairs having coffee, which made her and all of us feel very sad. After the funeral attended by many friends, my mother, brother, and I accompanied the funeral car to Fort Wayne, Indiana, where my father was buried in the Brandriff family plot in Lindenwood Cemetery with big beautiful oak trees nearby.

That same year, 1957, Bill had hernia surgery in the Grand Canyon Hospital, performed by Dr. Bill Henry. And the following year, after repeated bouts of indigestion as a result of the infectious hepatitis I had suffered after we left Spur Cross Ranch and before we went to work at the Bard Ranch, I had gallbladder surgery performed by Dr. Barnes in the Williams Hospital.

Also during the 1950s the boys had the usual childhood diseases, including chickenpox, measles, and mumps, colds and 'flu; and Monty broke his left arm three separate times, requiring trips to the Williams Hospital so that Dr. Barnes could keep patching him up. It was a worry, especially when Monty climbed to the top of the big water tower at Grand Canyon, almost losing his grip when his hands landed in fresh bird droppings. An adventurous type, he had been dared to climb by one of his little Hopi friends!

In 1959, looking forward to eventual retirement, we answered an ad in the Arizona Republic, and bought a beautiful but waterless acre lot in Stagecoach Acres subdivision, not far from the lovely little frontier town of Prescott in the pine-and-juniper-covered foothills of the rugged Bradshaw Mountains, where Bill eventually built us a four-room-with-bath home. Part of the ancient Butterfield Stage road, overgrown with fragrant cliff rose, is still visible running through the south side of the property.

We lost no time that fall making camp there for two weeks, doing preliminary work, first building an outdoor toilet complete with bucket of dry lime; it was hidden behind small trees and bushes; then Bill fenced the acre in anticipation of the horse we hoped to have some day. He built a small frame shed to hold tools and supplies, giving us a place while camping to take sponge baths and change clothes. We also had a ramada for shelter from storms and to rest under during the heat of the day while we ate lunch.

We were sleeping under the ramada one stormy night, the boys in the station wagon, lightning striking the hills all around, when suddenly I saw a bolt strike the radio tower several hundred yards below our place, a perfect lightning rod to protect our home! What a blessing! We never put the tent up, as Bill and I preferred sleeping out in the open under the wide expanse of star-filled sky where we could watch the grand silent procession of the constellations when we awoke at intervals during the night.

At that time there were few houses in the area, and we were right up against the wilderness of coyotes, mountain lions, foxes, and lynx, a thrill to all of us when we would hear wild cries in the night. It was a beautiful spot to camp, with views unparalleled of Granite Mountain, the Sierra Prietas, and Thumb Butte (Prescott's landmark) to the West.

As there was no water line to our acre, we had to make dry camp, nothing new to us. We hauled all of our water in jugs, canteens, and a big five-gallon milk can. I cooked over a campfire and sometimes the gasoline campstove. For light, we had the sun, moon, and stars, flashlights, kerosene and battery lanterns. Who could ask for more?

In the meantime, Aunt Florence and I had been planning a trip together to San Francisco, she to travel by train from Escondido, and I would go by train from Grand Canyon. So I decided to earn some money toward that end. In the spring of 1960, during the days while the boys were in school, I became baby-sitter for Dr. and Mrs. Lacy's family, their little boy Markie and baby girl Sylvia, while the doctor and his wife were busy at the Grand Canyon Hospital, until the two older children came home from school.

When school vacation time came, and as Monty and Sandy were old enough to leave at home on their own, I got a job as a maid at the El Tovar Hotel for a few weeks, at a wage of sixty-six cents an hour, plus lunch, plus tips which were too negligible to make much difference. I had around twenty-five rooms to take care of, most with two beds, and bathrooms with tubs. I was also expected to clean one of the public bathrooms for women guests. Not easy work by any means.

The other maids were Supai and Hopi women who seemed rather puzzled that a white woman would want to do that kind of work, but as it was nothing new to me, I managed to perform satisfactorily. Except for one time when I neglected to clean under a bed, and I was tipped a whole nickel the next morning. The hotel wasn't air-conditioned at that time, making it pretty uncomfortable by afternoon, so I was glad to quit near the end of summer, having saved my earnings toward my San Francisco venture with Aunt Florence.

In April of 1961 she and I were having the time of our lives, staying at the Roosevelt Hotel, exploring the sights of gloriously interesting San Francisco, riding cable cars, taking boat excursions, eating fish chowder at Fisherman's Wharf, shopping at the wonderful downtown stores, and eating our meals frugally at drugstore and dime store counters. I also got a new hairdo with permanent wave by a male Hawaiian hairdresser at Macy's store, which Bill and the boys didn't approve of after I returned home. They preferred the "old Clara/Mama." It grew out eventually. I liked it, but it was too hard to take care of, so no regrets. I always take care of my own hair except for an occasional permanent wave, in my same old style.

While I was away, Monty had been having health problems, tonsil infections, so we had him admitted to the Williams Hospital for a tonsillectomy by Dr. Barnes. After we brought Monty home, he developed ether pneumonia, so back down to Williams we went, and I stayed with him for a week until he recovered. Unfortunately, that was the week my mother and brother came to visit us before their trip to San Francisco, so when Monty and I returned by bus to the Canyon, I had only a brief visit with my very disappointed mother and brother before they left, but it couldn't be helped.

Later in 1961, more trouble. Bill had to have serious colon cancer surgery performed by Dr. Barnes at the Williams Hospital, but fortunately, no colostomy necessary. Bill made a good recovery while we camped on our acre that summer when we decided it was time to think about retiring and building our new home before it was too late to enjoy it together.

After Bill's sixty-fourth birthday in October, 1961, he became semi-retired, on Social Security. As I was fresh out of the Williams Hospital after a week's bout with pneumonia, I stayed at Grand Canyon with the boys while Bill moved down to our acre to start putting together our new home in earnest, returning to the Canyon on weekends to visit us and to drive "relief stage" bus between the Canyon and Williams where he had left our car.

Building a house without power tools wasn't going to be easy, but as Bill had done it before, on our Cave Creek place, putting up two cabins, he knew what he was doing. However, it turned out to be a cold, wet fall which made things very difficult for Bill, camping on our concrete slab, cooking for himself on the campstove (mostly canned stew or beans), sleeping on the cot inside of two sleeping bags, wind and rain blowing in on him. Even though the frame and roof were up, the walls were not, so Bill got very little rest.

By November I felt well enough to travel, so I insisted that the boys and I join him and all of us live in two rooms with kitchenette at the Juniper Motel in Prescott, not far from our acre, so that he could get proper care while doing so much hard work, and we could help him with it. Monty and Sandy transferred reluctantly from the Grand Canyon schools to the Prescott Junior and Senior High Schools to which they became adjusted after a while.

Until we had a structure suitable, into which we could move our furniture, we were permitted to leave it in our house at Grand Canyon. By the middle of February the outside walls of our new house were up and covered with tarpaper, and windows and doors were installed. Even though there was no running water or plumbing or insulation as yet, we had a fuel oil heater installed in the corner of the little "study" which had been the utility building and was now part of our house. And Bill, with the help of friend Joe Hartman, constructed a fireplace and chimney made of brick from the old Grand Canyon powerhouse chimney which had been torn down, plus extra fire brick purchased at Humboldt, and this stood grandly in one corner of our living room.

For cooking, I had a new Butane gas range in the kitchen end of our 12 foot by 24 foot main room. And as electricity and a telephone were hooked up, we decided to dispense with the motel expense and move into our little home. We felt sure we could manage, just as we did when camping.

After Bill and friend Bill Cook brought our furniture down from the Canyon in a borrowed truck and crowded it into the unfinished house, we moved out of the motel. The resultant clutter was appalling and funny. Piles of gray paper-covered roll-type insulation next to the dining table were dubbed the "elephants," and it was a circus act I never wanted to perform in again. Other building materials and ladders leaned against inside and outside walls, mud and sawdust were tracked in from the working area outdoors, and I gave up trying to be a tidy housewife for the duration.

With only tarpaper and roll roofing on top of roof boards and no insulation so far anywhere, the house chilled rapidly as soon as the sun disappeared behind the distant Sierra Prietas. When there was sun. On the frequent cold, cloudy, rainy, and snowy days, and during the evenings, we stoked up the fireplace. At night the inadequate fuel oil heater kept us from freezing, and we had to use sleeping bags covered with blankets, for the indoor temperature was in the forties and fifties in the morning until we had the fireplace and two electric heaters going.

The fuel oil heater ran out of fuel a couple of nights, and it was thirty-eight degrees in the house when we awoke. Bundled in sweaters and jacket, I fixed breakfast while the fireplace, electric heaters, and gas range, all going full blast, finally warmed the place up to the mid-fifties. It was only temporary, an adventure, something to talk about later, like a camping trip.

Even though our septic system was in, our plumbing wasn't. We still had no running water, and frost was thick inside our "Chic Sales" in the morning, but we made light of it. Below the kitchen sink a bucket served for draining dish water to be thrown into the bushes later. I heated water for dishes, clothes, and sponge baths on the gas range, washing our clothing each day by hand, the wash water dipped out of rusty rain barrels. Sometimes the water looked so dark that I seemed to be recycling dirt, but the clean rinse water from doing dishes was useful for rinsing clothes, so our wearing apparel looked reasonably respectable, and none of us worried about it. "Casual" was the byword.

In March we were still hauling all our water from an obliging gas station next to the Juniper Motel, and Bill made sure that we had sufficient water on hand whenever he left for his weekend relief job as stage driver. But early one Saturday afternoon when I returned on foot from my temporary part-time job making beds at the Juniper Motel, Sandy met me with a long face. He had a half-filled pan of dirty snow in his hands, and he woefully explained that his Dad had phoned from Williams that he had accidentally taken the canteens and jugs with him in the car and had told the boys that they would have to collect snow to melt for our water supply for the weekend while he was away.

The trouble was that the snow had melted to such an extent that it was impossible to gather enough for any practical purpose. I looked around the kitchen and had to laugh. We had less than a half gallon of water to last until Sunday evening, for washing, drinking, cooking, and dishes. The rain barrels were each about one-third full of very rusty water. So it was going to be an easy weekend for me. I would use paper dishes, I wouldn't wash clothes, we'd wash our hands in rusty water.

The boys were stunned at my reaction and decided I didn't realize the seriousness of the situation. So I sent them to the Mayfield house about a half mile away down in Government Canyon for some of their well water, about a gallon, and we settled down to an easy-going weekend.

Having made many a dry camp, I knew how to conserve on water. On camping trips when the boys were small, I would save the clean warm rinse water from doing dishes and pour it into a wash basin to wash my feet. After one such trip Monty merrily reported to his second grade teacher and little classmates, "My Mom washed her feet in the dishwater!"

Later that spring a thousand-gallon water tank and piping were installed on the upper end of our hillside, and we had water delivered by rancher Boyd Tenney's sons with their tank truck for a penny per gallon, the price going up in subsequent years. But we never took our wonderful running water for granted, nor did we waste it. With care, our family of four could make a thousand gallons last nearly three weeks, and even then we felt as though we had all we needed for quick shower baths, our indoor toilet supplemented during the day by the "Chic Sales"; and cooking, drinking, and washing small items of clothing by washboard. Larger things such as jeans, sheets, and towels, we took to the laundromat, drying everything in the sun.

Even with insulation in the walls, our house still wasn't warm enough on cold nights, so Bill added aluminum panels over the roll roofing, and that helped to hold the heat in and made the house cooler in summer. A good grate made our fireplace more efficient, and later Bill put glass doors on it to keep the heat from rising up the chimney once the fire died down at night.

In 1968 the natural gas line came in, so we converted from Butane, installed a gas wall heater in the hallway next to the bathroom and service closet, and finally had a comfortably warm house and cozy bathroom at night. The fuel oil heater was saved for emergencies only.

At last, the best thing of all—in March, 1973, we had a well drilled, over 300 feet deep, and even though it produced only a half gallon of water per minute, that equaled 720 gallons per 24 hours, and it was not only adequate for our needs, but it seemed like a miracle, that wonderful cold, pure, non-chlorinated water. So we could have a little garden, a patch of lawn, and a small portable washing machine. We were coming up in the world.

After a few years of driving stage between Grand Canyon and Williams on weekends, Bill quit that job to drive the Prescott-Whipple stage bus that went out to the V.A. Medical Center and back to town, for about three or four years. In April, 1967, he began to write his weekly column "Under the Southwest Sun" for the Prescott Courier, now called The Daily Courier, informing interested readers locally and subscribers all over the country about his experiences in and knowledge of the Southwest, including people he had met, adventures he had had, animals, birds, insects, geology, astronomy, baseball. You name it, he wrote about it. He had one of the busiest retirements on record.

We also continued with our camping trips, one very special one to Toroweap on the west end of Grand Canyon. We traveled by way of the Navajo country, crossing over to Jacob Lake by way of the Vermillion Cliffs, on to Fredonia, and then onto a bad dirt road that led to Mt. Trumbull, which is over 8,000 feet high and whose slopes seemed to be covered with clouds of big black flies, and finally we reached Toroweap over an even worse, rocky, rutted road. But what a sight! The clean, rocky sweep of the esplanade overlooking the Colorado River which was more than 2,000 feet below us, nearly straight down, in marvelous isolation, nobody else around except for Ranger John Riffey back in his ranger station.

Mr. Riffey very kindly drove his van down to our camp and presented us with a big canteen of water to supplement the supply we had brought with us, and when we were commenting on the bad road, he said he called his vehicle a "Canardly" because he can hardly get it out of its tracks.

We had been having a lot of car trouble with Horizon Hunter II, but Bill had babied it along somehow through the rough country while we were hoping and praying that it would take us out of Toroweap when it came time to leave. In the meantime, we were enjoying the magnificent scenery until Monty scared us silly by jumping casually from one big rock overhang to another, right at the edge of the precipice. One mishap and . . . well, he made it, and he didn't try it again. Our nerves couldn't take it, and I stayed away from the edge of the cliff from that moment on, with my knees shaking.

We did make it out of Toroweap successfully, drove past fly-infested Mt. Trumbull again without stopping this time, and that night we spent sleeping out in the open on our cots on the Shivwits Plateau where a mockingbird serenaded us all night long in the moonlight. A glorious memory. Next morning after breakfast we drove slowly but steadily along the rough dirt roads of The Strip country, until we decided to make a brief side trip to Colorado City, formerly known as Short Creek, where the Mormon polygamists live. We bought some ice cream, tried not to be nosy, then retraced our route home, taking our own sweet time, exploring, prospecting, and enjoying ourselves, reaching home finally, worn out but satisfied.

24

Monty Edward Parks
1947–1984

Toroweap was the last long trip we all took together. It had been a lot of fun and interesting, camped under the huge overhang and experiencing a new and very different aspect of our Grand Canyon, but Monty and Sandy were growing up and finding other things to do on their own.

Monty, my first born, was a sweet, delightful little boy, interested in everything in Nature. The Canyon, his birthplace, was very special to him and to all of us; its inhabitants including the deer that wandered through our yard, the squirrels and chipmunks scrambling in our trees, the birds which serenaded us as we worked and played, and the insects, especially the butterflies which he and Sandy collected for a while until they became conscience-stricken and stopped. Now, whenever I see a butterfly flit by me, I say a silent, loving "Hello, Monty." He is no longer with us, murdered at the age of thirty-six in the prime of his life.

Monty was an avid reader and student of everything he could get his hands on. I had started reading to him from the time he was ten months old when he acted as though he could understand everything I said. If he misbehaved as a toddler, all I had to say was, "If you don't behave, I won't read to you at bedtime," and that was all it took; books were that important to him. An excellent student in school, his main interest became mathematics when he won prizes in competitions. In his senior year in high school, he tested himself to the limit, taking on six subjects, staying up until three o'clock in the morning studying math, physics and chemistry, Russian language, American history, and English, too much for anyone, Bill and I thought, but he succeeded, with top grades. However, after he graduated, in 1965, he needed a change of pace and answered a call for melon workers in Yuma in southwest Arizona. Bill drove him down there to one of the fields where he worked in extreme heat for three weeks until he became ill from bad food and water and could work no longer. So Bill drove down to the field camp to rescue him and bring him home to cool Prescott and proper doctoring.

When Monty felt strong again, he began to hike in the mountains all around Prescott, backpacking, camping out alone overnight, sometimes for several nights. One time the weather turned cold and wet with dense fog in the hills, and Bill and I became very worried that Monty might be lost, so Bill drove out on the Walker road east of Prescott to try to find him, but without much hope, until, like a miracle, here came Monty striding out of the forest fog near the road, not lost, not needing rescue, sure of where he was, but, as he was tired and the weather too disagreeable for further camping, he let his Dad bring him home for home-cooking and rest. An answer to our prayers. We tried not to worry about him any more, and he never did become lost in the wilderness. He took after Bill who always knew his landmarks while hiking and was never lost; at least, not for long. They both had an instinct for travel in the wild. Not true of Sandy and me, unfortunately, but we tried.

In the fall of 1965 Monty entered Arizona State University with scholarships which paid his tuition and other expenses. Once again his main subjects of interest were advanced math—notably number theory—science, and Russian. He was also involved in Physical Education and ROTC which helped build up his strength. During his free time he did a great deal of running to help him relax after long arduous periods of study.

Restless and dissatisfied with school, in spite of excellent grades, he dropped out of ASU. in his sophomore year and signed up with the Navy, taking boot camp at San Diego in his stride, after which he entered the Navy's electronics school. Bored with that and wanting action, he transferred to the deck force and was stationed on the USS *Bradford* in Honolulu in 1967 where he became very ill. He was admitted to Tripler Hospital before being flown to the mainland and admitted to Camp Pendleton Hospital. After seven months he was given an honorable discharge and sent home to Prescott, looking ill and gaunt and feeling depressed, having suffered severe side effects from the medications he had been given. Eventually he was hospitalized at the Veterans Administration hospital in Phoenix for several weeks, and when he finally returned home he was treated as an outpatient at the V. A. Medical Center in Prescott.

When he felt well enough, he began to do different kinds of work, including tutoring children in Math, driving a taxi and acting as dispatcher at times, doing yard work, and also helping Bill with chores around our place. When he started computer training at Yavapai College in Prescott, he purchased a computer. His main interest in life continued to be advanced mathematics, number theory in particular, where he became very creative, writing to math professors about his theorems and other ideas. He wanted to study for a while at the University of Arizona's math department, so Bill obligingly drove him down to Tucson where he studied for a few weeks, after which Bill drove down to bring Monty home.

We bought Monty a secondhand Volkswagen "bug" so that he would be free to travel wherever he wanted to camp out, and when he was returning from one such trip, he fell asleep, ran his car into a ditch in Chino Valley 15 miles north of Prescott and was pinned inside so that the "jaws of life" had to be used to rescue him. The little car was wrecked beyond repair, and Monty was in the Prescott V. A. hospital for six weeks recovering from his injuries, including a broken hip. He received excellent care and made a good recovery. Later on he bought a used Ford LTD.

Wanting to live on his own, he rented a little shack for ninety dollars a month near downtown Prescott, but it was such a miserable hovel, we bought him a small clean trailer in Chino Valley. After a few months he became lonely for Prescott, so we sold that trailer and used the money to buy him another one, this time in a nice trailer park across town from us, which pleased him.

In the meantime, he had become acquainted by mail with a nice Malaysian Chinese girl who called herself Rina, not her Chinese name, who was attending school in Canada. After she came to Prescott to visit Monty, they fell in love and decided to get married. But first she returned to her home in Malaysia to visit her family and settle her affairs. The year was 1984. Monty was thirty-six years old.

On Sunday, March 18th, Monty hiked across town in the early morning hours, too early to stop by our house which was on the way, and climbed to the top of Badger Mountain (which is also called "P" Mountain for the painted "P" which represents Prescott High School) in the Bradshaws, where he lay down on the bare ground to rest and fell asleep. While he was asleep, some person or persons came upon him and beat his head in, killing him instantly according to Dr. Philip Keene, the Medical Examiner at that time; and Monty was robbed of his wallet, his I.D., watch, jacket, everything. No witnesses.

The following Tuesday morning, March 20th, Bill and I heard on the radio about the murder on the mountain of an unknown man, and from the description given of the clothes he was wearing, we felt immediately that it could be Monty, as that was one of his favorite areas for hiking. Bill phoned the Sheriff's office, and they notified the two deputies who were still on top of the mountain investigating the murder. They stopped by on their way down. One of them was Deputy Gordon Diffendaffer. When we described Monty, six feet tall, around 165 pounds, dark blond hair, brown eyes, dressed in hiking clothes, Diffendaffer said, "It sounds like it's your son."

I went to pieces. They offered to get someone to stay with me, but I rejected that idea. I wanted to be alone. They drove across town with Bill to Monty's trailer where they hoped to find clues, but there was nothing there to indicate what had happened to Monty. Several Silent Witness notices were published in the Prescott Courier, but no one ever came forward with information. Perhaps some day the person or persons who killed Monty will have a fit of conscience and confess, but it won't bring Monty back.

Later some neighbors who lived on the mountain near the road told us that they had seen Monty go by that Sunday morning while they were eating breakfast by their window overlooking the road. Shortly after that they saw two rough-looking men go by, headed in the same direction. No one came down off the mountain that morning.

And neighbors of Monty's at the trailer park told Bill and the deputies that a tough-looking man had visited Monty at his trailer the day before he was killed, and Monty had left the man there on his porch, drinking coffee, while he went to help the park manager, Mrs. Wade, with some yard work, but nothing came of that lead.

The Thursday before Monty died, he went on a long hike up Granite Mountain, then came clear across town on foot to see us. He told us very emotionally how much he loved us, what a happy childhood he had had, a "paradise" he called it. On Saturday morning I talked to him on the phone, and he sounded sweet and cheerful, saying he hadn't slept much but had had a restful night anyway. That was the last time we spoke.

Sandy sent a telegram to Rina, Monty's fiancee, and she flew back to Prescott, too late as Monty had already been cremated. Bill hiked up the trail on Granite Mountain, one of Monty's favorite places, to put his ashes there on the slopes where mountain lions might rest, while I stayed in the car and cried, listening to a canyon wren nearby in the granite boulders sing its haunting melody, the memory of which still brings tears to my eyes. Rina promised to write to me after she returned to Malaysia, but she never did.

Bill was very strong throughout the ordeal, helping me to get through it, but then he broke down, threw himself on our bed, and wept bitterly. He was never a person to cry, and that broke my heart all over again. And to spare me, he had had to identify Monty's body, suffering from nightmares for years afterward. Being a homicide, the case is still open, but there seems to be little or no hope that it will ever be solved. This is something I will never get over so long as I live. Sometimes I dream about Monty, and he is happy and well, and that gives me some comfort at the time.

25

William Sandelin Parks

Darling Sandy, our second handsome, brown-eyed little boy, cheerful, artistic, bright, and charming, forever drawing funny sketches and cartoons, painting pictures, of which several are framed and adorn the walls in my home. After my short story "Tiger in the Closet" about two little boys appeared in the *Ladies' Home Journal* in 1951 and I had an ongoing correspondence with the editors, they said they would be pleased to publish one of Sandy's cartoons which depicted his "future wife" tying his shoelaces. The drawing was made in response to my admonition that he had better learn how to do it himself, or his wife would have to do it for him some day. Eventually the editors changed their minds, so Sandy didn't get the showing hoped for. Life is full of little disappointments, as we all learn and must accept.

As with Monty, Sandy did excellent work in school. He won a spelling contest while at Grand Canyon, competing later in Flagstaff, not winning there but pleased, as we all were, at his having had the experience. And I still have a newspaper picture of him taken with other contestants after he won first prize in a county-wide math contest for Prescott Junior High students.

Sandy received top marks while in Prescott High School except for French class during his senior year where he rebelled at doing the homework. Although he was awarded A's on the exams, his teacher failed him for the course, his only low mark during all the years of his schooling. Bill and I didn't reproach him, as we never put pressure on the boys, just advising them to learn the "basics," reading, writing, and math, assuring them that the rest would come to them much more easily, which proved to be true.

To give Sandy something else to think about apart from school I suggested that he take accordion lessons. He agreed, so we bought him a secondhand accordion with which he made lovely music until he graduated from high school, gave it up, and bought himself a 1957 Chevrolet station wagon with money that had accrued from an insurance policy paid for by my mother. He soon discovered that the car had a cracked block and a pitted windshield, not revealed to him by the local car dealer who had unloaded it on him.

Bill and Sandy found a secondhand windshield to fit the car, and I raised cain with the dealership, talking them into replacing the windshield at a cost of only ten dollars, which they did. The old one was used later as a wind-break above the feed trough in the shed by the corral where we kept our eighteen-year-old horse named Tumbleweed, a beautiful Appaloosa which Bill bought and rode in one of Prescott's Fourth of July parades in the early 1970s, as well as on the back roads in our subdivision, Stagecoach Acres, later having to sell the horse when increased traffic made it too dangerous to ride on those curving roads.

After graduation Sandy wanted a change, so he drove north to Flagstaff, rented a room, and got a job in a nearby restaurant washing dishes. Bored with that he then went down to Phoenix to work in a resort kitchen and stayed there until he fell ill and returned home, cheated out of his final paycheck and disillusioned with that kind of work. Later on he worked at U. S. Motors as a coil winder, and eventually he worked at Quality Plastics evenings making plastic containers. Bill and I never tried to influence him or dissuade him from changing jobs. It was up to Sandy to try different things in order to discover the kind of work he liked and was best suited for. After all, that was what Bill had been doing most of his life, so how could we object?

Finally Sandy made up his mind to get further education and entered the University of Arizona at Tucson in 1970, majoring in geology, for two years. Tired of that, he then went to Maricopa Technical College (now called Gateway) in Phoenix and received an Associate in Arts degree in automotive technology while working as a clerk in the college's tool room from 1973 to 1978, also serving as a part-time automotive and hydraulics instructor evenings, all invaluable experience.

From 1978 to 1980 he studied at Arizona State University in Tempe and was awarded a Bachelor of Science degree in Communications Science, summa cum laude, with a 4.0 grade average, the highest. Not wanting to continue in that field and needing an income, he worked off and on from 1980 to 1984 at a small electrostatic painting company where he became secretary on the board of directors and served as foreman. He also became a telephone market researcher, along with inventing a small type of high-voltage electrostatic equipment for dry paint coating and was president of a business venture to market it but so far without success. What a busy life! And much more to come, new horizons!

While Sandy was at Maricopa Tech, one of the other instructors, John Vetnar, told him about his lovely young woman cousin, Dusanka Atanackovic, living in Yugoslavia, who wanted an Americain pen pal, so from 1977 to 1981 they corresponded. Dusanka invited him for a visit, and in the summer of 1981, Sandy flew to Yugoslavia to be with her. They had a wonderful time together, and before the visit was over, they decided to get married, whereupon Sandy flew home to break the news to us. We gave him our blessing and the plane fare to return to Yugoslavia, so, on December 27, 1981, Sandy became a married man, but soon after the wedding he had to return to America to make a living.

As Dusanka's mother was suffering from cancer and Dusanka was caring for her, she couldn't join Sandy in America, but she did come for a two-week visit in Phoenix at his downtown apartment, and he brought her to Prescott to meet us before they went on to Grand Canyon for Sandy to show her where he was born, in the most wonderful place in the world. Monty was still alive at that time, and I remember his coming into the kitchen and greeting Dusanka in Russian which she understood and which made us all smile. After a too-brief overnight stay, the newlyweds went up to the Canyon before Dusanka returned to Yugoslavia.

Sandy worked briefly at a Tempe service station until he found a job more to his liking in Reno, Nevada, at Precision Rolled Products in their metallurgical laboratory as a technician where he worked in quality control of aerospace materials. While in Reno, Sandy received a visit from Dusanka whose mother had died, they decided to live together in Yugoslavia where Dusanka had inherited her mother's house in Srbobran, and she owned an apartment in Sremska Kamenice near Novi Sad where she was chief accountant for two department stores, with eleven other accountants answerable to her.

After she returned to Yugoslavia, Sandy drove home to Prescott for a visit and to leave his 1962 Chevrolet sedan for us to sell for him. Then he left for Yugoslavia in March of 1986, right when the accident at Chernobyl in the Ukraine was spewing radioactivity over the area, giving us something to really worry about. As Sandy had become a "born again"

Christian while attending Faith Evangelical Free Church, now called Faith Church of Tempe, after having been an atheist for much of his life (not our doing), he served as a "tentmaker" missionary, becoming fluent in the Serbian language, so much so that he translated scientific papers, tutored students in English, and also translated and wrote subtitles for a Yugoslav television documentary. It was a demanding but rewarding and interesting time.

Most importantly, for all of us, he and Dusanka became parents of a darling baby girl on June 25, 1988, whom they named Tamara Rose and who became an American as well as a Yugoslavian citizen. Bill and I were very happy and excited to be grandparents for the first time and looked forward eagerly to darling pictures we received of the new addition to our family, a beautiful dark-haired, brown-eyed charmer whom we looked forward to meeting some day.

And that day came in December, 1989, when Tamara was eighteen months old, a delightful age. Bill and I could hardly take our eyes away from her for even a moment during their visit with us in Prescott. We hovered over her as she walked on the uneven ground around our house, delighting in everything she said and did, wishing that our little family would settle in Prescott.

But as Dusanka had Serbian relatives and friends living in the Phoenix metropolitan area, and Sandy's church was in the Valley at Tempe, they decided to live down there and rented an apartment at first until finally they started to buy a nice two-story townhouse in Mesa. Naturally, the question of making a living became paramount, and for a while Dusanka had a small day-care business in their home while Sandy worked for a few months on a temporary project as U. S. Public Schools Coordinator for Films for Christ in Mesa. He wrote advertising copy and magazine articles, proofread and helped promote the second edition of the bestselling *Illustrated Origins Answer Book* by Paul Taylor, did research for promotional purposes, and advised the Production Director, Mr. Taylor.

Following that, Sandy became Assistant Director at the Center for Scientific Creation in Phoenix, with his primary responsibilities being to market Dr. Walter Brown's book *In the Beginning* to Christian bookstores nationwide and to help promote his creation-science seminars across the United States, using a word processor to write letters, articles, and ad copy, and doing layouts for promotional materials. He assisted Dr. Brown in writing some technical papers, and he managed the office as well as doing most of the organization's accounting and secretarial work. This work lasted frcm April 1990 until February 1991.

From September 1991 until August 1992 Sandy worked as a salesman at a store called Watchworks in Tri City Mall, where he sold watches, installed watch batteries and bands, and kept inventory, later working part-time at that job until 1996 along with evenings as a janitor, with Dusanka's help, at their church. Needing a full-time, permanent position, he was hired in January, 1993, by a company located in Phoenix called POS Systems as customer service representative and technical support specialist.

As for his main interest in life, his writing, for which Bill and I admired and deeply respected Sandy's talent, he wrote and edited a monthly newsletter for his church; wrote articles or editorials for *The Christian Reader, The Christian Communicator, Confident Living* (formerly *Good News Broadcaster); The Forerunner, Creation Research Society Quarterly; The Arizona Republic; Mesa Tribune;* and *U. S. News and World Report.* In addition to all this, his article "Why Won't Our Schools Teach Scientific Creationism?" was published by *The Arizona Republic* in Phoenix, won a thousand dollars, an Award of Outstanding Merit, by the Amy Awards in 1990, which was very gratifying and encouraging. Such articles have to mention some wording from the Bible and must be published in a secular newspaper or magazine.

Sandy has also written three books, the first one on evangelism called "Have You Told Anyone about Christ Today?" unpublished so far and for which Multnomah President Dr. Joseph Aldrich wrote a foreword and endorsement. His second book *How to Teach Your Children Creation Science* is to be advertised by the Institute for Creation Research of San Diego; while his third book *Introduction to the Trinity* was published by Ecumenical Theological Education by Extension in Billings, Montana.

I might mention that in former years he became President as well as Vice President of a Toastmasters public speaking club in Phoenix; a volunteer reader for Recording for the Blind, and a reader for a fellow A.S.U. blind student, Susan Schaffer; a volunteer office worker for Food for the Hungry; judge at high school speech tournaments; and he appeared on Phoenix television as one of the panelists in a program on automotive maintenance. In connection with his religious faith, he designed an evangelistic billboard poster and coordinated its printing and posting on a billboard next to a freeway in Phoenix, and debated an evolutionist on a KFYI radio program. He now has a computer to help him do even more!

Bill and I were always happy to have Sandy and his lovely little family pay us visits here in Prescott, but some day they wish to live part of the year in Yugoslavia where Sandy wants to return to his "tentmaker" missionary work. But at least we have met and fallen in love with Dusanka and Tamara. They were heart-broken when Dad/Grandpa Bill died June 15, 1995, in the Prescott V. A. Medical Center Nursing Home at age 97. They have been a joy and a great comfort to me, all three of my dear children.

Before Dusanka had become an American citizen, she and Sandy decided they wanted to have a church wedding which would be a very important and more meaningful ceremony to them than the civil wedding which had taken place in Novi Sad, Yugoslavia, on December 27, 1981. So, on January 12, 1992, Sandy and Dusanka were married before a full church of their friends with their Pastor Nathan Lutz officiating, Dusanka wearing a lovely beige silk gown with jacket, and Sandy solemn and handsome in a business suit, with their darling little three-year-old daughter Tamara standing happily and proudly by their side, dressed in her best. So now they have two wedding anniversaries to celebrate each year. Although Bill and I were unable to attend either ceremony, photos, vivid descriptions, and a videotape of the church wedding helped to satisfy our interest, and we were with them in our hearts, as always.

26

The Last Horizon

I am alone. Alone with my memories and a sweet, funny little semi-neurotic cat named Sunshine, a golden-striped tiger with a two-inch quirk of a tail, whom we adopted out of the boulders in a nearby hill on Thanksgiving 1993. I am living in a trailer situated in a lovely mobile home park, my lot closely surrounded by eleven huge Ponderosa pine trees and several interesting gnarled oaks, all much older than I am. They are a joy and a comfort to me, even though they give me lots of yard work to do, raking up and bagging dead needles and leaves. Good exercise, I assure myself.

Alone but not lonely. I find that I can enjoy my solitude, my books, my writing, accompanied by soft, pleasing music from a local radio station. But most of all my thoughts and memories, relived lovingly with my late husband Bill, son Monty, and surviving son Sandy with his little family. At eighty-three years of age, I am pretty healthy, blessed with excellent vision and hearing, able to be quite active, having achieved well over 22,000 miles on my exercise bike, riding at least five miles a day while reading *Guideposts* and *Reader's Digest*, magazines small enough to be held easily. And I walk to town a mile and a half once a week to get groceries, taking a taxi or bus home with my load, as it is mostly uphill on the return trip. I could take the bus to town, but I enjoy the pleasant walk, smiling and greeting everyone I meet whether I know them or not, a small town custom which I enjoy. How much longer Prescott will remain a small town with its rapid growth and increasing traffic is something I don't like to think about.

Looking back, life was so simple and uncomplicated when Bill and I first started out together in April, 1941. Just a matter of finding a good campsite, or a job and a cheap place to live while working, enough money for a simple diet, gas, oil, and repairs for the '28 Chevy. No bills coming in, no phone, no set address for any length of time, just the prospect of possible hardship as the price we were willing to pay for our life of freedom and adventure, the excitement and pleasure of seeking and finding new and fascinating horizons. But when the time came, we didn't regret giving up our wandering life to settle down to raise our two sons Monty and Sandy who gave us the greatest joy of our lives.

Inevitably we had several medical problems while living at Grand Canyon and later at Prescott. Bill's two successful colon cancer surgeries and appendectomy, two for hernias, one for benign prostate trouble back in the 1960s, and in the late 1970s surgery on his right carotid artery after several transient ischemic attacks. Besides my gall bladder operation with appendectomy while at Grand Canyon along with the bout with pneumonia, I had to undergo a hysterectomy in 1965 at Williams Hospital while living in Prescott, which led to osteoporosis five years later.

With my bones deteriorating rapidly in the winter of 1970–1971, I felt pain in my legs and back until one early morning while making Monty's bed, my spine suddenly felt as though it were crumbling. Frightened, I walked into the living room, sat on the sofa, and wondered what to do. Finally, needing action, I made an appointment with an elderly osteopath named Dr. Parson in downtown Prescott. After an examination and careful manipulation, he had me go to the hospital for X-rays which revealed that I did indeed have osteoporosis. Dr. Parson saved my life. He prescribed Stilbestrol (DES), calcium, and exercise, a regimen I followed faithfully, but after seventeen years I could no longer get the tiniest .1 mg. dose of Stilbestrol as that size was no longer being produced, so I was forced to change over to Premarin which I continue to take in the smallest dose, a .3 mg. pill cut in half, five days a week for three weeks, quit for one week, then resume for another three weeks, and so on. I can't take a larger dose of Premarin as it causes side effects. And even though doctors claim that osteoporosis can't be reversed, I seem to have done so. I continue to take calcium, around 1200 mg. per day, and I exercise daily, even before I get out of bed in the morning; also while I watch television in the evening or while I wait for meals to cook, doing my own version of Tai Chi at times. It works!

After we were well settled in our home in Prescott and the boys had gone their own ways, Bill and I continued to take little trips, usually day-long picnics once or twice a week to gather dead wood for our fireplace. As we had been taking in stray cats and having them neutered and given the necessary shots, we felt tied down, responsible for these little lives, so we couldn't go off for more than two or three days at a time. We enclosed and screened the ramada, and we left plenty of dry cat food and bowls of water inside, with a small curtained cat door so that they could come and go as they pleased.

And cats came and went, sometimes grabbed in the night by prowling coyotes or big owls even though the ramada gave the cats safe haven. One was run over by a car, one killed by a big dog. They couldn't resist roaming outside when they heard mice and pack rats rustling in the dry grasses, weeds, and leaves. Our first cat was a gray tiger with white feet we called Dusty, followed by Orphan Andy, Orphan Annie, Paddy, Susie, Tommie, and finally beautiful black-and-white Sally and her four kittens I named Teeny, Meany, Miney, and Mosey, all black except for Mosey who was a lovely Siamese mix but without the "voice," just a cute little squeak.

Sally had appeared in our corral one day looking for food, and we noticed that she was a nursing mother, gaunt and desperate. After we fed her until her sides bulged, she would disappear to feed her kittens, returning again and again, deflated and hungry, until her babies were satisfied for that day and Sally could rest with them in their nest which Bill discovered down in Government Canyon. One day she brought them with her, the scaredest little mites, running through the bushes, leaping over weeds, and hiding whenever they saw us until finally they decided we could be trusted and became friends, rolling in the dust and letting us tickle their fat tummies. Sally herself was still just a kitten only six months old, but she was the best little mother, very protective, knowing instinctively how to care for her babies, calling them with sweet little trills to nurse until finally one day she decided they were big enough to be on their own and eat just cat food and catch their own mice, so she told them to knock it off in spite of their pleadings for "just once more." Teeny and Mosey, both females, sweetly accepted Sally's edict, but the males Meany and Miney pestered Sally for a long time afterward. In the meantime we had had Sally spayed to prevent further problems, and when it came time, the kittens were also altered and vaccinated, much to their dismay at being hauled off in carriers but ever so happy to be home again after their "terrible ordeal."

During this time two sad events occurred, one when my mother died on March 18, 1971, at age seventy-nine, in Toledo where I flew to be with my brother Alfred Brandriff Lukens for the funeral and later the burial service in Fort Wayne, Indiana, next to our father's grave in the Brandriff plot. Bill and I invited Alfred to come to Prescott to live, but he decided he'd rather stay in the family home which my mother had deeded to him in the early 1960s.

In late 1971, after we visited Aunt Florence in Vista, California, where she was living with her son James and his family, she had a bad fall, breaking a hip, and later died in a nursing home in July, 1972, when she was nearly ninety-two years of age. While visiting us ten years earlier in Prescott, she told me that she was "failing fast." I disputed it, wouldn't listen to her, so she lived another ten years during which time we had some wonderful trips together. Besides the one to San Francisco back in 1961, she treated me to visits by the beach in Carlsbad, California; San Diego where we stayed at the Churchill Hotel and had fun shopping and visiting the Zoo and the beaches; and Wilmington so that we could take the boat over to beautiful Catalina Island. She was a great friend and companion, interested in everything, someone for me to emulate in my later years. I still miss her.

Even though our cat family of seven depended on us, Bill and I wanted to take a vacation, so we decided in the spring of 1982 to take separate trips to San Diego to visit the Zoo and Sea World. He went over and back by bus for his week, and after he came home, I traveled by bus to Phoenix to take a plane over. I had planned to stay two weeks, but after the Churchill Hotel started some remodeling work and wanted to move me to another room, I decided I had had enough after a week's stay. I had visited the Zoo, Sea World, and La Jolla, among other things, so I flew back to Phoenix and from there returned to Prescott in a single-engine plane which I loved, a new adventure for me, making me feel more like flying than being in a big plane, even though we hit some turbulence when the little plane felt as though it were running over big rocks. The pilot apologized which was very unnecessary so far as I was concerned.

One lovely morning that same year, Bill decided that at last I must see Monument Valley. With no wind and sand storms threatening this time, we took off with our camping gear for a three-day trip. Monty was available and willing to look after our place and the seven cats, so off we went with clear consciences and joyful anticipation.

The first night we camped by a big, empty, isolated Navajo corral, setting our folding cots with air mattresses and sleeping bags under the stars as we always had in nice weather, looking forward to a peaceful night's rest. After we were asleep, a Navajo pickup truck roared by on the dirt track past our camp, waking us and frightening me, although the truck continued on and around the corral and up a small hill where it disappeared around a curve.

I found it impossible to get back to sleep, as I kept expecting the truck to return, so by morning I was feeling pretty ragged. Bill decided they were probably Navajo police looking for bootleggers, but who knows? They could see by our old Plymouth station wagon and camping gear that we weren't of their tribe, so I guess that was why they didn't stop. If they had had evil intentions, we had no weapons and were completely vulnerable.

After a good breakfast in the cool air, I began to feel more alive, and when we drove on to see the colorful glories of Monument Valley with its fantastic formations, the incident of the night before became meaningless, just one of our memories, an adventure that didn't happen, something to wonder about occasionally. We always loved the Navajo country and its gentle, kind, and interesting people.

Later that year we took a morning trip to climb Glassford Hill east of Prescott, an extinct volcano, formerly called Bald Mountain by some newcomers until they learned better. From a distance it looks rather bare, but it is covered with rough lava rocks and cinders, making a very rugged climb. Even though Bill was eighty-five years old, but still strong and active, he climbed clear to the top so that he could look down into the crater. While I, at age sixty-eight, stopped three-fourths of the way up, content to sit on a sun-warmed rock and take in the scene below, Lonesome Valley which is now called Prescott Valley and is very built-up with hundreds of houses and businesses.

Sometimes our picnic trips took us north to Chino Valley and on to Hell Canyon where there are picnic tables and a convenient rest room. It is a beautiful spot by the steep and colorful canyon which is crossed on a long, sturdy bridge. One day as we were eating our lunch at a table not far from the bridge, we saw a tall man walking by, dressed in a long white robe of homespun material and sandals, carrying a small blanket and little else. He had long dark hair and a beard which made him look like pictures we had seen depicting Jesus Christ. As we watched, he strode onto the bridge and stopped half-way over, looking down for a long time at the presently dry bottom of the steep canyon.

"He must be looking for water," Bill said. "But the creek is dry, no chance there." We had finished our lunch by then, and I said, "Let's take him some water." We had a quart plastic bottle that was still full; I always took along more water than we might need on our trips, and we wouldn't need this for the drive home.

After stowing our picnic things onto the back seat of our station wagon, we drove across the bridge to where the man had stopped by the side of the road. He made no move to try to thumb a ride or ask for help, and I rolled down my window to ask him, "Do you need water?"

Looking at me with gentle dark eyes, he said, "Yes." So I gave him the quart bottle from which he drank thirstily, his head tipped way back. When he tried to return the bottle to me, I said, "Keep it, you'll need it."

Then I asked him, "Do you need food?" Again he said yes, so I gave him a full package of hamburger buns which I had bought in Chino Valley to use for our supper that night. Thanking me quietly, he retreated to the dirt bank a short distance from the road to eat.

Bill made a U-turn on the deserted highway so that we could head for home, and we never saw or heard of the man again. Who was he? Where was he from? Where was he going? No one else reported seeing such a person.

Even though that highway is a fairly busy one, no other cars had come by. It was so quiet and peaceful, just the three of us there on that sunny afternoon. We had asked him no questions, felt no need or impulse to invade his privacy. It felt almost as though we had had a "vision," and we were grateful at having been there to help him, whoever he was.

Several years later Bill wrote one of his "Under the Southwest Sun" weekly columns about the incident, which aroused quite a bit of interest among his readers, but no one came up with any answers or reports of similar encounters, either at Hell Canyon or anyplace else.

Our worst memory, of course, was when Monty was murdered on March 18, 1984, about which I have already written. And I have told about Sandy's trip in 1986 to live with his wife Dusanka in Yugoslavia where their baby girl Tamara Rose was born on June 25, 1988, and their return to America in the fall of 1989.

Even though Bill was in his early nineties, he continued to be active, working around our place, even climbing a ladder up to our roof top to clear snow off in winter. He also drove to town every other day to get mail and groceries until on November 21, 1991, while on his way to the bank, he fell backward from a steep downtown curb onto the street and broke his left hip, a disaster. I wasn't with him, but a nearby pedestrian called 911, an ambulance came and took Bill to the Prescott V.A. Medical Center, and the man kindly brought Bill's car home and drove me to the hospital to be with Bill.

I saw him after he came out of the X-ray room when he was in a great deal of pain and in anguish as to what this meant for his, and my, future. The doctors decided to send Bill to the Phoenix V.A. hospital for surgery, and I learned later that he had almost died when he reached Phoenix and had to be revived with electric shock treatment.

That evening Sandy drove up to Prescott to get me, and after an overnight stay at his home, I visited Bill who urged me to return to Prescott to look after our place and the cats. He would be sent back to the Prescott V.A. in a few days where I could visit with him as much as I wanted to.

After a winter spent in the hospital, receiving excellent care and much physical therapy at the Prescott V.A. Medical Center, Bill was brought home in March, 1992, with plenty of loaned equipment for his care, including a folding wheelchair, a walker, a quad cane, hold bars for bathroom and bedroom, several medications and vitamins, and a huge box of Attends. The V.A. also arranged for Bill to attend a care center for continued physical therapy weekdays when he was picked up and delivered by a special van. He couldn't have received better care anywhere, and the V.A. doctors and staff couldn't have been kinder or more interested in Bill's welfare. And they respected his having served in the U. S. Army in France during World War I which made him eligible for the care.

Bill tried desperately to follow orders and become stronger and more active, but he was still in pain from his hip, and it bothered him greatly that he could no longer drive or even get into the driver's seat of our car. And it was difficult for me to take care of him, our place, and all the errands as I don't drive and was too old to learn. The thought of coping with the increasing traffic in Prescott had unnerved me in earlier years. As Bill was tired of sitting in his wheelchair all day, I bought an electric lift chair which proved to be a wonderful piece of furniture, allowing him to lie back and nap when he wished, also rise easily. He did have a couple of falls when I had to phone 911 for help, but even though it was traumatic for both of us, no more bones were broken. Bill had been a milk drinker all his life, so his bones were quite strong for his age. We felt that breaking his hip was a stroke of bad luck that shouldn't have happened.

As it was getting too difficult for me to handle everything by myself, regretfully we decided to sell our place and move into town closer to stores and Post Office to make things easier for me. Houses were too expensive, so I found an older but nice 12-foot-by-60-foot Fleetwood mobile home with a fine screen porch, two bedrooms, one-and-a-half baths, plus a small study which, with the porch, sold me on the place.

I had a taxi take Bill and me over to see it for his approval, and Wally, the cab driver, was kind and gentle, guiding Bill up the porch stairs and all through the house while the owner and I stayed behind to await Bill's decision. He approved, so we bought it.

We put our house and acre up for sale, and by November it was sold to a lovely young single woman named Erin who loved the place, its million-dollar view of the mountains and the wide expanse of sky above, the privacy, the birds, and even our cats which she agreed to take care of. We had thought we might take Sally and Mosey with us, but we decided we couldn't take them away from their wonderful freedom and shut them up in a house or even the screened porch. We understood how they might feel, as we felt the same way ourselves.

It was a big job getting our house ready to sell, during which we gave away to the Friends of the Prescott Library hundreds of books we had garnered over the years; to the Salvation Army, clothes and other things; and useless junk we had hauled to the dump. Over fifty years' worth of stuff, as Bill had been a regular pack rat, never wanting to part with anything. Myself, I was always ready to get rid of anything I hadn't been using or wearing for a couple of years.

Well, it was all up to me, but I finally won out, and then I had to pack and sort, sort and pack, for the big move. After the movers had come and gone, with the key and instructions for our mobile home, a taxi took Bill and me and many small items and artifacts to our new dwelling.

Bill was helped into the home and to his lift chair, and then, after the movers had left, to my dismay, he burst into tears. I looked at him and then to the awful mess the movers had left for me to cope with, and I couldn't help telling Bill to stop crying, I had too much to do, it was all too much for me, and I just couldn't take it.

After he stopped weeping, I had to get busy and start clearing out the kitchen which was piled high with boxes and equipment, after which I found that the movers had stuffed four huge "wardrobe" boxes full of our clothing into my little study, although I had told them to put the large ones on the porch. It was almost more than I could take, but I had to. There was no one else to help, so I did it.

I had purchased the mobile home partly furnished, and as there was one big chair that I didn't need or want (it was in the way of Bill's lift chair and my little maple rocking chair), I had told the movers to take it to the Salvation Army. Too late, I remembered that a sleeping bag stuffed into a big plastic garbage bag had been on that chair, and they took both away before we arrived, also a similar sleeping bag that had been in my little study, and a fluorescent lantern I had stowed in one cardboard box.

I looked everywhere for them, but they were gone. I phoned the moving company, but nothing was ever done. No recourse. We couldn't camp out any more, but I had wanted to give the sleeping bags to Sandy and Dusanka to use for the church "retreats" they attended once a year in camps in the pines around Prescott. And I needed the lantern during power failures which sometimes happen during lightning storms here in the big trees. Irked, I bought a new one, but it wasn't the same, not as good.

Gradually Bill became adjusted to our new home after I had put everything away and placed our pictures and artifacts around to make the place homey and familiar. And in nice weather he could sit out on the screened porch and watch the birds come to the feeders I hung for them on one of the oak trees nearby. Sandy brought us a bird bath which Bill could watch from his lift chair when the big front door was open.

Every few weeks Bill had to be taken by taxi to the V.A. Medical Center for checkups, prescriptions, and more huge cartons of Attends. There were co-payments of $2.00 per prescription we had to pay, a bargain indeed! We were very grateful for the good care and help provided by the V.A.

Bill also continued to write his column "Under the Southwest Sun" for the *Courier,* typing it himself until it became too difficult for him to sit at his desk, so I took on the job after he hand-wrote it. Each Monday morning I would walk to town to turn it in, for publication on Friday. Then I would load up on groceries and other necessities for the week and take a cab home. Sometimes I would walk up the hill a half mile from here to a supermarket to get extra bread, milk, and whatever else we might run out of. While I was away, I would leave a cordless phone with Bill with which he could call for help in case he fell or became ill.

On Thanksgiving, 1993, after we had been in the trailer for a year, I learned from a neighbor, Harriet, of a little tiger cat stray living in the boulders at the top of her hill where her mobile home was situated. As she couldn't take care of it, I told her, "I'll take it," knowing that Bill missed our cats and would love to have one for company. While Harriet was visiting her family for Thanksgiving, I hiked up the hill and called, "Kitty, kitty, here kitty!" And out from the boulders crept the cutest little golden striped cat with only a two-inch-long tail, at an angle like a Japanese Bob-Tail cat. She was very timid but let me pick her up and carry her down the hill, although she tried to get loose once or twice until I carried her into the porch, up the steps to the landing, and into the house. Bill was thrilled. He loved that little creature, and she loved him, snuggling down beside him in his chair to sleep. One afternoon when he was napping, she crept up onto his chest and touched her nose to his, and he never awoke. I wish that I could have taken a picture of the incident to show him, but I did tell him about it later. It meant a lot to him to have her there with him, and she gave him lots of laughs when she would lie on her back on my lap and fight with my hands and pretend to bite me.

Taking care of Bill during those years wasn't easy for me, but I didn't mind, as he never complained or fussed at me about his disability or anything else. He ate whatever food I served, let me dress or undress him, making it as easy for me as possible, and was resigned to his lot. He tried to exercise, but his hip made it too painful, so his days were spent in his lift chair, reading, sleeping, and watching television, mostly baseball games, Nature programs, and "Western" movies which I would turn on for him before I went anywhere. We had a black-and-white set, without "remote," as Bill preferred it to color.

He liked to watch any and all baseball games, but the Chicago Cubs were his big favorite, and during the baseball strike in 1994, he began to lose heart and slept most of the day. He did perk up, however, when the Hubble telescope was launched into space until it was found to be defective. It was a big disappointment until they finally repaired it, and he could see some of the pictures it sent back to Earth.

Astronomy was one of Bill's big interests, although he always rejected the "Big Bang" theory and wrote two or three columns about his own ideas. He was such an interesting man, able to converse on many subjects including geology and mining; animals, birds, and insects; people he had met, jobs he had held; his adventures all over the West; politics; religion; sports; archeology; flowers, weeds, and trees. Name it, he could talk about it and write his columns about it. Even though he hadn't gone past eighth grade, he was self-taught through both reading and experience, always eager to learn. Sometimes I think back to my college days and try to remember what my boy friends and I had talked about, and I just can't think of anything interesting we may have discussed. I feel so lucky that I found Bill for my lifetime partner. He had awakened my mind and helped me mature and become interested in so many things. He was also a wonderful father to our sons, willing to discuss everything and anything with them.

Taking care of Bill gave structure and purpose to my days, but I got a scare one night when I awoke around one A.M. with my heart beating like crazy, irregularly, and I couldn't get it to behave. I had been taking a tiny dose of Lanoxin for irregular heartbeat for a few months, including one that night, but I knew I didn't dare take any more. And I didn't dare to call 911 for help, as I couldn't leave Bill alone, so I put on my warm robe and sat in his lift chair the rest of the night, my heart still acting wild. By morning I was very weak when I went to get Bill out of bed and help him to the bathroom. I told him what had happened, minimizing the problem, and then went to the kitchen to fix myself a cup of coffee and some toast, hoping it would give me some strength, which it did. Suddenly my heart started beating normally, and even though I was very weak, I was able to dress and feed Bill and do my chores. I never took Lanoxin again and haven't had any more trouble. Very mysterious. Very encouraging. Now when I have checkups for my health, everything is normal!

I had been setting my alarm for two A.M. to take Bill to the bathroom. He was getting weaker every day, with little appetite, and on January 11, 1995, he could hardly get out of bed even with my help, and while we were returning to his bed, he suddenly collapsed. It was impossible for me to help him up, so I had to phone for an ambulance. As is customary, they contacted the Prescott Fire Department, and pretty soon there were seven big strong young people entering our house. They walked down the hall to the bedroom where Bill was lying on the floor, covered with his robe, and propped up with the pillows I had set at his back, and they were so kind and gentle and concerned that I was filled with gratitude, reassured that we were in very good hands.

They took Bill's vital signs, noted his medications, then put him on a stretcher to take him to the V.A. Center as I told them I couldn't take care of him any longer. I was eighty years old and not strong enough. The time had come for others to take over.

It was after three a.m. by that time and raining hard, so they asked Bill if it would be okay to cover his head with a blanket to protect his head. Of course, it was okay! I told Bill I'd see him in the morning, and after the ambulance and big fire truck left, I returned to bed for the rest of a sleepless night filled with unhappy thoughts.

Next morning after breakfast I went by taxi to the V.A. Medical Center to see Bill who was settled into a comfortable bed with one of those pulsing air mattresses under him to prevent bed sores. He was in a room with three other patients, and all were receiving excellent care. So I was reassured that what I had done was for the best. I had no alternative, and I told Bill right off that I couldn't take care of him any more. He accepted that, didn't complain, made everything as easy as possible for me, as always.

I continued writing his *Courier* columns for him, using his material, reading the final product to him for approval before turning it in each week, but we decided by April when it would be exactly twenty-eight years since he had started writing it, that we should call it off, so I composed one last column, with his help and approval, turned it in, and that was that.

The *Courier* published the final column along with a beautiful editorial and article with a picture of Bill in his World War I uniform, which had been taken in France on a postal card and which I had had copied and enlarged, placing one 8 by 10 on the bulletin board by his bed in the V.A. Nursing Home after he was transferred there from the main hospital building. The Courier also published appreciative letters from readers of Bill's column, with regret that he had had to stop writing it. Others sent him cards and letters telling him how much his column had meant to them. This made Bill and me feel better about having had to end it.

Bill made me cut my visits to him to every other day to make it easier for me, and after two months in the hospital during which he almost died from pneumonia, he was taken to the nursing home nearby where, again, the care was excellent, and I, also, was treated with kindness. The staff tried to build Bill's strength back with therapy, but he began to get weaker and lose appetite, unable to walk even with a quad cane, confined to wheelchair and bed, until finally he went into a coma when he wasn't expected to live.

Alarmed, Sandy and family came to visit him along with a preacher from their church who prayed over Bill who came out of the coma after two or three days, although he was very weak, unresponsive, and unable to eat beyond a few spoonsful of pudding or Ensure. I visited him then every day and sometimes at night, realizing the end was near but not willing yet to say goodbye.

One morning when I was preparing to catch the bus to go to the hospital nursing home after Bill had been there for three months, an elderly man I had met briefly at the nursing home some time previously, knocked at my trailer door and told me that he had wondered where I lived so came to find out. I invited him in as he told me he would drive me to the hospital. While I was in the bathroom getting ready, I found when I returned to the living room that he had been nosing around, looking over my possessions, as he commented on some of them, including my family's two big genealogy books and the hunting knife which I had stuck in a corner of my magazine rack. I told him that I also had a gun.

While he was driving me to the hospital, he remarked, "I'm going to be your family from now on."

Surprised and shocked, I didn't reply, thinking to myself, "Nobody is going to take Bill's place." I thanked the man for the ride but I didn't mention the incident to Bill. I never saw that man again. I guess he got the "message." Sometimes silence can be more eloquent than words.

On the morning of June 15, 1995, Bill's kindly Nurse Practitioner Vivian phoned me that Bill had died that morning. Then she called Chaplain Bentley who came and drove me to the nursing home to be with Bill for a while. The doctors and nurses and other staff members were very kind and comforting, hugging me and telling me how sorry they were. They didn't offer any platitudes, for which I was grateful. They knew, as I did, that Bill's death at ninety-seven was inevitable, ending his suffering. I will be forever grateful to them for all they did for Bill and for me.

Chaplain Bentley walked me to the office at the V.A. to make final arrangements there, and I was presented with a beautiful American flag folded in the customary triangle, in honor of Bill's service in the United States Army in World War I, after which Mr. Bentley drove me to the funeral home to arrange for cremation and an airplane flight over Granite Mountain which Bill had requested in his will, and verbally to me in previous years, similar to my own wish for myself when I die.

Several days later I went along in the small single-engine plane when Bill's ashes were scattered over the mountain at the other end of where Monty's ashes had been placed by Bill over eleven years before. My last horizon with Bill.

At the end of June, there was a lovely memorial service conducted at the V.A. Nursing Home for the veterans who had died that month, during which we widows or other survivors were asked to speak. When it came my turn, I tried to be calm, but suddenly I couldn't bear it, and I began to wail, no doubt embarrassing the others, and a kind elderly woman volunteer came and put her arms around me as I subsided in tears.

The Prescott daily paper, the *Courier*, published an editorial saying that Prescott "will be a lesser place without Bill Parks," and there were other columns and several letters expressing regret over his death. And then a wonderful cartoon by author/artist Jim Willoughby depicting Bill driving a little bus up toward "The Great Beyond" with the heading "God go with you, storyteller" and a lovely verse: "They say that where I'm going is really nice. Where I'm coming from has been like Paradise! The time comes, though, when we've got to go—We'll meet again . . . so, friend, until then . . . Adios!" At the bottom is a little drawing of a man, "Buckey O'Prescott" printed on his shirt, and he is saying "Vaya Con Dios, Bill!"

When I saw that on the editorial page of the *Courier*, I began to laugh and cry at the same time, after which I phoned Jim, getting his answering machine to which I expressed my appreciation for the wonderful thing he had done. Later he phoned me and offered to bring me the original drawing, which he did, and I had it framed and placed it on my living room wall in back of Bill's lift chair. It makes me happy and sad at the same time to look at it. And I have Jim Willoughby's cartoon books, beautifully drawn with clever captions, called *Cowboy Cartoons*, *Quick on the Draw*, and *A Dude's Guide to the West*—the latter by Jim and his wife Sue—generously autographed to me personally, with love, warming my heart forever.

I received many kind cards and letters expressing sorrow over Bill's death, which gave me a lot of comfort, and now I was alone with no one else to care for except my little cat Sunshine who, like most cats, is easy to care for, but is good company for me, yet undemanding most of the time. I have little to worry about except my own health which is good, and the upkeep of my trailer. I am satisfied with my modest little home. It is cozy, cool in the summer with an efficient evaporative cooler, even during humid weather; and warm in the winter with my new furnace which I had to get when my old one gave out. I also had to get a new water heater and have the outside of my trailer painted and the roof coated to forestall possible leaks.

I feel safe here, safer than I would be in a large house where I might have to worry about someone trying to break in at a distant door or window.

One would think that having undergone rather extreme privation during the earlier years with Bill that I would crave luxury, but that's not the case. I prefer the simple life which makes few demands on me, so that I can think, work on my writing, read what I please, go where I choose. I have wonderful neighbors who respect my privacy but would be glad to be of help to me, as I would be to them. We watch out for each other.

I have always been a resilient, optimistic person, giving other people the benefit of the doubt, hoping for the best in the world regardless of how bad the news might be. I know there is crime, as it has touched my family with the murder of Monty and other young people in our community. But I also know that the good people are in the majority in the world, especially when I read *Guideposts* magazine with its heartwarming stories, and the accounts in *Reader's Digest* of the good things that take place everywhere. I refuse to be downhearted or depressed, and I guess that is why my health remains good at eighty-three years of age. Possibly I could live to be one hundred years old, and that wouldn't be a bad thing if I could remain well and active as I am. My weight and vital signs are all normal, and even my hair hasn't turned white, just a few streaks of gray along with the "dishwater blonde," making me look younger than my years, or so I am told.

Sandy, Dusanka, and Tamara have urged me to come to Mesa to live with them, there or in Yugoslavia some day when they plan to return to that country, but I decline, as I treasure my independence, knowing that I would lose strength if I let them take care of me and my needs. And they have their own lives and interests, so I don't want to interfere. We are a loving family, we are friends, we talk often on the phone, and occasional visits are always a delight.

Even though I am too busy to feel lonely, I miss Bill and Monty and think about them every day, especially when I see butterflies and birds, rainbows and sunsets, television programs about nature, travel, space, and the Hubble telescope with its fascinating and beautiful pictures of the Universe and colliding galaxies, and Stephen Hawking, with his brilliant ideas about time and space that make our minds expand with wonder. Bill and Monty would be so excited about the advances in space exploration since they saw men walking on the moon. But maybe they already know?!

"As Bill always says when the going gets tough, we'll be eatin' the bark off the trees if something doesn't turn up pretty soon." That was the first sentence in my *Ladies' Home Journal* article "Horizon Hunters" over fifty years ago. Well, it never came to the point where we had to eat bark, but we did eat an awful lot of potato soup those early years of our marriage.

Although Bill wasn't a big man, never weighing more than 155 pounds, he was one of the strongest people I ever knew, willing to take on any kind of work, confident that he could handle it, from cotton picking to guide work at Death Valley and the Grand Canyon to building three houses without power tools to writing novels and short stories and his *Courier* column "Under the Southwest Sun" to being a good father to our two sons, and all the other things I have mentioned in this account of our life together.

The summer after Bill died, I re-typed the 100,000 words of his novel "The Seventh Horizon" about the Navajos, a "people story" which I am sure they would enjoy reading themselves. I made changes and corrections Bill had wanted, and I have been trying to find a publisher for his book, also for a collection of his best columns "Under the Southwest Sun" which many of his readers have requested. When I work on these projects in Bill's memory, I feel that he is still here with me, and I am inspired to continue. So I really don't feel that I am alone after all.

Printed in the United States
83876LV00008B/130-138/A